RESEARCH IN URBAN POLICY

Volume 2 • 1986

Part A

FISCAL AUSTERITY AND URBAN MANAGEMENT

EDITORIAL BOARD

RESEARCH IN URBAN POLICY

A Research Annual

FISCAL AUSTERITY AND URBAN MANAGEMENT

Editor: TERRY NICHOLS CLARK
The University of Chicago

VOLUME 2 • 1986
PART A

JAI PRESS INC.

Greenwich, Connecticut *London, England*

55 Old Post Road, No. 2
Greenwich, Connecticut 06830

JAI PRESS LTD.
3 Henrietta Street
London WC2E 8LU
England

ISBN: 0–89232–534-A
ISBN: 0–89232–729–4 (set)

Manufactured in the United States of America

CONTENTS

EDITORIAL INTRODUCTION

This is an exciting volume. The subtitle, "Fiscal Austerity and Urban Innovation," is also the name of a project joining many contributors. In just three years the Fiscal Austerity (FA) Project has become the most extensive study of local government and fiscal management in the world. An overview was published in Volume 1 of *Research in Urban Policy* (*RUP*) (Clark 1985).

Using standardized methods, project participants have surveyed mayors, council members, and administrators in all U.S. cities over 25,000. Twenty-six teams collected data in their state areas. The surveys were then merged and combined with census and other data by Robert Stein at Rice University, and all teams were sent back tapes and documentation. The first results appear here, some analyzed by state or region, others nationally. Twenty-five other teams are conducting analogous surveys in as many countries.

Several papers were discussed at Project conferences; such continuing professional contacts have sharpened and focused these efforts. Fiscal austerity is salient around the world, and innovative solutions keep appearing. A major Project activity is documenting and assessing innovations to help them spread. Interested social scientists, policy analysts, and public officials are welcome to participate in Project activities, which are reported in newsletters and other publications.

One message emerges clearly from the volume: Austerity is widely experienced, but responses are richly diverse and often innovative. We are seeing more lists of new practices (indeed, several efforts at storing them in computerized data banks), but far less about how cities should choose among them. No one approach is generally right or wrong, but some policies are more appropriate in some locales than others. The Project is distinct in emphasizing fiscal, political, and administrative concerns which make policies feasible for a given locale.

The Abstracts and Commentaries summarize specific themes paper by paper, so I comment here only on a few more general issues.

NATIONAL URBAN POLICIES, LOCAL AUTONOMY, AND THE FUTURE OF THE WELFARE STATE

Major shifts in national-local relations are under way or are discussed in several countries. In the United States, the Reagan administration proposed a New Federalism, little of which was implemented. It was widely interpreted as too much a traditional Republican policy, stressing decentralization and less intergovernmental aid (cf. Mollenkopf 1983). Local officials often supported or opposed intergovernmental aid in this partisan manner.

Yet this left-right characterization of national urban policies may be too simple (Clark 1983). Some international comparisons are illuminating. In Yugoslavia, national-local relations have been reorganized multiple times since World War II, despite continuities in national leadership. And in France, Italy, and Spain major changes have come from the left. In Italy and Spain many local governments have seen Communist majorities in the last decade. What is striking is how much they pursued a Eurocommunist line, breaking openly with the Leninist-Stalinist state centralism of the Soviet and French parties. The degree to which state centralism was no longer orthodoxy was illustrated by some Italian Communist cities that invited American civic leaders to consult on how to contract out with private firms for social services.

These Italian and Spanish examples were discussed at a conference of the Fiscal Authority Project held in 1983 at the University of Paris-Nanterre. The French case, considered there in more detail, was in some ways even more striking. The French participants suggested the conference title so as to reflect a central concern for the new Socialist government: "Questioning the Welfare State, and the Rise of the City."[1] More specifically, how devolve basic functions of national welfare to local government, where services may be performed more democratically and at lower cost? This reform has become the vanguard issue of the Mitterand government, fundamentally differentiating it from both the authoritarian right tradition from Napoleon through DeGaulle, and the authoritarian left of the French

Communist Party. Yet the reforms are close in spirit to the Reagan proposals! The major difference, of course, is that the French reforms were adopted. What lessons does this suggest for other countries considering national urban policy changes?

A major issue at international urban conferences is local autonomy. In the past, at least, some argued that U.S. cities had more local autonomy and thus were not comparable to European cities (Clark 1974). This view reflects a constitutional and legal perspective that has been fundamentally challenged as studies of actual local policy making have been conducted in country after country, from the United Kingdom (cf. Newton and Sharpe 1984) through Italy (Martinotti 1981) and Yugoslavia (Jambrek 1975). The French case is especially critical as it is widely cited as having the least local autonomy of major European countries. Becquart-Leclercq (1976, 1977) challenged this view in the first major study of French local power. She found that within the formally centralized structures, entrepreneurial mayors often developed informal contacts with national party, legislative, and administrative officials to get what they wanted for their cities. A further counterintuitive result came from a careful comparison of British and French cities by Ashford and Thoenig (1981): French local officials have more (yes, more!) local autonomy than their British counterparts.

In his paper below, Thoenig builds on these past findings to interpret the recent Decentralization Reforms. As his title suggests, master plans have systems effects, which are often complex and unanticipated. He cautions that it is still early to draw conclusions, but he indicates that changes to date are far less than suggested in part since local officials already had far more autonomy than many (national) observers had appreciated. Thus, in many areas, the reforms simply recognize in law what already had occurred in practice. Thoenig elaborates this and other points that should provide food for thought for observers in the United States and elsewhere pondering fundamental changes in national urban policy.

French decentralization occurred simultaneously with sluggish economic growth; local governments thus receive greater legal autonomy, and more freedom in using intergovernmental grants, but fewer francs. The Yugoslav, Italian, Spanish, and French cases suggest that decentralization and less funding need not come from the right. Does the fact that such policies emerge from such different types of national governments suggest a more general questioning of the adequacy of national centralization as a condition of efficient state organization?

Dissatisfaction with large-scale organization is not limited to government. Recent work in the United States (by Birch 1979) and Germany indicates that about two-thirds of all new jobs are created by firms with 20 or fewer employees. Thus, large, hierarchical corporations—like large governments—seldom innovate like little, nimble ones. In Japan, some data suggest that small firms may be as much as twice as important as in the United states or Western Europe. And some large firms like Honda create highly autonomous subsections to similar effect.

Increasing world interdependence, and questioning of hierarchical and ideological traditions, encourages innovation by decentralization. Results from France indicating more decentralization than meets the legal eye are similar in spirit to U.S. studies suggesting more local autonomy than is articulated in state capitals or Washington. Papers below by Saltzstein, Sonenshein, and Ostrow on Los Angeles; Saltzstein on Proposition 13; and Schecter's Commentary elaborate this theme.

NOTES

1. Some 170 persons attended the conference, most of whom presented papers. Three volumes of conference papers have been published. Papers on Austerity and Innovation are available from Gerd-Michael Hellstern, Freie Universitat Berlin, Inst fur sozialwissenschaftliche Forschung, Sarrazinstr. 11–15, 1000 Berlin 41, West Germany. Papers on National-Local Relations and Citizen Participation are available from Dan Ferrand-Bechman, Institut D'Administration Economique et Sociale, Domaine Universitaire de Saint-Martin-d'Heres, Batiment Sciences Humaines et Mathematiques, Universite des Sciences Sociales de Grenoble, 47 X 38040 Grenoble, France.

REFERENCES

Ashford, Douglas, and Jean-Claude Thoenig, 1981. *Les aides financières de l'Etat aux collectivités locales en France et á l'étranger*. Paris: LITEC.

Becquart-Leclercq, Jeanne. 1976. *Les Paradoxes du Pouvoir Local*. Paris: Presses de la Fondation Nationale des Sciences Politiques.

———. 1977. "French Mayors and Communal Policy Outputs." Pp. 79–120 in Ronald J. Liebert and Allen W. Imershein, eds., *Power, Paradigms and Community Research*. Beverly Hills: Sage.

Birch, David L. 1979. *The Job Generation Process*. Cambridge, Mass.: MIT Program on Neighborhood and Regional Change.

Clark, Terry Nichols. 1974. *Comparative Community Politics*. New York and Beverly Hills: Wiley-Halstead; Sage.

———. 1983. "Local Fiscal Dynamics under Old and New Federalisms," *Urban Affairs Quarterly* 19 (September): 55–74.

Frémontier, Jacques. 1984. *Les cadets de la droit*. Paris: Seuil.

Jambrek, Peter. 1975. *Development and Social Change in Yugoslavia*. Lexington, Mass.: Lexington Books.

Martinotti, Guido. 1981. "The Illusive Autonomy." Pp. 63–124 in L. J. Sharpe, ed., *The Local Fiscal Crisis in Western Europe*. London and Beverly Hills: Sage.

———. 1983. "I Modelli per il Sindaco," *Corriera de la Serra* (November 28).

Mollenkopf, John. 1983. *The Contested City*. Princeton, N.J.: Princeton University Press.

Newton, Kenneth, and L. J. Sharpe, 1984. *Does Politics Really Matter?* Oxford, Eng.: Oxford University Press.
Sorman, Guy. 1984. *La solution liberale*. Paris: Fayard.

Terry Nichols Clark
Series Editor

INFORMATION FOR CONTRIBUTORS TO *RESEARCH IN URBAN POLICY*

EDITORIAL PROCEDURES:

We welcome manuscripts up to about 20 double-spaced typed pages although longer papers will be considered. Papers in any style will be accepted for review, but *RUP* style must be respected for final publication. All papers deemed appropriate for the *RUP* are sent out to readers. The editor relies heavily on the judgments of those readers but is not bound by them. Manuscripts are accepted for publication subject to editing with the understanding that the *RUP* has the right of first publication. Submission of a manuscript to the *RUP* is taken to indicate the author's commitment to publish in the *RUP*. No paper known to be under consideration by any other journal will be reviewed by the *RUP*. Upon publication, all rights, including subsidiary rights, are owned by JAI Press. Authors retain the right to use their articles without charge in any book of which they are the author or editor after it has appeared in *RUP*.

Four copies of the manuscript and abstract, on white paper, must be submitted. Manuscripts should be addressed to Terry Nichols Clark, editor of *Research in Urban Policy*, 1126 East 59th Street, The University of Chicago, Chicago, Illinois 60637. *Manuscripts are not returned to authors.*

PREPARATION OF COPY

1. Use only good-quality opaque white paper, 8 1/2 x 11, type on one side and number consecutively from start to finish.
2. Type *all* copy—including indented matter, footnotes, and references—double-spaced, allowing a one-inch margin at top, bottom, and sides of pages.
3. Type each table on a separate page. Refer to each table in numerical order in the text. Prepare tables without vertical lines.
4. Clarify all symbols with words in the margin of the manuscript. Circle these and other explanatory notes not intended for printing.
5. Draw figures on white paper in ink. Original or glossy print of each figure will be required if manuscript is accepted. Figures should be identified with the name of the author and the number of the figure on the back or in the margin.
6. All figures and tables should be gathered together at the end of the manuscript.
7. All footnotes should be numbered including acknowledgment footnotes. Subscript references or footnote numbers should be typed after a period or comma.
8. Include an abstract of approximately 150 words summarizing the findings.
9. Include four copies of a biographical sketch of approximately 10 typed lines.
10. Enclose a self-addressed stamped postcard, containing the manuscript title, to obtain acknowledgment of manuscript receipt. No other acknowledgment will be sent.

Format of References in Text

Reference lists should be triple-spaced. Each reference should be double-spaced. All references to monographs, articles, and statistical sources are to be identified at the appropriate point in the text by last name of the author, year of publication, and page number where appropriate, all within parentheses. Footnotes are to be used only for substantive observations. Specify subsequent citations of the same source in the same way as the first one; do not use *ibid*, *op. cit.*, or *loc. cit.*

1. When author's name is in the text: Kain (1959); When author's name is not in the text: (Allen 1963).
2. Page numbers follow year of publication: (Lipset 1964: 261–265).
3. For more than three authors, use "et al."; for institutional authorship, supply minimum identification from the beginning of the complete citation: (U.S. Bureau of Census 1963: 117).
4. With more than one reference to an author in the same year, distinguish them by use of letters (a, b) attached to the year of publication: (1965a).
5. Enclose a series of references within a single pair of parentheses, separated by semicolons.

Format of References Section

List all items alphabetically by author (providing the full list of multiple authors), and, within author(s), by year of publication, in an appendix titled "References." Examples follow.

Davis, Kingsley. 1963a. "Social Demography." Pp. 124–137 in *The Behavioral Sciences Today*, ed. Bernard Berelson. New York: Basic.

———. 1963b. "The Theory of Change and Response in Modern Demographic History," *Population Index* 29: 345–366.

Goode, William J. 1967. "The Protection of the Inept," *American Sociological Review* 32: 5–19.

Moore, Wilbert E., and Arnold S. Feldman. 1960. *Labor Commitment and Social Change in Developing Areas*. New York: Social Science Research Council.

Sanford, Nevitt, ed. 1962. *The American College*. New York: Wiley.

Weber, Max. (1921) 1968. "Society's Problems." Pp. 12–16 in *Economy and Society*, ed. Guenther Roth and Claus Wittich. New York: Bedminster.

Terry Nichols Clark

PART I.

POPULATION TRENDS AND ECONOMIC DEVELOPMENT

COMMUNITY AND COLLECTIVE GOODS:

HOW SUNBELT CITIES RESPOND TO AUSTERITY

Lynn M. Appleton and Bruce A. Williams

ABSTRACT

We empirically examine Florida cities' responses to the fiscal problems posed by rapid growth. Different factors affect each of the two main kinds of possible responses—raising taxes and cutting costs.

We argue that a city's willingness to raise taxes rests upon its sociopolitical characteristics: particularly, on the degree to which it is a "community." However, the nature and extent of a city's use of cost-cutting strategies is more sharply affected by its political culture. Our analysis suggests that recent patterns of regional migration have important consequences for cities' abilities to respond to problems of growth.

INTRODUCTION

This paper investigates some elements of the social and political significance of migration from "snowbelt" to "sunbelt" states. At a more general level, it analyzes social and political ramifications of the market forces that have shaped the sunbelt.

The paper is divided into six sections or subsections. First, we discuss

Research in Urban Policy, Vol. 2, pages 3–24.

ISBN: 0-89232-534-8

problems posed for the urban political system by shifts in population from snowbelt to sunbelt. Second, we discuss the possibility that the construction of "community" (Suttles, 1972) in sunbelt cities may help to resolve these dilemmas. Third, we discuss facets of sunbelt development that may militate against such construction in the South's boom towns. Fourth, we discuss Florida, the setting for our preliminary empirical analyses. Fifth, we discuss our data collection and our procedures for analysis. Finally, we discuss our findings and their implications.

SNOWBELT/SUNBELT SHIFTS

Much attention has recently focused on movement of jobs and population from the old industrial heartland to the South and Southwest (Perry and Watkins 1977; Bluestone and Harrison 1983; Sawers and Tabb 1984). Most of this literature focuses on the movement's consequences for declining cities and states; less attention has been paid to implications of this shift for sunbelt cities.

For two reasons, more attention to the sunbelt is warranted. First, sunbelt cities face many pressing problems—albeit associated with growth rather than decline: roadways and utilities that are overwhelmed by the pace of population increase; police and fire departments that are inadequate to population sprawl. Thus they may be as subject to fiscal strain as their northern counterparts (Clark and Ferguson 1983; Feagin 1984). Such problems are likely to increase in severity if aid to states and localities continues to bear the brunt of federal budget cutters. However, while a great deal of scholarly literature has focused on policymaking in northern cities (e.g. Banfield 1961; Banfield and Wilson 1963; Dahl 1961; Sayre and Kaufman 1960; Yates 1977), much less attention has been paid to the ways in which sunbelt cities are governed. We suggest that, for a variety of reasons, the politics in sunbelt cities may differ dramatically from those found in more frequently studied northern cities. Therefore, it is difficult to anticipate the ways in which sunbelt cities are likely to respond to their new problems.

Second, when people move between locations, their incorporation into community decision-making systems is always problematic. Rapid in-migration, such as that to the industrial cities of the early twentieth century, strains the capacity of extant social and political organizations to absorb the newcomers (Mandelbaum 1965; Warner 1968, 1972). We believe that the recent migration to the sunbelt has placed—and will continue to place—similar strains on politics and society in this region.

It is easy to see why migration would place strains on government. In a private-market economy, government is called upon to provide "public goods" that will not be adequately produced by the private sector: education, police services, sewers, transportation, etc. (Bish 1971). To produce public goods requires overcoming the "free rider problem": those who enjoy the benefits of such goods must be compelled to contribute to their provision—even when the benefits received for such contributions are not immediately apparent (Downs 1960).

In a democracy, a certain level of trust in government is required in order to get people to contribute to the provision of services that they may not use themselves. That is, individuals must be willing to trust that, even if they don't always get what they want or "their money's worth" in a given case, they will receive their fair share over the long run. Thus, pluralist political theorists have emphasized the importance of citizens' sharing a "democratic creed" that legitimates the rules of the game (Ricci 1971). Even when citizens do not agree with a particular decision, they must generally concede that the process of decision making is fair (cf., Dahl 1956, 1961); further, they must share some minimal set of beliefs about what constitutes a collective good (Harvey 1973).

The origins of such beliefs are multiple, but one important source is attachment to and participation in the affairs of the local community (Polsby, 1963; Janowitz and Street, 1978). In the sunbelt, as in the frostbelt, community may serve as a partial antidote to the individuation of modernity.

Communities and Markets

Following the first great wave of Western industrialization and urbanization, a variety of different theorists predicted that "community" would be swept away by the forces of modernity and the market (cf. Engels 1962; Tonnies 1957; Wirth 1938). Urban, industrial society would consist of relentlessly self-interested and self-absorbed individuals, bereft of significant ties of blood and affection. The "death of community" became a commonplace of twentieth-century sociology.

Nevertheless, the position always had its critics. As early as the 1920s, Chicago sociologists (cf. Thomas and Zaniecki 1958; Park and Burgess 1921; Park, Burgess, and McKenzie 1925) found evidence of "community" in the heart of that fast-growing industrial city. Later, theorists of "the community of limited liability" offered both a critique of idealizations of pre-industrial community and a theory of the determinants of community in modern urban settings (cf. Greer 1962; Hunter 1975; Janowitz 1951; Kasarda and Janowitz 1974; Lee et al. 1984). Community, they suggested, develops out of the shared interests and amiable interactions that are a consequence of long-term residence in an area. Although urbanites cannot attain the all-encompassing *gemeinschaft* described by early sociologists, their local life is not necessarily anomic and Hobbesian. Seemingly, geographical mobility dissolves community; *ceteris paribus*, community is constructed when mobility slows.

However, as institutional economist Karl Polanyi (1944) stressed, market systems require a mobility that perennially threatens community. True market systems require that society's resources be allocated via the pricing mechanism that emerges from competition between buyers and sellers. Markets require that their constituent elements self-interestedly respond solely to prices and opportunities for profit. For this to occur, land, labor, and capital must be transformed into commodities whose use and movement are determined by their exchange value. The dominance of the market produces a distinctive kind of society: one characterized by highly anomic individuals restlessly seeking advantage in exchange relationships. In such a society, the possibility of community is severely constrained.

However, Polanyi argues that the values of the marketplace are unable to completely establish their dominance. The consequences of the market's operations are such that its ascendancy always generates resistance to its outcomes. For example, an area's residents often form community associations that attempt to intervene in the market's impersonal assignment of value: They organize to oppose proposed new construction, to demand improved roads, to stop "red-lining," or to prevent sales to "undesirables." Not only do residents sometimes attempt to intervene in the market's assignment of value, they also "step outside of the market" when they value their communities for characteristics that are irrelevant to housing value. Through these same community associations, they can clarify and reaffirm their commitments to the area; in this manner, they crystallize and clarify their understanding of their community's nature. The formation and function of community associations illustrates Polanyi's argument that those adversely affected by markets tend to organize politically to resist the negative effects of market dominance.

Contemporary scholars have compared the advantages and disadvantages of market and nonmarket mechanisms for the provision of goods and services. Douglas and Wildavsky (1982), for example, compare and contrast market and bureaucratic models as alternatives for regulating risk in a society. Ostrom (1973) and Bish (1971) have critically analyzed the advantages and disadvantages of provision of public goods and services through large, centralized bureaucracies as opposed to their provision via smaller, decentralized governmental institutions operating in a competitive market. From a less normative perspective, the work of Clark and Ferguson (1983) analyzes the effect of a city's political culture on the extent to which government will provide public goods, thus limiting the degree to which markets are the sole distributors of goods and services. In order to understand politics in newer sunbelt cities, it is important to analyze the ways that they strike a balance between market and nonmarket mechanisms for the allocation of goods and services.

Polanyi's arguments, as well as theorizing about "the community of limited liability," lead us to characterize many sunbelt cities as experiencing the ascendancy of the market and a concommitant dimunition of community. Certainly, community may develop and, out of community, the organizational base and the sense of shared fate that are prerequisites to the attainment of collective goods. If so, then sunbelt cities will eventually come to resemble their northern counterparts. To estimate the probability of such convergence, our task in the next section will be to discuss the conditions under which community develops and the likelihood that these conditions will be met in sunbelt cities.

Constructing Community

In the sunbelt, community development in boomtown urban areas faces formidable obstacles due to the ascendancy of market forces in that region's development. In this section, drawing on contemporary theories of "communities of limited liability," we outline a set of factors that affect the development of community attachment and community associations. Then, considering these factors, we discuss the likelihood that sunbelt cities will develop community institutions on a scale adequate to their problems of political and social integration.

As Hunter (1975) recognized, "community" is variously conceptualized in the sociological literature: as a location that serves to meet sustenance needs, as a network of social interactions, and as a unit of collective identity. To capture all three dimensions, the following factors must be considered in analyzing the likelihood of community's emergence. First, we must consider the degree to which residents' economic status is bound up with the community's fate. In the United States, people rarely work close to their homes (cf. Katznelson 1982). Area residents' primary economic tie to their neighborhoods is in terms of housing's value; for many persons, their home is their most significant asset. If they believe that they are unlikely to move, they are much more likely to involve themselves in community activities and associations seeking to maintain or improve that home's value.[1] Second, do residents have friends and family in the area, or must they create new associational networks? Does the physical layout of the area facilitate neighborly interactions? Do community associations exist that they can readily join? Third, does this locality have a distinctive identity available to newcomers? In this regard, a just-completed development starkly contrasts with an established urban neighborhood. Moreover, we must consider residents' reasons for residing in a particular locality. Do they have anything to do with its unique cultural identity?

It is useful, for illustrative purposes, to contrast the effects of immigration and rapid population growth on sunbelt cities with their effects on northern industrial cities. From our perspective it seems that the boom towns of the sunbelt may face many more barriers to community's emergence than did the northern urban boom towns of the early twentieth century. Certainly, both were produced by changing patterns of demand for labor and opportunities for capital. Both are examples of the ways in which the market demands that factors of production respond to price signals. However, the degree to which market forces could drive out nonmarket values differs significantly between the two migrations.

In both migrations, the speed of population change and the segregation of migrant areas rendered extant community incapable of "assimilating" newcomers (Kasarda and Janowitz 1974). In sunbelt cities, growth is in peripheral areas rather than the inner city; such cities are bordered with newly developed sections that were pastureland only a few years back. Residents of such areas are effectively barred from existing community systems that are geographically distant.

To be sure, the language and religious and cultural diversity of early-twentieth-century migrants posed substantial problems not faced by sunbelt cities (except in cities that have attracted immigrants from Latin America and the Carribean, e.g. south Florida, Texas, and southern California). Nevertheless, as turn-of-the-century urban political systems faced isolated areas dominated by newcomers, they had two major advantages over sunbelt cities: First, their urban political machines had incentives and methods to incorporate these areas into their operations; second, these areas were populated by groups rather than a heterogenous collection of dissimilar individuals. Early-twentieth-century urban migrants often came as ethnic groups and settled in ethnic "villages." They brought culture containing values inconsistent with those of the market; they brought their kin and their traditional associational forms (cf. Gans 1962; Glazer and Moynihan 1970). Often, political machines were able to use these ethnic groups' institutions (e.g., the Irish pub, the church) to integrate them into the urban political system (Merton 1968; Lewis 1973). Moreover, even without an available political machine, an ethnic neighborhood with strong interactional ties could more readily develop community organizations (and community attachment) than will the sprawling and individuating housing developments of the sunbelt (Jacobs 1961; Markusen 1984). Moreover, the early urban political systems faced an immigration population that had little expectation of availing itself of an "exit" option if the neighborhood became unpalatable; this starkly contrasts with the apparently ready mobility of the sunbelt population. Thus, despite frostbelt and sunbelt cities' equal inability to assimilate urban newcomers into existing communities, community sentiment and community organization were more likely to arise in the latter than in the former setting.

Of course, community can be constructed in areas without preexisting identities as communities. According to Kasarda and Janowitz's (1974) path-breaking work, length of residence is the most important determinant of community attachment. So if sunbelt newcomers remain in their new homes, they may create communities—albeit with a bit more difficulty than the newcomers to the old industrial heartland's cities.

However, such community construction faces major barriers: actual and anticipated geographical mobility, and the private delivery of services. Rapid population change, in particular, militates against the interactions and attitudes necessary to community's emergence. Lee et al. (1984) stress the "political" roots of community associational life. Residents create community associations to influence city government to improve neighborhood conditions; these associations then increase the frequency of solidary interactions and thereby reinforce community sentiment.[2] However, we would argue that the creation of such community associations is more likely when residents believe that they are unlikely to move, and that such a belief may not be characteristic of the newcomer population of sunbelt cities. The greater the degree to which mobility is anticipated, the greater the "free rider" problem in the construction of community associations—and the less the likelihood of community construction. Further, lacking a basis of social ties, residents of such areas are less likely to overcome the cost of organization that poses such formidable barriers to "latent" groups' pursuit of collective goods (Olsen 1965). Finally, many new developments have some "condo" component—that is, a significant proportion of roads, services, and amenities are provided by a private association in which the residents purchase "citizenship." With such private production of previously public services, residents' associational energies may be exhausted in struggles to influence condo decision making. Largely private already, the area may remain politically and interactionally isolated from the rest of the city. The sense of "shared fate" may stop at the boundaries of the development.[3]

For these reasons, we suggest that sunbelt cities' politics will reflect the ascendancy of the market in the near future and perhaps indefinitely. Consequently, urban governments will have difficulty garnering the resources and authority necessary to produce public goods—ranging from coherent development policies to adequate roads and lighting. As they approach government, newcomer citizens will use "market values" to evaluate competing proposals for government action; in accord with these values, they will seek to minimize taxes and governmental interference in their private decision making. Therefore, *ceteris paribus*, the larger the proportion of a city's population that consists of newcomers who live in community-inhibiting settings, the greater the resistance to raising taxes for providing government services and the greater the support for cutting services as a method of dealing with fiscal problems.

In the next section, we describe the setting for our examination of the implications of the preceding argument; for a variety of reasons, the state of Florida is well-suited to be a starting point for empirical inquiry into these matters.

NATIVES AND NEWCOMERS IN A SUNBELT STATE: THE CASE OF FLORIDA

Analysis of urban politics in Florida provides a good initial test of our general approach to the relationship between community's extensity and the provision of public goods. Because we are examining a single state, many problems of cross-state comparisons are avoided. All Florida cities, for example, have council-manager plans, thus holding government structure constant for our entire sample. Further, state fiscal contributions to cities are all governed by the same statewide formula, thus simplifying our analysis.

In most respects Florida is a characteristic sunbelt state. As is true in the rest of the sunbelt, Florida's economy has grown at a much faster rate than that of the nation as a whole over the past 20 years. Its unemployment rate is significantly below the national average. Further, economic growth has been increasingly concentrated in those areas that have been projected to be the fastest growing areas in the American economy for the foreseeable future: electronics, service and retail trades, health care, real estate, and defense contracting. Thus, Florida's economic growth has come in the areas identified by Sale (1974) as the pillars of the southern rim. This growth has attracted large numbers of migrants in search of the job opportunities offered by Florida's rapid growth; in 1980, Florida's population growth was almost four times the national average (Fernald 1981:82), and its net migration rate in the past decade was 39.9%.

This rapid population change is likely to overwhelm existing networks of community associations that provide support for the provision of public goods via government. Further, for the reasons noted above, large numbers of newcomers, moving as individuals or nuclear families and living in newly created neighborhoods, are unlikely to quickly develop a sense of community or shared fate. Thus, rapid population change in Florida creates large numbers of newcomers with little attachment to the community or each other, who are unlikely to support increased provision of public goods by government. Rather, just as this population change is largely determined by the forces of market exchange—the "push" of declining job opportunities in the North and the "pull" of opportunities in the sunbelt—so too would we expect sunbelt city politics, more than politics in cities with more stable populations, to be shaped by market forces.

Interestingly, for the purposes of our analysis Florida has, in addition to great numbers of young job seekers, another large group of immigrants: retirees. Florida's climate has long attracted retirees from northern states (Fernald 1981:103). Two significant characteristics distinguish these migrants from their younger counterparts. First, they have moved to Florida solely because of its "pull" of a balmy climate and its image as a retirement playground. Further, they have not been uprooted from their existing communities by the forces of the market; their move is largely voluntary. Second, their pattern of settlement is remarkably similar to the immigrants of the early twentieth century: They live in ethnically homogenous settlements—albeit condominiums and trailer parks rather than neighborhoods and tenaments; moreover, their settlements are also age-homogenous. These settlements resemble the "natural communities" so frequently described but so rarely found in the study of the community: The overwhelming bulk of residents' interactional life is contained within the area; the area has a distinctive cultural identity; residents rarely leave, except to die.

Our analysis examines the responses of urban governments in Florida to fiscal problems posed by demands for increased services and decreased (or constant) taxes. Florida is an extremely low-taxing state. It ranks between 49 and 46 in per capita taxation, depending on the methods used to calculate tax rate. Nevertheless, the state has been the scene of much agitation aimed at reducing the tax burden.[4] At the same time, the growing population of the state has led to pressures to expand government services.

We would argue that as pressures mount on Florida cities to provide higher levels of services while cutting or not raising taxes, cities' responses will be shaped by two different sets of factors: demographic characteristics of the population and political culture of the city. The ability of governments to simply raise taxes in order to provide increased services will be determined by the rate of population change they experience and the proportion of newcomers who are retirees. As noted above, we believe that citizens' willingness to contribute to the production of public goods is a function of the degree to which they see themselves as members of a community with a shared set of economic and sentimental interests. Long-time residents and retirees are more likely to live in community-enhancing settings than are the market-responsive new migrants. Therefore, we would expect cities with large populations of retirees and/or slower rates of population change to be most likely to increase taxes in order to maintain present levels or secure higher levels of government services. Conversely, we would expect that rapid population growth would be most closely associated with resistance to tax increases and with support for cuts in city budgets.

Our predictions run contrary to Floridians' common wisdom about the origins of support for tax cutting in the state. Retirees and long-time residents are generally assumed to support reductions in tax burden and government services. It is often argued that retirees oppose raising taxes to pay for expanded government services: They live on fixed incomes; they believe that they have already supported the provision of public services in their former homes; they have no children in the schools; overall, they lack a long-run commitment to their new state. It is often argued that long-time residents, particularly native Floridians, oppose increased taxes to pay for expanded government services because, as part of a traditionalistic political culture of the South (Elazar 1972), they are accustomed to minimal government interference in their lives. Further, they are reportedly hostile to the hordes of newcomers whom they see as the primary causes of increasing taxes and expanding government. In contrast, those who move to Florida from more liberal and higher-taxing northern states are often viewed as the strongest source of support for increasing taxes to pay for expanding government services: They expect a higher level of government services than is available in Florida; they are used to paying a higher proportion of their income in taxes; they tend to have children, thus increasing their demands for quality public education. Nevertheless, for reasons outlined above, we believe that a very different pattern of support for and opposition to increased taxes and government will be revealed in our analysis of the taxing and spending behavior of Florida cities.

In addition, once the issue of increased taxation is resolved, we believe that a different set of factors is important for explaining the ways in which governments allocate scarce public funds. Especially in cities where raising taxes is precluded for the reasons we outline, government must still respond to the increasing demands for services generated by rapidly growing populations. Drawing on the work of Clark and Ferguson (1983), we examine the influence of political culture on the strategies adopted by cities in their allocation of increasingly scarce public funds.

Data

The data were gathered as part of a nationwide project on fiscal austerity that is coordinated by Terry Nichols Clark of the University of Chicago and involves researchers across the United States. The project has collected information on fiscal practices and political climates in all American cities with 1980 populations of 25,000 or more. This preliminary analysis, however, will focus only on the Florida data collected in the last half of 1983. At that time, we contacted the mayors, chief administrative officers, and a leading council member in all eligible cities; to each of these we sent one or more mailings of our questionnaire. We received responses from at least one of our target informants in all but three of the 45 eligible cities.

Dependent Variables. Cities can respond to fiscal problems in three basic ways: They can increase monies that flow in, they can decrease monies that flow out, or they can increase the efficiency with which they use the monies that are available. A wide range of strategies are available to meet these objectives. In all Florida cities, the chief administrative officer (CAO) was asked to rank the dollar importance of 33 strategies that are frequently reported in the literature on urban financial policy. These rankings are the basis for our dependent variables.[5]

We first look at the extent of a city's reliance on tax increases as a method of coping with fiscal problems: TAXES is indicated by the CAO's ranking of the dollar importance of that strategy over the past six years. A high score indicates heavy reliance on tax increases; a low score, little reliance.

Next we turn our attention to cost-cutting or program-cutting measures. We use two summary measures. The city's reliance on cost cutting is indicated by a weighted sum of the CAOs' responses to questions about the dollar importance of a broad range of tactics that reduce expenditures without eliminating functions (CUTBACK): cutting all departments; cutting least efficient departments; laying off personnel; decreasing administrative expenses; decreasing work force by attrition; decreasing expenditures for travel, equipment, and supplies; improving productivity with management techniques; improving productivity with labor-saving techniques; keeping increases below inflation levels; early retirements; reducing overtime; joint purchasing agreements.[6] The extent of a city's reliance on eliminating services (CUTFUNC) is indicated by a weighted sum of responses to questions about functional changes: selling assets, shifting responsibilities to other governments, contracting out services to other governments, contracting out services to the private sector, decreasing services funded with local revenues, decreasing services funded with intergovernmental revenues. For both CUTBACK and CUTFUNC, a high score indicates extensive use of the strategy. We also include a broad range of additional strategies that are not so readily categorized: alternative sources of local revenue and of intergovernmental revenue, increased user fees, lowered surpluses, deferred payments on loans, increased long- and short-term borrowing, decreased employee compensation, frozen wages and salaries, frozen hiring, decreased capital expenditures, joint purchasing agreements, deferred maintenance of capital stock, control of new construction. For all of these items, a high score means little or no use of this strategy. Table 1 reports the intercorrelations of the dependent variables.

Independent Variables[7] Two variables are directly relevant to our ar-

Table 1. Fiscal Management Strategies:
Zero-Order Correlations of Summary and Individual Items (N = 35)

	TAXES[1]	*CUTFUNC*[2]	*CUTBACK*[3]	*Local Revenue*[4]	*Intergov'l. Revenue*[5]	*Lower Surplus*	*Sell Assets*
TAXES	1.000	.212	.126	−.151	−.263	−.003	−.006
CUTFUNC	.212	1.000	.449	−.269	−.229	−.302	−.709
CUTBACK	.126	.449	1.000	−.655	−.637	−.324	−.276
Local Revenue	−.151	−.269	−.655	1.000	.505	.255	−.030
Intergov'l. Revenue	−.263	−.229	−.637	.505	1.000	.309	.212
Lower Surplus	−.003	−.302	−.324	.255	.309	1.000	.187
Sell Assets	−.006	−.709	−.276	−.030	.212	.187	1.000
Defer Payment	−.395	−.248	−.540	.267	.432	.076	.203
S.T. Loans	−.259	−.424	−.472	.352	.337	.295	.308
L.T. Loans	−.244	−.321	−.195	.177	.268	.597	.154
Cut Pay	.044	−.758	−.258	.004	−.042	.044	.656
Freeze Wages	−.338	−.521	−.530	.230	.371	.213	.429
Freeze Hiring	−.528	−.150	−.294	.240	.218	.032	−.005
Eliminate Programs	−.178	−.465	−.512	.430	.377	.180	.344
Defer Maintenance	−.137	−.597	−.465	.421	.326	.519	.540
Control Growth	−.255	−.284	−.525	.212	.491	.188	.342

[1]See footnote 6. For TAXES, CUTFUNC, and CUTBACK, a high score means a heavy reliance on the strategy. For the remainder, a high score means a low reliance on the strategy.
[2]See footnote 6.
[3]See footnote 6.
[4]"Seek new sources of local revenue."
[5]"Seek new sources of intergovernmental revenue."
[6]"Increase short-term borrowing."
[7]"Increase long-term borrowing."

gument. First, we use a measure of the cities' population change between 1970 and 1980: a logged ratio of the 1980 and 1970 population. The face validity of this indicator is supported by its strong zero-order correlation (−.63) with a measure of the proportion of city residents who were born in Florida; further support is provided by its strong zero-order correlation (.93) with a measure of the proportion of the city's housing stock that was built during the 1970s.

Second, we will use the cities' median age as an indicator of the size of their retiree populations. Median age has a zero order correlation of .94 with a measure of the proportion of the population over 65 but is available for more cities. The variable is normally distributed, and there are no substantial outliers.

We also examine the effect of political culture on the strategies adopted to cope with fiscal strain. As noted above, while we expect population characteristics to affect the ability of government to raise taxes, political culture is also expected to be an important determinant of the particular

Table 1. Continued

Defer Payment	*S.T. Loans*[6]	*L.T. Loans*[7]	*Cut Pay*	*Freeze Wages*	*Freeze Hiring*	*Eliminate Programs*	*Defer Maintenance*	*Control Growth*
−.395	−.259	−.244	.044	−.338	−.528	−.178	−.137	−.255
−.248	−.424	−.321	−.758	−.521	−.150	−.465	−.597	−.284
−.540	−.472	−.195	−.258	−.530	−.294	−.512	−.465	−.525
.267	.352	.177	.004	.230	.240	.430	.421	.212
.432	.337	.268	−.042	.371	.218	.377	.326	.491
.076	.295	.597	.044	.213	.032	.180	.519	.188
.203	.308	.154	.656	.429	−.005	.344	.540	.342
1.000	.770	.386	.144	.653	.427	.340	.198	.766
.770	1.000	.639	.206	.520	.211	.532	.385	.627
.386	.639	1.000	.046	.273	−.015	.343	.380	.484
.144	.206	.046	1.000	.296	−.015	.179	.402	.048
.653	.520	.273	.296	1.000	.490	.526	.460	.638
.427	.211	−.015	−.015	.490	1.000	.286	.107	.394
.340	.532	.343	.179	.526	.286	1.000	.564	.432
.198	.385	.380	.402	.460	.107	.564	1.000	.266
.766	.627	.484	.048	.638	.394	.432	.266	1.000

strategies adopted by politicians to allocate scarce tax dollars. Clark et al. (1984) constructed four indices of political culture (Democratic, Republican, Ethnic, New Fiscal Populist) by variously combining five dimensions of city decision makers' political beliefs. While we would have liked to use these indices, our pattern of missing data made it impossible. If we had used them, we would have faced a severe reduction in degrees of freedom. As an alternative strategy, we decided to examine the impact of each of the dimensions on the likelihood of a city's adopting particular fiscal strategies.

The first dimension of political culture is fiscal conservatism (FISCAL), a combination of mayors' responses to questions about spending preferences and tax burdens. The social liberalism dimension (SOCIAL), is a combination of mayors' responses to questions about gun control, sex education, and abortion. The third dimension taps beliefs about accountability to constituents (POPULISM), a combination of mayors' responses to questions about how often government responds favorably to individual citizens' spending demands and mayors' own beliefs about the propriety of taking positions unpopular with constituents. The fourth dimension (ORGN) measures governmental responsiveness to various organized groups. It is based upon mayors' responses to a series of questions about the frequency with which city government favorably responded to the spending preferences of 10 organized groups (public employee unions, low-income housing residents, homeowners' groups, neighborhood groups, civic groups, minority groups, taxpayer groups, business groups, the elderly, church and religious groups). A fifth dimension was designed to tap beliefs about the general desirability of providing public goods. It was based upon mayors' responses to a single question about the propriety of "breaking the rules" to provide the public good of "helping people." However, Clark et al. (1984:5) note that this item "is less than ideal." We were forced to drop this dimension from our analysis due to missing cases and lack of interpretability.

Cities' fiscal decisions are always made within the constraints of their past decisions' consequences. Therefore, we include an indicator of the extensity of each city's functional commitments; FUNC is the simple number of functions assumed by the municipality, logged for normalcy. Ideally, we would use a measure that weighted such functions by their importance (i.e., percentage of the budget allocated to each function). However, such a measure was not available for this analysis. Further, we include an indicator of the city's 1981 per capita expenditures (PCEXP), logged for normalcy.

Finally, cities' fiscal decisions are always made against a backdrop of urban needs. Unarguably, one significant indicator of need is the size of a city's population; urban population in 1980 (POP80) is therefore also included as a control. See Table 2 for the intercorrelation of the independent variables.

DATA ANALYSIS

Ordinary least-squares regression of TAXES on the first set of independent variables produces an R^2 of .32 and an adjusted R^2 of .19 (see Table 3).[8] The only significant coefficients to emerge are for population change and median age. The propensity to increase taxes to respond to fiscal problems is significantly and negatively affected by the amount of recent population change, and is significantly and positively affected by the city's median age.

This result supports our argument that rapid population change tends to militate against increasing taxes to provide for the provision of collective goods through government. Further, contrary to the common wisdom but consistent with our argument, we find that the presence of a substantial retiree population leads to greater reliance on increased taxation as a response to increased demands for the provision of public goods.

Note that the cities' present fiscal commitments (as indicated by its functional breadth and per capita expenditures) do not determine its taxing policies. Our indicator of need (1980 population) is similarly unimportant. Sociopolitical considerations matter; "objective" indicators of what the city does and what it needs don't seem to make a difference to its reliance on a taxing strategy.

Next, we rotated each of the set of political culture variables into the

Table 2. Intercorrelation Matrix of Independent Variables

	ETHNIC	*ORGI*	*POPULISM*	*SOCIAL*	*FISCAL*	*POP80*	*AGE*	*CHPOP*	*EXP*	*NFUNC*
ETHNIC	1.0000	−.6313 P = .03	.5568 P = .02	.1157 P = .34	.5416 P = .02	.2026 P = .23	−.4187 P = .06	−.4025 P = .08	.4058 P = .11	.5485 P = .02
ORGI	−.6313 P = .03	1.0000	−.6582 P = .01	.3310 P = .16	.0179 P = .48	−.3408 P = .11	.2408 P = .19	.2906 P = .16	−.3331 P = .15	−.6182 P = .01
POPULISM	.5568 P = .02	−.6582 P = .01	1.0000	.1681 P = .28	.2123 P = .18	.0378 P = .44	−.3310 P = .08	−.3892 P = .05	.2657 P = .16	.3441 P = .07
SOCIAL	.1157 P = .34	.3310 P = .16	.1681 P = .28	1.0000	−.2075 P = .22	−.2652 P = .16	.0996 P = .36	−.1323 P = .32	−.0132 P = .48	−.0826 P = .38
FISCAL	.5416 P = .02	.0179 P = .48	.2123 P = .18	−.2075 P = .22	1.0000	−.0832 P = .36	−.4076 P = .03	−.0458 P = .42	.1796 P = .24	.2866 P = .10
POP80	.2026 P = .23	−.3408 P = .11	.0378 P = .44	−.2652 P = .16	−.0832 P = .36	1.0000	−.2259 P = .10	−.2625 P = .07	.2463 P = .10	.6267 P = .01
AGE	−.4187 P = .06	.2408 P = .20	−.3310 P = .08	.0996 P = .36	−.4076 P = .0 3	−.2259 P = .10	1.0000	.5451 P = .01	−.4020 P = .01	−.5120 P = .01
CHPOP	−.4025 P = .08	.2906 P = .16	−.3892 P = .05	−.1323 P = .32	−.0458 P = eq .42	−.2625 P = .07	.5451 P = .01	1.0000	−.3550 P = .03	−.5365 P = .01
EXP	.4058 P = .11	−.3331 P = .15	.2657 P = .16	−.0132 P = .48	.1796 P = .24	.2463 P = .10	−.4020 P = .01	−.3550 P = .03	1.0000	.5906 P = .01
NFUNC	.5484 P = .02	−.6182 P = .01	.3441 P = .07	−.0826 P = .38	.2866 P = .10	.6267 P = .01	−.5120 P = .01	−.5365 P = .01	.5906 P = .01	1.0000

Table 3. Regression of TAXES on the Sociopolitical and Political Culture Variables (N = 35)

R^2/*adj.* R^2	*Standardized Partial Regression Coefficients*
.32/.19	−.54 CHPOP* +.51 AGE* −.14 EXP −.11 FUNC +.07 POP80
.33/.18	−.57 CHPOP* +.55 AGE* −.14 EXP −.16 FUNC +.005 POP80 +.12 FISCAL
.36/.22	−.55 CHPOP* +.51 AGE* −.15 EXP −.21 FUNC +.10 POP80) −.22 ORG1
.32/.17	−.53 CHPOP* +.53 AGE* −.14 EXP −.08 FUNC +.05 POP80 −.04 POPULISM
.40/.27	−.50 CHPOP* +.54 AGE* −.15 EXP −.25 NFUNC +.16 POP80) +.32 ETHNIC
.32/.18	−.56 CHPOP* +.52 AGE* −.14 EXP −.12 FUNC +.07 POP80 −.07 SOCIAL

* = significant at .01 or better.

set of independent variables that we regress on TAXES. (See Table 3.) Significant increments to R^2 were not produced by any of the political culture variables except the measure of the salience of religious and ethnic cleavages (ETHNIC). This serves to buttress our argument: The less important are these bases of cleavage in the community, the more likely that fiscal problems will be addressed by an increase in taxes. The bulk of the political culture variables, however, do not add to our ability to explain variation in the adoption of tax increases. An increase in taxes to deal with fiscal problems is such an easy solution that it is considered by decision makers in all political cultures. The acceptability of this solution is determined by the sociopolitical organization of the citizenry, not by the political culture of the city's decision-making elite. When the city has some of the characteristics of a community, decision makers are able to attain collective goods in the easiest of all possible ways: by levying a tax. As cities lose the characteristics of communities, decision makers must deal with an increasing inability to cope with fiscal problems through taxation. They must turn to alternative solutions.

Next, we regressed our sociopolitical and political culture variables on the remainder of the set of dependent variables: the two summary measures (CUTFUNC and CUTBACK) and 13 individual measures of the use of nontaxing strategies. Neither the population change nor the population age measures attained significant coefficients; the control variables (i.e., functional breadth, per capita expenditures, 1980 population) were similarly unimportant determinants of these alternative fiscal strategies. In general, any variance explained was a consequence of the political culture variables. In particular, the measure of mayoral social liberalism proved to be important. For example, the measure of social liberalism has the same significant and negative relationship to the measure of general budgetary cuts (CUTBACK) and to the measure of functional cuts (CUTFUNC): The greater the social liberalism of politicians, the less likely are

Table 4. Regression of CUTBACKS on the Sociopolitical and Political Culture Variables (N = 35)

R^2/adj. R^2	Standardized partial regression coefficients
.17/.02	.26 CHPOP +.30 AGE +.05 EXP +.33 NFUNC +.05 POP80
.18/.01	.21 CHPOP +.36 AGE +.05 EXP +.27 NFUNC +.10 POP80 +.16 FISCAL
.17/–.01	.26 CHPOP +.30 AGE +.04 EXP +.35 NFUNC +.05 POP80 +.04 ORG1
.21/.04	.32 CHPOP +.42 AGE +.05 EXP +.55 NFUNC –.04 POP80 –.27 POPULISM
.19/.02	.28 CHPOP +.32 AGE –.04 EXP +.25 NFUNC +.11 POP80 +.20 ETHNIC
.34/.21	.15 CHPOP +.36 AGE* +.06 EXP +.28 NFUNC +.04 POP80 –.44 SOCIAL*

* = significant at .01 or better.

budgetary or functional cuts. (See Tables 4 and 5.) Similarly, the greater the social liberalism of politicians, the less likely are pay cuts and wage freezes for city workers.

Overall, our results indicate that population characteristics only affect the propensity of government to raise taxes as a way to meet increasing demands for public goods via increased taxes. Apart from the issue of reliance on taxation, however, population characteristics do not affect the choice of alternative strategies for dealing with increased service demands. Consistent with the findings of Clark and Ferguson (1983) and Clark et al. (1984), our analysis indicates that urban political culture provides a set of "transformation rules" that affect the ways in which political systems perceive and respond to the limits set by social and economic characteristics of the city. Thus, factors external to the political system shape its ability to adopt a taxing strategy; factors internal to the political system determine its choice among the broad range of nontaxing strategies that are available to deal with fiscal problems.

Table 5. Regression of CUTFUNC on the Sociopolitical and Political Culture Variables (N = 35)

R^2/adj. R^2	Standardized partial regression coefficients
.10/–.05	.09 CHPOP –.05 AGE –.20 EXP +.46 NFUNC –.32 POP80
.13/–.06	.04 CHPOP +.02 AGE –.20 EXP +.39 NFUNC –.27 POP80 +.19 FISCAL
–.11/–.08	–.30 CHPOP –.05 AGE –.21 EXP +.41 NFUNC –.31 POP80 –.10 ORG1
.10/–.09	.07 CHPOP –.09 AGE –.20 EXP +.41 NFUNC –.30 POP80 –.06 POPULISM
.12/–.06	.11 CHPOP –.04 AGE –.20 EXP +.39 NFUNC –.27 POP80 +.17 ETHNIC
.42/.30	–.06 CHPOP +.03 AGE –.18 EXP +.39 NFUNC –.34 POP80 –.58 SOCIAL*

* = significant at .01 or better.

To this point, the data analysis seems to support our model. However, it is prudent to examine the major alternative explanation for our findings. Slow-growing cities may be poor cities and may therefore have weaker tax bases and a larger dependent population than do cities that have grown rapidly. In such a situation, tax increases might be forced by the magnitude of urban problems and the demands of a large dependent population. However, the data do not support this alternative explanation. First, there is no evidence that slower growing cities are poorer cities. The zero-order correlation between population change and the proportion of families below the poverty line is a nonsignificant −.10. Second, there is no relationship between our measure of population change and CAOs' reports of the extent of problems with the city's tax base ($r = -.24$).[9] Moreover, a general index of the number and extent of the city's fiscal problems has no significant relationship to population change (.17).[10] Additionally, this measure has insignificant correlations with our dependent variables, suggesting that these policy outcomes are not narrowly determined by cities' "needs." Therefore, there is little evidence that slower growing cities are poorer cities or are cities with more fiscal problems. Moreover, we find additional evidence that fiscal problems do not lead automatically to strategic responses. Rather, perception and response are mediated by a series of social and political factors. Overall, then, we find a pattern of support for the implications of our argument and we find little support for alternative explanations of our findings.

CONCLUSIONS

In this paper, we began the task of investigating the impact that migration is likely to have on the governance of sunbelt cities. We suggested that such migration, driven by market forces, is likely to result in a style of sunbelt city politics dominated by norms of market exchange. Such a political style is likely to reduce government's ability to tax for the purposes of providing public goods and services.

This paper has launched an investigation of the degree to which new migrants to the sunbelt have been—and will be—able to construct communities that will limit the dominance of market values. We have found that cities with community-enhancing characteristics—such as slow rates of population growth, in-migrant communities that resemble northern cities' "urban villages"—are more likely to use tax increases than are the more market-dominated boomtown communities. Market-dominated cities have community-inhibiting characteristics: rapid population growth, a younger population of individuated migrants who move to heterogeneous residential areas, greater use as "bedroom" communities. In such cities, we found a greater reluctance to increase taxes—despite Florida's generally low tax rates and woefully inadequate city services. Our findings, while preliminary, offer support for our argument. If confirmed by further analysis, they could have important implications for the study of the social and political organization of high-growth states.

Much of the sociological literature suggests that, as length of residence increases, individuals tend to create communities in new areas. Our findings may be simply an artifact of the recency of population growth in Florida. If this is so, then eventually we will find greater convergence between urban political systems in the snowbelt and sunbelt cities. However, for a variety of reasons, these differences may be more enduring than the extant literature would predict. First, patterns of housing development (i.e., privately supplied services, layout) in newer cities may make the creation of community difficult (Jacobs 1961). Second, newcomers' expected and actual mobility may make it unlikely that they will develop sufficient stake in a particular area to sacrifice short-run individual self-interest for longer run collective interests. In Hirschman's (1970) terms, as "loyalty" to an area declines, "exit" will become a much more modal citizen response than "voice." In such a case, urban government may develop and maintain a very different style in the growing sunbelt states than it evolved in the older industrial states. We plan to explore these questions more fully in our future work.

ACKNOWLEDGMENTS

A revised version of a paper prepared for presentation at the 1984 meetings of the Midwest Sociological Society, Chicago, Illinois. Please do not quote or cite without permission.

The authors thank the FAU/FIU Joint Center for this Study of Environmental and Urban Problems for its support of this research. We thank Terry N. Clark, Lance DeHaven-Smith, and Bruce London for their helpful comments on earlier drafts.

NOTES

1. We may also speak of the size of a person's rent as a way in which his or her economic status is bound up in the place of residence. Renters, as well as homeowners, may mobilize to advance their interests in a residential area.

2. We would argue that Lee et al.'s (1984) use of "political" is a bit of a misnomer. In their article, they are referring to neighborhoods' use of community associations to seek to persuade city government to improve neighborhood conditions. If an area has a large proportion of homeowners, such activity is as aptly labeled "economic" (or "sustenance") as "political": It identifies and defends homeowners' collective economic interests in the preservation and increase of what (for most of them) is their sole bit of wealth.

3. The "going private" of previously public services is a theme that we will be pursuing in future research. Many of the large PUDs (planned unit developments) that cover the

sunbelt have effectively supplanted city government: For a monthly "maintenance" or "membership" fee, they provide police protection, recreational amenities, parks, zoning ordinances and appeals boards, street signs and lights, etc. Under these circumstances, residents have no incentive to support city service delivery in any of these functional areas. After all, *their* needs are adequately provided by their development.

4. If the state supreme court had not ruled that its wording was unconstitutional, last November's ballot would have presented a stringent amendment to the state's constitution that would roll back government revenues to their 1980–81 levels and limit future increases to 2/3 of the inflation rate. This amendment is uniformly regarded as much more severe than California's Proposition 13.

5. Each city's chief administrative officer was given a list of 33 strategies for dealing with fiscal problems. S/he was asked to "please indicate the importance, in dollars, of each strategy (since January 1978)." For TAXES, we use CAO ranking (on a five point scale) of the importance of the strategy "Increase taxes."

6. Although responses to these items are highly intercorrelated, varimax rotation of a principal factor analysis of the set of 12 items suggests two general factors. One factor includes items unlikely to stir spirited intragovernmental conflict: to introduce labor-saving devices; to improve productivity through better management techniques; to peg expenditure increases to inflation; to save money through joint purchasing agreements; to reduce expenditures for supplies, equipment, and travel. A second factor involves items more likely to arouse controversy because, although they do not involve a service's elimination, they affect the pocketbooks of many government workers: the imposition of across-the-board cuts in all departments, cutting the budgets of the least efficient departments, laying off personnel, early retirement, reduction of overtime, the shifting of responsibilities to other units of government. Together, these factors account for roughly 3/4 of the variance in this set of variables; their ready interpretability assures us, in the absence of a sufficient number of cases to permit factor analysis of the entire set of 33 items, that we have not constructed an untrustworthy scale.

7. With the exception of FUNC and the political culture variables, all of the variables in this analysis are drawn from the 1983 County/City Data Book, Table C. FUNC, which is logged for the analysis, is constructed by counting those functional areas for which a city had service responsibility in 1977; the functional area data is from the U.S. Bureau of the Census (1977). In the regression analyses, we have used the conservative practice of substituting variables' means for their missing value.

8. Adjusted R^2 is a conservative estimate of the proportion of explained variance; it adjusts for the number of cases in the analysis (Pedhazur 1983:147–149).

9. CAOs were given a list of 11 possible sources of urban fiscal problems and asked, "In the last three years, how important have each of the following problems been for your city's finances?" Each possible problem source was ranked on a five-point scale of importance. The variable to which the text refers was based on the CAOs' ranking of the importance of the problem of a "declining tax base."

10. This scale of the extent of the city financial problems is a simple weighted sum of CAOs' responses to the above-cited question about 11 possible sources of urban fiscal problems: loss of federal revenue; loss of state revenue; inflation; unemployment; declining tax base; rising service demands from citizens; state tax, revenue, or expenditure limits; pressure from local taxpayers to reduce taxes and spending; failure of bond referenda; mandated costs from federal and state governments; pressures from municipal employees. Each possible problem source was ranked on a five-point scale of importance.

REFERENCES

Banfield, Edward C. 1961. *Political Influence*. New York: The Free Press.

Banfield, Edward C., and James O. Wilson. 1963. *City Politics*. New York: Vintage Books.

Bish, Robert L. 1971. *The Public Economy of Metropolitan Areas*. Chicago: Markham.
Bluestone, Barry, and Bennett Harrison. 1982. *The Deindustrialization of America*. New York: Basic Books.
Clark, Terry Nichols, Margaret Burg, and Martha Diaz Villegas de Landa. 1984. "Urban Political Cultures and Fiscal Austerity Strategies." Paper presented at the 1984 Annual Meeting of the American Political Science Association, Washington, D.C.
Clark, Terry Nichols, and Lorna Crowley Ferguson. 1983. *City Money: Political Processes, Fiscal Strain, and Retrenchment*. New York: Columbia University Press.
Dahl, Robert A. 1956. *A Preface to Democratic Theory*. Chicago: University of Chicago Press.
———. 1961. *Who Governs?* New Haven, Conn.: Yale University Press.
Douglas, Mary, and Aaron Wildavsky. 1982. *Risk and Culture*. Berkely: University of California Press.
Downs, Anthony. 1960. "Why the Government Budget Is Too Small in a Democracy," *World Politics* 12:541-563.
Elazar, Daniel, J. 1972. *American Federalism*. New York: Thomas Y. Crowell Co.
Engels, Friedrich. 1962. *The Condition of the Working Class in England in 1844*. London: Almeyer.
Feagin, Joe R. 1984. "Sunbelt Metropolis and Development Capital: Houston in the Era of Late Capitalism." In *Sunbelt/Snowbelt*, ed. Larry Sawers and William K. Tabb. New York: Oxford University Press.
Fernald, Edward A., ed. 1981. *Atlas of Florida*. Tallahassee: Florida State University Foundation, Inc.
Gans, Herbert. 1962. *The Urban Villagers*. New York: Free Press.
Glazer, Nathan, and Daniel P. Moynihan. 1970. *Beyond the Melting Pot*. Cambridge, Mass.: The M.I.T. Press.
Greer, Scott. 1962. *The Emerging City: Myth and Reality*. New York: Free Press.
Harvey, David. 1973. *Social Justice and the City*. Baltimore: The Johns Hopkins University Press.
Hirschman, Albert O. 1970. *Exit, Voice, and Loyalty*. Cambridge, Mass.: Harvard University Press.
Hunter, Albert. 1975. "The Loss of Community: An Empirical Test through Replication," *American Sociological Review* 40:537–552.
Jacobs, Jane. 1961. *The Death and Life of Great American Cities*. New York: Vintage Books.
Janowitz, Morris. 1951. *The Community Press in an Urban Setting*. Chicago: University of Chicago Press.
Janowitz, Morris, and David Street. 1978. "Changing Social Order of the Metropolitan Area." In *Handbook of Contemporary Urban Life*, ed. David Street and associates. San Francisco: Jossey-Bass.
Kasarda, John D., and Morris Janowitz. 1974. "Community and Attachment in Mass Society," *American Sociological Review* 39:328–339.
Katznelson, Ira. 1982. *City Trenches*. New York: Pantheon Books.
Lee, Barrett A., R. S. Oropesa, Barbara J. Metch, and Avery M. Guest. 1984. "Testing the Decline-of-Community Thesis: Neighborhood Organizations in Seattle, 1929 and 1979," *American Journal of Sociology* 89:1161–1188.
Lewis, Eugene. 1973. *The Urban Politic System*. Hinsdale, Ill.: The Dryden Press.
Lindblom, Charles E. 1977. *Politics and Markets*. New York: Basic Books.
Mandelbaum, Seymour J. 1965. *Boss Tweed's New York*. New York: John Wiley and Sons.
Markusen, Ann R. 1984. "Class and Urban Social Expenditure: A Marxist Theory of Metropolitan Government." In *Marxism and the Metropolis*, ed. William K. Tabb and Larry Sawers. New York: Oxford University Press.
Merton, Robert K. 1968. *Social Theory and Social Structure*. New York: Free Press.

Olsen, Mancur. 1965. *The Logic of Collective Action*. Cambridge, Mass.: Harvard University Press.

Ostrom, Vincent. 1973. *The Intellectual Crisis in Public Administration*. University: University of Alabama Press.

Park, Robert E., and Ernest W. Burgess. 1921. *Introduction to the Science of Sociology*. Chicago: University of Chicago Press.

Park, Robert E., Earnest W. Burgess, and Robert D. McKenzie, eds. 1925. *The City*. Chicago: University of Chicago Press.

Pedhazur, Elazar. 1982. Multiple Regression in Behavioral Research. New York: Holt, Rinehart and Winston.

Perry, David C., and Alfred J. Watkins, eds. 1977. *The Rise of the Sunbelt Cities*. Beverly Hills, Calif.: Sage Publications.

Polanyi, Karl. 1944. *The Great Transformation*. New York: Rinehart and Co.

Polsby, Nelson W. 1963. *Community Power and Democratic Theory*. New Haven, Conn: Yale University Press.

Ricci, David M. 1971. *Community Power and Democratic Theory*. New York: Random House.

Sale, Kirkpatrick. 1974. *Power Shift: The Rise of the Southern Rim and Its Challenge to the Eastern Establishment*. New York: Random House.

Sawers, Larry, and William K. Tabb, eds. 1984. *Sunbelt/Snowbelt*. New York: Oxford University Press.

Sayre, Wallace S., and Herbert Kaufman. 1960. *Governing New York City: Politics in the Metropolis*. New York: Russell Sage Foundation.

Suttles, Gerald D. 1972. *The Social Construction of Communities*. Chicago: University of Chicago Press.

Thomas, W. I., and Florian Zaniecki. 1958. *The Polish Peasant in America*. New York: Dover.

Tonnies, Ferdinand. 1957. *Community and Society*. trans. Charles P. Loomis. East Lansing: Michigan State University Press.

U.S. Bureau of the Census. 1977. *Census of the Governments: Government Finances*. Washington, D.C.: Government Printing Office.

———. 1983. *County/City Data Book*. Washington, D.C.: Government Printing Office.

Warner, Sam Bass, Jr. 1968. *The Private City*. Philadelphia: University of Pennsylvania Press.

———. 1972. *The Urban Wilderness*. New York: Harper and Row.

Williamson, Oliver. 1975. *Markets and Hierarchies*. New York: Free Press.

Wirth, Louis. 1938. "Urbanism as a Way of Life," *American Journal of Sociology* 44:3–24.

Yates, Douglas. 1977. *The Ungovernable City*. Cambridge, Mass.: The M.I.T. Press.

ECONOMIC DEVELOPMENT POLICY AND COMMUNITY CONFLICT:
A COMPARATIVE ISSUES APPROACH

Paul Schumaker, John M. Bolland, and Richard C. Feiock

ABSTRACT

The formulation of municipal policies concerning 12 recent economic development issues in Lawrence, Kansas, is examined to test hypotheses about the composition of pro-growth and anti-growth coalitions and about the relationships between coalitional characteristics and policy outcomes. Although the characteristics of pro-growth and anti-growth actors generally conform to the models developed by Mollenkopf and others, significant variation in coalition characteristics across issues is found. Pro-growth coalitions are most successful when they are led by a mayor acting as a developmental entrepreneur and when the pro-growth coalition is composed primarily of upper-stratum actors. But pro-growth coalitions are likely to be defeated when these conditions are absent and when large anti-growth coalitions are mobilized, expanding the scope of conflict. These results provide elaborations upon prevailing theories that stress the importance of "political entrepreneurs" and the presence of "systemic bias" in community conflict over economic development policies.

City governments have a strong interest in promoting economic development in order to generate jobs, increase tax revenues without increasing

Research in Urban Policy, Vol. 2, pages 25–46.

ISBN: 0-89232-534-8

taxes or tax rates, and thus enhance the quality of municipal services. But whether or not economic growth constitutes a "unitary interest" of the city has been a subject of recent debate among urban scholars (e.g., Peterson 1981; Fainstein et al. 1983). Most economic growth policies, especially those involving the development of a city's export economy, no doubt have consequences, due to the multiplier effect, that serve the public interest understood in utilitarian terms. However, it is also clear that many economic development policies have adverse consequences that are contrary to the interests of some residents and thus prompt their mobilization; these adverse effects include residential displacement, environmental stress, and the opportunity costs associated with investing in capital goods rather than in social consumption. As a result, policies seeking to promote economic development usually generate extensive conflict within communities.

Such conflict is the focus of this paper. In part 1 we argue that prevailing models of community conflict concerning economic development policies are suggestive of general, or modal, tendencies; but these models fail to observe the presence within communities of extensive variations in the compositions of pro-growth and anti-growth (or slow-growth) coalitions and in policy decisions. In part 2 a methodology is outlined facilitating a comparison of coalitional characteristics and policy outcomes across a small sample of economic development issues within Lawrence, Kansas. In part 3 the modalities and the variations in coalitional characteristics for 12 economic development issues in Lawrence, are presented. In part 4, variances in the characteristics of pro-growth and anti-growth coalitions are related to policy outcomes. These results are then discussed in terms of their implications for conflict theory and for the theories of "political entrepreneurship" and of "systemic bias," which are widely cited descriptions and explanations of economic development policy outcomes.

PREVAILING VIEWS ABOUT COMMUNITY CONFLICT ON ECONOMIC DEVELOPMENT

Building on the earlier foundations of Dahl (1961), Williams and Adrian (1963), Salisbury (1964), and others, the theoretical literature on community conflict surrounding economic development policies has expanded dramatically during the past 10 years. (See, for example, Wolfinger, 1974; Mollenkopf 1975, 1983; Molotch 1976; Stone 1976, 1980; Peterson 1981; Trounstine and Christensen 1982; Fainstein et al. 1983; Fosler and Berger 1983; Jones, Bachelor, and Wilson 1986.) Two general types of questions have been particularly addressed in this literature: (1) What types of actors are most likely to support or oppose economic growth policies? Or, more generally, what are the characteristics of pro-growth and anti-growth (or slow-growth) coalitions within communities? (2) Which types of actors usually win in community struggles over economic development? Why? And under what conditions do anti-growth forces succeed in halting economic growth projects?

Perhaps the most ambitious effort to define the "city trenches" (Katznelson 1981) or "fault lines" (Fainstein et al. 1983) dividing communities over economic development policies is that of Mollenkopf (1983), who suggests a relatively universal pattern of pro-growth and anti-growth actors. Believing that economic growth constitutes a collective good and contributes to electoral success, mayors and other elected officials take the initiative in creating a pro-growth coalition. (See also Dahl 1961; Salisbury 1964). Public administrators also play a key entrepreneurial role in pro-growth coalitions, for they view economic growth as a necessary means of enhancing revenues and thus enhancing program budgets (Claggett 1983). Local business interests—including bankers, downtown merchants, realtors, and newspapers—all see the opportunity for increased trade in economic growth and are generally active participants in pro-growth coalitions (Morlock 1974). Public-sector employees tend to view wage increases as dependent on increased tax revenues generated by economic growth, and they may also participate actively. In addition, middle-class residents, especially those living in newer neighborhoods, who are insulated from the costs of economic development but dependent on its benefits to achieve upward mobility, are likely to be mobilized in support of economic development. These diverse actors are normally mobilized in support of growth policies by the Democratic Party in large cities and by the Republican Party in suburbs and middle-sized communities.

In contrast, anti-growth forces are generally led by neighborhood organizations and ad hoc protest groups composed of displaced blacks and ethnics as well as other interests threatened by specific economic development programs. In addition, ecologically oriented upper-middle-class professionals are often mobilized in an anti-growth coalition (Fainstein et al. 1983).

While this descriptive model of pro-growth and anti-growth coalitions may hold in many cases, its limitations have been implicitly suggested by Clark and Ferguson (1983), who find that cities vary dramatically in their political cultures and thus in the kinds of actors involved in and supportive of various economic and budgetary policies. The detailed case studies of urban redevelopment in specific cities provided by Fainstein et al. (1983), Fosler and Berger (1982), and Fleishman and Feagen (1985) reinforce this notion of significant cross-community variations in the patterns of community conflict on growth policies. Even within communities, specific economic development issues can spawn conflicts within the business community or within the middle class, between core and peripheral areas or neighborhoods of the city, between groups seeking capital accumulation and those wishing social consumption, and even among lower-income neighborhoods (Fainstein and Fainstein 1983:255). If there is such great diversity of cleavages within communities on economic development issues, caution must be exercised against overgeneralizing about the characteristics of pro-growth and anti-growth coalitions. Simple models depicting conflict on urban economic policy as involving business interests versus neighborhood interests may be theoretically limited and thus provide a faulty guide to political action.

In response to the question, "Who wins on development issues?" Stone (1980) has suggested the presence of "systemic bias" in favor of pro-growth interests, due to the dependence of public officials on the resources, status, and organizational involvements of upper-stratum, pro-growth actors.

Just as one can concede Mollenkopf's modal pattern of community conflict, one can concede Stone's depiction of the modal pattern of policy outcomes. Yet policy outcomes, like coalitional characteristics, exhibit important variations. It can be argued, for example, that economic development policies may sometimes fail without the support of various types of actors considered to be influential by alternative models of community power: elected officials (Eulau and Eyestone 1968; Dahl 1961), public administrators (Lineberry 1977; Newton 1976), private elites (Hunter 1953; Domhoff 1983), policy activists (Verba and Nie 1972; Zeigler and Tucker 1978:5-7), interest and protest groups (Lowi 1979; Yates 1977), and voters (Hoffman 1976; Clark and Ferguson 1983).

To achieve the necessary support of such actors, the presence of a "policy entrepreneur" may be crucial (Eyestone 1978; Mollenkopf 1983). Salisbury (1964) and Jones, Bachelor, and Wilson (1986) suggest that mayors are in a strategic position to act as entrepreneurs and lead pro-growth coalitions because of their base of electoral support and ability to mobilize public opinion through their control of information, their central positions in the networks of communication between public and private interests, their control over the professional planning bureaucracies, and their capacity to mobilize private and public—including state and federal—resources. Salisbury (1964) and Claggett (1983) suggest that a city manager may also be able to play the role of policy entrepreneur, although Jones, Bachelor, and Wilson (1986) suggests that the manager is much more restricted in this role. In short, economic development initiatives may fail in the absence of a supportive and strong mayor or, perhaps, city manager.

If pro-growth forces can fail when adequate leadership is lacking, anti-growth forces may be able to overcome systemic bias under certain conditions. For example, both Mollenkopf (1983) and Fainstein and Fainstein (1983: 258-268) argue that anti-growth forces were more successful in the 1970s than either previously or subsequently. And Henig (1982) suggests that successful neighborhood mobilization can occur, especially under such conditions as cultural homogeneity, the presence of preexisting neighborhood organizations, and a competitive balance of power within a community.

In general, a neopluralist perspective (Manley 1983) on community conflict would suggest that both pro-growth and anti-growth coalitions have a variety of potential resources available to them, and the resolution of specific issues is strongly influenced by the ability of each side to mobilize these resources. However, the most critical resources needed by each side are only vaguely suggested in the literature. As suggested above, the success of pro-growth coalitions seems to depend upon the leadership of "policy entrepreneurs" and the presence of upper-stratum actors. For anti-growth coalitions, however, the critical resources may be different. According to conflict theory, relatively disadvantaged groups must expand the scope of conflict to be successful (Schattschneider 1960), mobilizing the support of other influential "third parties" (Lipsky 1970) and public opinion (Schumaker 1975). Building a large and diverse coalition against the project through legitimate means of public protest may thus be critical to the success of anti-growth forces (Gamson 1975:51).

In short, prevailing models of community conflict provide useful depictions of the type of actors that generally support or oppose economic development policies and useful descriptions and explanations of policy outcomes. But they do not adequately relate coalitional patterns to policy outcomes. In this paper, we expand on these models by testing the following four hypotheses dealing with coalitional patterns and with the relationships between coalitional characteristics and economic development policy outcomes.

Hypothesis 1: The composition of pro-growth and anti-growth coalitions follow *general* patterns defined by the positions, attitudes, and demographic characteristics of their members. Pro-growth coalitions typically attract members with the following characteristics:

a. elected officials
b. public administrators
c. local business interests and private elites
d. upper-status activists
e. residents of newer neighborhoods having higher property values
f. public sector employees
g. Republicans, at least in medium-sized communities.

Hypothesis 2: Despite these *general* patterns, there will be large variations in the composition of pro-growth and anti-growth coalitions on specific economic development issues. There will be little overlap in coalitional membership across issues within a community, and, as a result, the dominant cleavages will vary across issues.

Hypothesis 3: The outcomes of economic development policies depend on the distribution of support for the project provided by several types of actors. The preferences and participation of public officials (especially mayors and city managers) and of issue-specific activists shape economic growth policies. But the preferences of broader publics are also important.

Hypothesis 4: The composition, hierarchical structure, and size of coalitions affect their success in achieving desired outcomes. Pro-growth coalitions are more successful when they are composed of a homogeneous group of upper-stratum actors. Anti-growth forces are more successful when they have heirarchical (i.e., centralized) leadership structures and when they are large.

TWELVE ECONOMIC DEVELOPMENT ISSUES IN LAWRENCE, KANSAS

This study is based on 12 economic development issues that have arisen and required policy decisions by the city commission during the past five years in Lawrence, Kansas. In addition to its convenience, Lawrence was selected because of its relatively liberal political culture (Schumaker 1984a:7) and its reformed institutions. According to prevailing theory, reformed institutions (principally the city management form of government with nonpartisan, at-large elections) are relatively responsive to business and other pro-growth interests (Banfield and Wilson 1963; Morlock 1974). However, the presence of a broad commitment to liberal values within a community might be thought to serve as a counterforce to reformed institutions, providing a receptive climate to anti-growth actors. The countervailing tendencies of reformed institutions and of a liberal political culture might thus provide a context where neither pro-growth nor anti-growth forces consistently prevail, resulting in considerable variation in the degree of success by pro-growth actors on economic policy issues.

This research is part of a larger study that examines the preferences of various community actors (e.g., elected representatives, administrative officials, private elites, various kinds of organized groups, activists, and voters) and the pressures these actors have exerted to influence policy outcomes on 30 community issues (Schumaker 1984b). Issues were selected for this larger sample because they were concrete manifestations of seven abstract policy concepts and because they exhibited diverse levels of controversy—thus avoiding the problems discussed by Bachrach and Baratz

(1962) of selecting only "key issues" (Schumaker 1984b:13). Two of these abstract concepts concern distributive policies and regulatory policies affecting economic development:

1. The Distributive Policy issue [SUBSIDY]: Should local government provide tax incentives, services, and other inducements to attract new industry to the community?
2. The Regulatory Policy Issue [LANDUSE]: Should property owners have the right to develop their land in accordance with market forces despite potentially adverse effects on neighborhoods and others in the community?

Of our original 30 issues, 13 appeared to be strong concrete manifestations of these two abstract policy concepts (Schumaker, 1984a:14). One of these issues has not yet been resolved, leaving 12 issues for analysis in this report. Each of these issues was selected prior to its policy decision being known, thus diminishing the chance of a biased sample. In Table I, these issues are listed along with data about the type of abstract concept they embody, their outcomes, and some characteristics about the pro-growth and anti-growth coalitions that developed around them.

For each issue, data were gathered concerning the preferences of elected and administrative officials, private elites, activists, and citizens, and the involvements of interest groups, protest groups, and task forces. Citizen preferences on the issues were derived from citizen surveys conducted during the springs of 1980, 1982, and 1984. The following sample sizes were obtained: for 1980, n = 532; for 1982, n = 269; and for 1984, n = 406.

Data on activists, private elites, and groups were obtained from 203 telephone and personal interviews, mostly conducted between July 1983 and June 1984. We began with three lists as the basis for these interviews: (1) those persons, other than formal decision makers, mentioned as active in our issues by newspaper accounts or minutes of meetings, (2) those heads of community groups possibly being involved in governmental issues, and (3) the 100 persons ranked as most influential in a modified reputational study of Lawrence (Bolland 1984). Over 600 persons were contacted about their involvement and less than 5 percent refused interviews. However, many persons, especially group leaders and private elites, were not ultimately included in our sample, as they claimed no or very little involvement on our issues.

Respondents were asked standard questions about their socioeconomic backgrounds, their broad philosophical orientations toward local government, and their organizational affiliations. Then, they were asked to describe their involvement on each issue in our sample and, if active, to estimate their success. On the basis of these responses, further questions

Table I. Twelve Economic Development Issues in Lawrence, Kansas. Outcomes and Some Coalitional Characteristics

	Abstract Issue type	*Outcome*	*Pro-Growth Coalition*		*Anti-Growth Coalition*	
			SIZE	*HIERARCHY*	*SIZE*	*HIERARCHY*
1. Development of Cornfield Mall (CORN)	LANDUSE	13	20	.371	38	.304
2. Development of JVJ Downtown Mall (JVJ)	LANDUSE SUBSIDY	15	22	.405	53	.350
3. Development of Sizeler Downtown Mall (SZLR)	LANDUSE SUBSIDY	13	28	.426	23	.504
4. Down-zoning in Oread Neighborhood (OREAD)	LANDUSE	39	22	.496	25	.452
5. Down-zoning in East Lawrence (EAST)	LANDUSE	14	23	.226	22	.468
6. The Bluffs Development (BLUFF)	LANDUSE	30	16	.468	18	.367
7. Develop Rail-Served Industrial Park (RAIL)	LANDUSE SUBSIDY	15	55	.378	20	.527
8. Develop Research Office Park (TECH)	LANDUSE SUBSIDY	49	51	.373	7	.300
9. Authorization of IRBs to Competing Firms (IRB)	SUBSIDY	35	24	.288	32	.205
10. Build Parking Lot at 600 Masasachusetts (PARK)	LANDUSE	50	11	.533	35	.413
11. Improve Airport (AIR)	SUBSIDY	47	24	.195	10	.091
12. Improve North 2nd St. (N2ST)	SUBSIDY	37	22	.498	6	0

were asked about those issues in which the respondent was most involved. During this battery of questions, activists were asked to indicate their principal allies and opponents on each issue, enabling us to determine the composition of both pro-growth and anti-growth coalitions. Activists were also asked if they acted as individuals or as members of a group on each issue. If interviewees indicated a group involvement, they were asked a variety of questions about group goals, activity, stability, size, cohesion, leadership, and membership.

Thirty-six elected and administrative officials were also interviewed in May and June 1984, with a 100 percent response rate being achieved.

Among other matters, officials were asked about their preferences and involvements in each issue, their justifications for personal and collective decisions, their perceptions of activist and audience (public) preferences, and their views of those individuals and groups most influential on each issue.

Measures of policy outcomes [OUTCOME in Table I] on each issue area were derived from both official and activist interviews. The success of pro-growth forces is conceptualized as a continuous variable ranging between 10 and 50. If all pro-growth proponents agreed that they were highly successful and all opponents agreed that they were highly unsuccessful, an outcome score of 50 was assigned. If all pro-growth proponents agreed that they were highly unsuccessful and all opponents agreed that they were highly successful, an outcome score of 10 was assigned. If proponents and opponents of economic growth had equal aggregated success scores, the intermediate outcome score (30) was assigned. The outcome scores of activists and public officials were highly correlated ($r = .95$), lending validity to OUTCOME. Our summary OUTCOME measures reported in Table I are the average scores derived from official and activist perceptions.[1]

For each of these issues, we have obtained measures of the following factors hypothesized to effect economic development policy OUTCOMES:

A. *The aggregated "net" preferences* of elected representatives [REPS], public administrators [ADMINS], private elites [ELITES], issue-specific activists [ACTIVES], and VOTERS. The net preference score for each type of actor on each issue is simply the percentage of persons holding unambiguous anti-growth positions subtracted from the percentage of persons holding unambiguous pro-growth positions.

B. *The "pressure"* exerted by previously organized interest groups [PERMGRP], ad hoc issue-specific protest groups [PROTEST], and issue-specific task forces [TASK]. Group support scores are based not only on the position of involved groups, but also the "pressure" each group has exerted in pursuit of its position. In other words, group demands were weighted, such that a large, highly involved, high-resource group would exert more pressure than a small, marginally involved, low-resource group.[2] Measures of net demands by various types of groups within each issue area were then calculated by subtracting pressure scores of anti-growth groups from pressure scores of pro-growth groups.

C. *Pro-growth and anti-growth coalition characteristics*. Data on the size, composition, and hierarchy of both pro-growth and anti-growth coalitions on each issue were generated from the interview data with activists and public officials. To determine "membership" in an issue-specific pro-growth coalition, we included all activists and officials indicating a pro-growth position, all persons identified by public officials as influential in supporting growth, all persons mentioned by pro-growth activists as their supporters, and all persons mentioned by anti-growth activists as their opponents. In a similar manner, we identified members of anti-growth coalitions on each issue. The SIZE of pro-growth and anti-growth coalitions is simply the number of persons so identified. The HIERARCHY of each coalition—indicating the extent to which visibility within the coalition is concentrated within a few persons or diffused among many persons—was determined using interval-level measures of reputed involvement. Each person in a coalition was given a score of reputed involvement equal to the number of times that person was mentioned by others as an influential or important supporter of the pro-growth (or anti-growth) position. Gini coefficients were then calculated for inequality of involvement.[3] To the extent that persons in a coalition are equally cited, a low gini coefficient was obtained, indicating a nonhierarchical or diffused coalition structure. To the extent that a few persons in a coalition were frequently cited while others were seldom cited, a high gini coefficient was obtained indicating a hierarchical or concentrated coalition structure.

Demographic and attitudinal data from interviewed coalition members were used to determine the characteristics of pro-growth and anti-growth coalitions in each issue. The following characteristics of coalition members are reported here: (1) socioeconomic status [SES], (2) mean property values of homes in their neighborhoods [PROPVAL], (3) self-reported ideological orientations [LIBCON], and (4) party identification [DEMREP]. Aggregating these data for all coalition members provided measures of central tendencies and variances on these characteristics within each coalition.

CHARACTERISTICS OF PRO-GROWTH AND ANTI-GROWTH COALITIONS

The typical composition of pro-growth and anti-growth coalitions is suggested by the data in Tables II and III. Table II reports correlations between some background characteristics of activists and their opposition or support for economic development issues (GROWINDX).[4] Table III summarizes the involvement and positions of such key actors as the Chamber of Commerce, the local newspaper, and political leaders on our 12 issues.

Hypothesis 1, which specifies the types of individuals and groups that typically participate in pro-growth and anti-growth coalitions, is generally supported by the data. The roles of various kinds of participants in these coalitions are elaborated upon below.

Elected Officials. As shown in Table III, various mayors and city com-

Table II. Background Variables and Involvement in Economic Development Issues (Zero-Order Correlations)

Background Characteristics	*Correlation with GROWINDX*
Public official standing (OFFICIAL)	.12
Elite standing (ELITES)	.15*
Reputational importance within elite (REPUT)	.35*
Network centrality within elite (CENTRAL)	.44*
Socioeconomic status (SES)	.05
Neighborhood mean property values (PROPVAL)	.41*
Employment in public sector (SECTOR)	−.11
Republican Party identification (DEMREP)	.32*
Ideological conservatism (LIBCON)	.09
Race (BLACK)	−.02

*$p < .05$.

Table III. The Involvement of Key Actors in Economic Development Issues (Number of Issues = 12)

	Involved	*Initated*	*Supportive*	*Opposed*
Incumbent mayor	11.0[a]	1.0	7.0	4.0
Other commissioners, 1980–1984 (averages)	7.9	0.1	4.5	3.4
City manager	11.0	1.0	10.0	1.0
Five top administrators in city government (averages)	5.8	0.2	4.0	0.8
Five most active business elites (averages)	6.0	0.8	5.6	0.4
Five most active neighborhood leaders (averages)	5.4	0	1.0	5.2
Groups				
Chamber of Commerce	9.0	4.0	8.0	1.0
Building trade unions	5.0	0	5.0	0
Lawrence *Journal World*	10.0	0	9.0	1.0
Neighborhood organizations	6.0	0	0	6.0
Organized developers/realtors/landlords	8.0	6.0	8.0	0
Task forces	4.0	4.0	4.0	0
Ad hoc protest	5.0	0	0	5.0

[a]Incumbent mayors were also involved in a twelfth issue (IRB), but the IRB issue had many resolutions over the five years of this study, with no consistent pattern of mayoral support.

missioners have been active on an average of two-thirds of the 12 issues. Elected officials generally were involved in those issues that arose while they served on the commission, and only occasionally were they involved in those issues that arose prior to or subsequent to their terms of office. However, Lawrence's mayors (as well as the commissioners) have varied in their level of support for economic development policies, as one mayor has tended to represent neighborhood interests and three others have not been consistently pro-growth. In general, elected officials do not differ significantly from other activists in the community in their level of pro-growth participation on economic development issues (r = .12 in Table II). Moreover, elected officials have not been initiators of pro-growth issues. The mayor and other city commissioners are important because of their formal decision-making powers, but their role is reactive (Stone 1980), as they attempt to balance the initiatives of developers, the Chamber of Commerce, and other pro-growth forces with the protests of those in the anti-growth coalition. In short, the weak mayors in Lawrence's council-manager form of government—who have few formal powers and who have no special electoral base due to their being selected by other commissioners on an annual basis—do not usually play the role of policy entrepreneurs.

Public administrators have been both less involved in and more supportive of economic development policies than elected officials. Seldom has any top administrator in city government opposed economic growth projects, and the city manager and director of the planning department supported all economic growth projects except for the Cornfield Mall. However, only these two officials were highly involved across our 12 issues.

Local business interests also participated to a high degree, and as hypothesized, they overwhelmingly supported pro-growth positions. Except for two down-zoning proposals, which were proposed by public officials and neighborhood organizations, the economic development issues were initiated by the Chamber of Commerce, businessmen, and developers. The Chamber was particularly important in initiating those issues involving multiple economic actors (e.g., AIR, N2ST, RAIL, and TECH). Developers, in contrast, initiated specific projects (e.g., CORN, JVJ, SZLR, BLUFF). In short, business interests were particularly influential in setting the agenda of economic development issues.

With respect to overall involvement, the Chamber of Commerce participated in the pro-growth coalition on nine of the economic development issues while opposing only one. The local newspaper was involved in 10 issues, taking the pro-growth side in nine of them. Area developers were unanimously in favor of those issues in which they participated, as were local bankers.

In general, activists identified as community leaders [ELITES] by a modified reputational analysis tended to be slightly more pro-growth than were other activists (r = .15). Indeed, the greater a leader's reputation [REPUT] and centrality [CENTRAL] within the elite network, the greater was his or her pro-growth involvement. (See Table II.)

Surprisingly, the *socioeconomic status [SES] of activists* is not related significantly to pro-growth involvement (r = .05). This suggests that many anti-growth activists also have higher incomes, educational attainments, and occupational positions.

As expected, the *neighborhood* where activists reside is related significantly to their general involvement in economic development issues. Residents of newer neighborhoods having higher average property values [PROPVAL] tend to be pro-growth while residents of older neighborhoods having lower average property values tend to be anti-growth. Indeed, neighborhood organizations representing older areas of the community have been active on half of the issues in the sample, in each case taking anti-growth positions.

Contrary to expectations, persons employed in the *private sector* [SECTOR] tended to be slightly more pro-growth than those in the public sector (r = −.11). This can be largely explained by two factors, however. First, municipal employees tended not to participate, and any pro-growth tendencies they might have exhibited were not registered. Second, many of the public-sector employees who did participate were staff and faculty members at the University of Kansas; as is true with many universities, the politically liberal tradition there may well have fostered an anti-growth position among its employees.

Republicans [DEMREP] were hypothesized to take pro-growth positions on economic development issues, and the data support this hypothesis. Although this finding conflicts with Mollenkopf's emphasis on Democratic support for economic growth, it may be explained by the difference between Lawrence and other larger cities with a substantial blue-collar population and labor union membership. Indeed, in Lawrence the building trade unions took pro-growth positions on five economic development issues. But Lawrence is primarily a white-collar community, with a low unemployment rate, and the New Deal Democratic coalition is probably not a very potent force there.

While these findings provide general support for the first hypothesis, the magnitude of the observed relationships between personal characteristics and pro-growth activism is sufficiently low to suggest important differences among issues. This is consistent with Hypothesis 2, which suggests that the membership of pro-growth and anti-growth coalitions changes across issues. This hypothesis is more directly supported by the data summarized in Table IV, which show the intercorrelations among coalition membership across issues to be generally small. Only in a few isolated cases did coalition membership show substantial overlap between issues. (E.g., the Cornfield

Table IV. Significant Overlaps among Actors Across Issue Areas (Pearson Correlations where $p < .05$)

	JVJ	*SZLR*	*OREAD*	*EAST*	*BLUFF*	*RAIL*	*TECH*	*IRB*	*ARK*	*AIR*	*N2ST*
CORN	.28	−.49	—	.12	—	—	—	−.16	−.15	−.11	—
JVJ		−.17	—	.25	.09	—	.18	.16	.26	.09	—
SZLR			—	−.16	—	.22	.09	.28	.11	.14	—
OREAD				.13	.12	—	—	—	.09	—	—
EAST					.16	—	—	—	.35	—	—
BLUFF						—	—	—	.17	—	—
RAIL							.50	.20	.12	.23	—
TECH								—	—	.20	—
IRB									.30	.22	.12
PARK										.26	.15
AIR											—

Mall [CORN] and the Sizler Mall [SIZE] were viewed by activists as competing projects with persons supporting one proposal often opposing the other; the rail-based industrial park [RAIL] and the office research park [TECH] were seen as complementary projects to enhance the economic base of the community.) In most cases, coalition formation seemed to be issue-specific.

The hypothesis is further supported by our findings concerning the bases of conflict, which vary across issues; these data are summarized in Table V. First, theoretically important bases of conflict—socioeconomic status [SES], neighborhood property values [PROPVAL], partisanship [DEMREP], ideology [LIBCON], and sector of employment [SECTOR]—were

Table V. Significant Cleavages Across Issues

Issue/Cleavage	*SES*	*PROPVAL*	*DEMREP*	*LIBCON*	*SECTOR*
CORN	−.29*	—	−.31*	—	.47*
JVJ	—	.33*	—	—	—
SZLR	.27*	—	—	—	—
OREAD	—	.42*	.47*	—	.36*
EAST	—	.37*	.45*	−.37*	.38*
BLUFF	—	—	—	−.62*	—
RAIL	—	.43*	—	—	.27*
TECH	—	.35	—	—	—
IRB	—	—	—	—	—
PARK	—	.61*	.53*	−.37*	—
AIR	—	.61*	.38*	—	—
N2ST	—	—	—	—	—

*Indicates existence of a cleavage. Cells with zero-order correlation entries only exhibit relationships that are significant at the .05 level but do not exhibit a cleavage.

related, using Pearson correlation procedures, with involvement on each issue.[5] Those correlations that are statistically significant ($p < .05$) are reported in Table V. However, it is important to realize that a significant relationship between the backgrounds of participants and their positions on issues does not necessarily indicate a cleavage with respect to that background characteristic. A cleavage exists only when the majority of one side (e.g., the upper stratum) prefers one outcome while a majority on the other side (e.g., the lower stratum) prefers the policy alternative. For example, Table V shows that residents of neighborhoods having higher property values [PROPVAL] are more supportive of the research park that are residents of poorer neighborhoods ($r = .35$). However, the majority of activists from all neighborhoods supported this project. It would thus be misleading to suggest that there is an important neighborhood cleavage on the issue.

The typical bases of conflict discussed under Hypothesis 1 thus are not frequently manifested on specific issues. Only six issues exhibited significant cleavages between residents of newer and older neighborhoods, and only five issues exhibited significant cleavages between Republicans and Democrats. Even fewer issues exhibited class, sector, or ideological cleavages. Moreover, the 12 issues in the sample exhibit a wide range of patterns of conflict and cleavage—as anticipated by Hypothesis 2.

FACTORS AFFECTING POLICY OUTCOMES ON ECONOMIC DEVELOPMENT ISSUES

According to Hypothesis 3, the support of several types of actors—elected officials, public administrators, policy activists, interest and protest groups, elites, and voters—may all be important in achieving pro-growth outcomes. The data in Table VI support this hypothesis by suggesting that economic development policy outcomes are responsive to the preferences and pressures of each of these types of actors.[6] Public officials [REP, ADMIN] appear to be especially important elements within pro-growth and anti-growth coalitions. Since outcomes have been moderately responsive to VOTER preferences ($r = .46$), the role of public (or audience) support is also suggested (Schattschneider 1960; Schumaker 1984a).

Of special interest is the role of public officials as potential "policy entrepreneurs." The data show that the incumbant mayor almost always was successful—as his or her preferences [MAYOR] are highly correlated with outcomes ($r = .67$). Figure I shows the distribution of "corrected" zero-order correlations[7] between policy OUTCOMES and the involvements of individual mayors, commissioners, and public administrators. It

Table VI. The Relationship between the Preferences of Various Types of Actors and Policy Outcomes (Zero-Order Correlations)

Elected officials [REP]	.68*
Incumbent mayors [MAYOR]	.67*
Administrative officials [ADMIN]	.50*
City manager [CM]	.24
Private elites [ELITES]	.17
Policy activists [ACTIVES]	.22
Public opinion [VOTERS]	.46*
Interest group pressure [PERMGRP]	.26
Chamber of Commerce [CHAMBER]	.63*
Neighborhood groups [NEIGH]	−.35
Protest group pressure [PROTEST]	−.36
Task force pressure [TASK]	0

*p < .05.

shows that generally these persons have been successful in their participation on economic development issues, suggesting some potential for strong entrepreneurial roles for public officials. But it is important to recall our discussion of Hypothesis 1 concerning the varied support among public officials for economic growth policies. The Cornfield Mall, JVJ Mall, Sizeler Mall, and the Rail-served industrial park all failed and in each instance the incumbent mayor took a strong anti-growth position, citing widespread opposition to the projects. In reality, the voters were strongly opposed to only the JVJ Mall and, indeed, strongly supported the industrial park. Lawrence mayors have thus had some potential to be policy entrepreneurs, and there is strong evidence that such entrepreneurship is essential to the success of pro-growth forces. But Lawrence mayors have retreated from that role when signs of opposition emerged.

The city manager, perhaps due to his greater isolation from public opposition, has been much more supportive of economic growth. But his involvement [CM] is less strongly related to policy outcomes ($r = .24$) than is the involvement of the incumbent mayors, thus suggesting that his potential entrepreneurial role is more limited. Thus, it is the Chamber of Commerce and other business elites who most often play entrepreneurial roles in Lawrence.

Rather than acting as political entrepreneurs, elected officials in Lawrence mostly react to political forces in formulating economic growth policies. Our fourth hypothesis suggests that the SIZE, HIERARCHY, and composition of pro-growth and anti-growth coalitions affect their decisions. As revealed in Table VII, the composition of pro-growth coalitions appears to be especially important. When pro-growth coalitions are composed of

Figure 1 The Success of Various Types of Actors: The Distribution of Zero-Order Correlations Between Involvements and Policy Outcomes Across Twelve Economic Development Issues

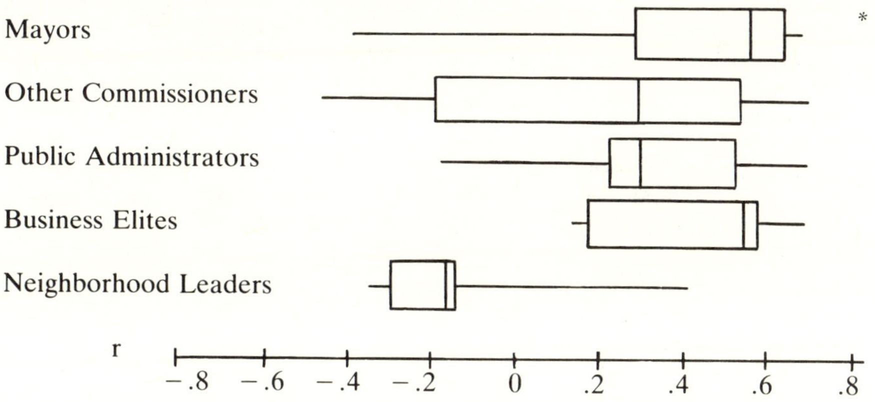

Boxes encompass all but the highest and lowest correlations for each group, which are indicated by the extended lines.

*indicates the correlation between OUTCOME and the preferences of the incumbant mayor.

ideologically conservative, upper-stratum Republicans, they are most successful. This finding is consistent with Stone's theory of systemic bias in favor of situationally advantaged actors.

For anti-growth forces, coalition composition is unimportant relative to coalition size and hierarchy. Anti-growth coalitions led by a few visable leaders have been most successful ($r = -.49$), as such leaders seem most able to mobilize other anti-growth activists. (The zero-order correlation between HIERARCHY and SIZE is .35.) And the greater the SIZE of the anti-growth coalition, the less successful are pro-growth coalitions in achieving pro-growth policies ($r = -.56$). The importance of size probably derives from the role of the public in community conflict, as public officials seem unwilling to offend large numbers of voters in pursuit of growth proposals. While the raw number of anti-growth activists constitutes a miniscule proportion of the voting public, protests by a large number of activists can increase both voter opposition to projects and official perceptions of voter opposition. The importance of group size is suggested by the strong negative correlations across the 12 issues between anti-growth co-

Table VII. Coalition Characteristics and Pro-Growth Outcomes (N = 12) (Zero-Order Correlations)

	Pro-Growth Coalition	*Anti-Growth Coalition*
SIZE	−.09	−.56*
Composition levels		
Mean SES	.40*	.37
Mean neighborhood PROPVAL	.19	−.44*
Mean party ID [DEMREP]	.59*	−.21
Mean conservatism [LIBCON]	.53*	−.07
Composition variances		
Variance in SES	−.56*	.13
Variance in neighborhood PROPVAL	−.36	−.69*
Variance in party ID [DEMREP]	.01	−.04
Variance in ideology [LIBCON]	−.13	−.10
Coalition HIERARCHY (gini coefficient)	.12	−.49*

*$p < .05$.

alitional SIZE and public support [VOTERS] (r = −.68) and between SIZE and commissioners' perceptions of public support (r = −.92).

CONCLUSIONS

Three principal conclusions emerge from this analysis. First, the study suggests the usefulness of a comparative-issues approach to the study of community politics and economic development policies (Schumaker 1981). This approach explains variation in policy outcomes in terms of intra-community variables involving such factors as the distribution of support, the presence of leadership, and the characteristics of competing coalitions. The wide intracity variance in coalitional characteristics both suggests an explanation for intracity variance in policy outcomes and suggests caution in cross-community comparisons of policy outcomes that ignore intra-community variation.

Second, the study contributes to Stone's theory of systemic bias. Like Stone (1976), we find public officials to be in reactive, adjudicatory roles rather than policy entrepeneurial roles. Elected officials are cross-pressured by elite-based pro-growth forces and anti-growth activists. But while Stone suggests a general tendency for officials to side with pro-growth forces based on their structural dependencies on elites, our findings suggest that the extent of such bias is variable. If elites do not dominate pro-growth coalitions—and they do not on a number of issues in Lawrence—pro-growth forces may fail. Thus elites must participate in and dominate pro-growth coalitions if they are to succeed.

Our third conclusion concerns the theory of political entrepreneurship. Like Mollenkopf (1983), Salisbury (1964), Eyestone (1978), and others, our study suggests that policy entrepreneurs are important to the success of growth policies. But such entrepreneurs may not always emerge. When mayors are not directly elected and when they have few formal powers—as is the case in Lawrence and many other smaller reformed communities—they may not have the resource base to put together pro-growth coalitions. The city manager, lacking an electoral base and cautious about overstepping his or her "administrative" position, may also be restricted in the role of policy entrepreneur. It is perhaps for this reason that a number of smaller reformed cities have recently changed governmental forms to strengthen the position of mayor (Jones, Bachelor, and Wilson 1986).

Advocates of strong mayoral systems should, however, understand the consequences of their proposal. If the analyses in this study are correct, strong mayors are important to political entrepreneurship which can achieve the collective goals associated with economic growth. However, to the extent that economic growth is achieved by a political entrepreneur, systemic bias will be enhanced and policy will be more responsive to advantaged sectors of the community at the expense of disadvantaged populations. Anti-growth coalitions should not be misled into believing that enhancing the position of the mayor would lead to economic growth policies more responsive to their interests.[8]

NOTES

1. These perceptions of OUTCOME appear to be very consistent with policy decisions made thus far by the city commission. However, the relationship between these perceived outcomes and policy impacts is more problematic. For example, while proponents of the research park have persuaded city officials to extend city services to the site location, only two major developments have been built this far. Similarly, opponents of the Cornfield Mall proposal have thus far persuaded city officials to deny the rezoning necessary for the project, but recent irritation with the lack of progress on downtown mall proposals may lead to a receptiveness to future Cornfield Mall proposals.

2. To measure the pressure exerted by each group on an issue, we considered (1) group size, (2) the number of group members active on the issue, (3) cohesion, or similarity of preferences on the issue among group members, (4) duration, or the number of years the group had been in existence, (5) the level of activity by group leaders on the issue, and (6) the importance of the issue to the group. Perceptions of group members on these variables were averaged, and standardized scores were calculated and added to yield a measure of pressure by each group.

3. Since the gini coefficient has a maximum value of (1 − 1/N), it is extremely sensitive

to small sample size. Each of the obtained gini coefficients was normalized by dividing them by (1 − 1/N); thus, each value of gini varies between zero and unity.

4. Each person received a score ($GROWISU_i$) for each issue (i) equal to the number of times he or she was cited as being in favor of the growth position minus the number of times he or she was cited as being opposed to the growth position. GROWINDX then sums these scores for the 12 issues in our sample.

The background characteristics reported in Table II are, for the most part, conventional or self-evident. ELITES is a dichotomous variable indicating whether or not each actor is among the top 100 leaders in the community, as measured by a modified reputational study. REPUT, or reputed importance, is a rank-order measure of leadership based on the frequency that each actor was cited as being important to the achievement of community goals. CENTRAL, or network centrality, is a measure of the number of other network members with whom each actor is directly or indirectly linked in the continuous flow of information (Bolland 1984:78). While various measures of elite standing and GROWINDX are based on frequency of citations, these citations were derived from independent surveys measuring very distinct concepts, thus minimizing the possibility of high correlations due to contamination.

5. Our measure of involvement on each issue is the $GROWISU_i$ scores discussed above in note 4.

6. See Schumaker (1984b) for an explanation of why the concept of responsiveness, but not necessarily the concept of influence, is indicated by significant zero-order correlations between preferences and policies. The negative correlations regarding protest group [PROTEST] and neighborhood group [NEIGH] pressures actually indicate positive responsiveness, since the greater the pressure of these groups (against growth policies), the less successful have been pro-growth policies.

7. Since the number of times an individual was identified as a participant on any given issue is a direct function of sample size for that issue, simple correlation coefficients may overestimate (or underestimate) the relationship between involvement and success. Nor is a partial correlation coefficient a viable alternative, since many people participated in a mixture of pro-growth and anti-growth issues (and the pro-growth and anti-growth sample sizes differed). As a compromise, corrected product moment correlation coefficients were calculated between outcomes and the probability that a person was identified as a pro-growth (or anti-growth) participant by each member of the sample of pro-growth (or anti-growth) respondents.

8. In Lawrence, 70 percent of the citizens indicated, in the 1984 survey, a preference for a directly elected full-time mayor. Anti-growth activists led an unsuccessful attempt to have such a mayor in 1977, and support for the change is still particularly strong among anti-growth forces.

REFERENCES

Bachrach, Peter, and Morton Baratz. 1962. "The Two Faces of Power," *American Political Science Review* 62: 947–952.

Banfield, Edward C., and James Q. Wilson. 1963. *City Politics*. New York: Vintage Books.

Bolland, John. 1984. "The Limits to Pluralism: Power and Leadership in a Nonparticipatory Society." *Power and Elites* 1: 69–88.

Claggett, William E. 1983. "Dallas: The Dynamics of Public-Private Cooperation." In *Public-Private Partnerships in American Cities*, ed. R. Scott Fosler and Renee Berger. Lexington, Mass.: Heath.

Clark, Terry N., and Lorna Ferguson. 1983. *City Money*. New York: Columbia University Press.

Dahl, Robert A. 1961. *Who Governs?* New Haven, Conn.: Yale University Press.
Domhoff, William. 1983. *Who Rules America Now?* North Scituate, Mass.: Duxbury.
Eulau, Heinz, and Robert Eyestone. 1968. "Policy Maps of City Councils and Policy Outcomes: A Developmental Analysis," *American Political Science Review* 62: 124–143.
Eyestone, Robert. 1978. *From Social Issues to Public Policy*. New York: Wiley.
Fainstein, Norman I., and Susan S. Fainstein. 1983. "Regime Strategies, Community Resistance, and Economic Forces." Pp. 245–282 in *Restructuring the City*, ed. Susan Fainstein et al. New York: Longman.
Fainstein, Susan, et al., eds. 1983. *Restructuring the City: The Political Economy of Urban Redevelopment*. New York: Longman.
Fleishman, Arnold, and Joe R. Feagen. 1985. "Political Institutions and the Politics of Urban Growth." Presented at the Southwestern Political Science Association, March 20–23.
Fosler, R. Scott, and Renee Berger. 1982. *Public-Private Partnership in American Cities*. Lexington, Mass.: Lexington Books.
Gamson, William. 1975. *The Strategy of Social Protest*. Homewood, Ill.: Dorsey.
Henig, Jeffrey R. 1982. *Neighborhood Mobilization: Redevelopment and Response*. New Brunswick, N.J.: Rutgers University Press.
Hoffman, Wayne. 1976. "The Democratic Response of Urban Governments: An Empirical Test with Simple Spatial Models." Pp. 51–74 in *Citizen Preferences and Urban Public Policy*, ed. Beverly Hills, Calif.: Sage.
Hunter, Floyd. 1953. *Community Power Structure*. Chapel Hill: University of North Carolina Press.
Jones, Bryan, Lynn Bachelor, and Carter Wilson. 1986. *The Sustaining Hand: Community Leadership and Corporate Power*. Lawrence: University of Kansas Press.
Katznelson, Ira. 1981. *City Trenches*. New York: Pantheon.
Lineberry, Robert. 1977. *Equality and Urban Policy: The Distribution of Municipal Public Services*. Beverly Hills, Calif.: Sage.
Lipsky, Michael. 1970. *Protest in City Politics*. Chicago: Rand McNally.
Lowi, Theodore J. 1979. *The End of Liberalism*. 2nd ed. New York: W. W. Norton.
Manley, John. 1983. "Neopluralism: A Class Analysis of Pluralism I and Pluralism II," *American Political Science Review* 77: 368–383.
Mollenkopf, John H. 1975. "The Post-war Politics of Urban Development," *Politics and Society* 5: 247–295.
———. 1983. *The Contested City*. Princeton, N.J.: Princeton University Press.
Molotch, Harvey. 1976. "The City as a Growth Machine: Toward a Political Economy of Place," *American Journal of Sociology* 82: 309–332.
Morlock, Laura L. 1974. "Business Interests, Countervailing Groups, and the Balance of Influence in 91 Cities." Pp. 309–328 in *Search for Community Power*, ed. Willis A. Hawley and Frederick M. Wirt. Englewood Cliffs, N.J.: Prentice-Hall.
Newton, Kenneth. 1976. "Feeble Governments and Private Power: Urban Politics and Policies in the United States." Pp. 37–58 in *The New Urban Politics*, ed. Louis H. Masotti and Robert L. Lineberry. Cambridge, Mass.: Ballinger.
Peterson, Paul. 1981. *City Limits*. Chicago: University of Chicago Press.
Salisbury, Robert H. 1964. "Urban Politics: The New Convergence of Power," *Journal of Politics* 26: 775–797.
Schattschneider, E. E. 1960. *The Semisovereign People*. Hinsdale, Ill.: Dryden Press.
Schumaker, Paul D. 1975. "Policy Responsiveness to Protest Group Demands," *Journal of Politics* 37: 488–521.
———. 1981. "Citizen Preferences and Policy Responsiveness." Pp. 227–243 in *Urban Policy Analysis: Directions for Future Research. Urban Affairs Annual Reviews*, vol. 21, ed. Terry Nichols Clark. Beverly Hills, Calif.: Sage.

———. 1984a. "The Policy Effects of Unstable Cleavages in Local Politics." Presented at the Midwest Political Science Association, Chicago. April 11–14.

———. 1984b. "Representative Democracy and Partisanship: An Application of a Pluralist Perspective to an Analysis of 30 Policy Issues in a Reformed Community." Presented at the American Political Science Association, Washington, D.C. August 30–September 2.

Stone, Clarence N. 1976. *Economic Growth and Neighborhood Discontent: Systemic Bias in the Urban Renewal Program in Atlanta*. Chapel Hill: University of North Carolina Press.

———. 1980. "Systemic Power in Community Decision Making: A Restatement of Stratification Theory," *American Political Science Review* 74: 978–990.

Trounstine, Philip J., and Terry Christensen. 1982. *Movers and Shakers: The Study of Community Power*. New York: St. Martin's Press.

Verba, Sidney, and Norman Nie. 1972. *Participation in America*. New York: Harper and Row.

Williams, Oliver P., and Charles R. Adrian. 1963. *Four Cities*. Philadelphia: University of Pennsylvania Press.

Wolfinger, Raymond E. 1974. *The Politics of Progress*. New Haven, Conn.: Yale University Press.

Yates, Douglas. 1977. *The Ungovernable City*. Cambridge, Mass.: The MIT Press.

Zeigler, L. Harmon, and Harvey J. Tucker. 1978. *The Quest for Responsive Government*. North Scituate, Mass.: Duxbury Press.

COMMENTARY:
THE POLITICS OF URBAN GROWTH

Roger Friedland

The politics of growth in a territorial community—whether city or nation-state—poses difficult problems of conceptualization. Economists treat institutions outside the economy, indeed sometimes those of the economy itself, as exogenous to the model. Increasingly we have watched while the logic of the market is exported analytically to all institutions—ranging from state to family—from decisions to support public policies to those to have children. The logic of the market has come to us via such theories as public choice and transaction costs. While such models might help explain why people do or don't join a social movement, or when activities are organized by the market or by hierarchy, the economist's models have not fared particularly well in explaining their central institutional concern—economic growth. Sociologists and political scientists also typically take the economy as an unobserved exogenous institution, without understanding how the structure of the economy generates the social problems and politics with which they concern themselves.

As economic growth increasingly depends upon the state, as production and distribution are increasingly organized within firms that are like states,

Research in Urban Policy, Vol. 2, pages 47–51.

ISBN: 0-89232-534-8

as distributional conflicts seem to imperil growth, as productivity increasingly depends upon the acquisition and organization of human skills, it is imperative that we construct a framework by which to understand the politics and sociology of economic growth. Territorial politics in the United States are important to that task in two ways. On the one hand, the U.S. government lacks an explicit industrial policy, save for the defense budget. The policy initiatives of state and local governments today constitute a vast range of "industrial policies," trying to shape the flows of capital and the organization of production within their boundaries. On the other hand, cities and states have become increasingly involved in trying to regulate the social costs of growth, whether in terms of pollution, displacement, employment change, or tax burdens. Thus growth is being politicized at the subnational level in the United States. While all communities wish to maintain their economic base, there are variations in the manner in which economic growth can be achieved. These variations suggest that urban growth per se is not a unitary interest, but an issue that is capable of politicizing urban and regional communities.

THE POLITICS OF ECONOMIC GROWTH

Schumaker, Boland, and Feiock's essay, "Economic Development Policy and Community Conflict," is a decided advance in our understanding of the politics of urban growth. Their analysis of the variable composition of coalitions favoring and opposing 12 growth-generating policies in Lawrence, Kansas, allows them to build on what surely remains one of the finest case studies of urban renewal politics in one city, that of Clarence Stone, *Economic Growth and Neighborhood Discontent* (1976). Stone's theoretical case study of renewal politics in Atlanta, across several mayoral administrations, demonstrates the operation of systemic bias. Growth politics are most amenable to neighborhood influence at the legislative stage and least amenable at the initiation and implementation stages. During these stages, the systemic power of business tends to be strong.

The Schumaker, Boland, and Feiock essay is an exemplary piece of empirical work within a pluralist framework (Alford and Friedland 1985). The authors demonstrate that elected officials and neighborhood groups did not initiate growth proposals, while business elites did. Especially active in the growth coalitions were the Chamber of Commerce, the newspaper, developers, and the local bank. Individuals who were central within the local elite network were most likely to participate. Participation is not highly correlated across the growth proposals. Business proposals do not always win, especially when there is vociferous protest by neighborhood groups, when the anti-growth coalition is relatively large, and when popular opinion is opposed.

The study assumes that participation is the major source and the conformity of preferences and outcomes is the most important indicator of political influence. Missing is some conception of interest on the one hand and benefit on the other. I would argue that the conformity of interest and benefit is a more appropriate way to measure systemic power. Power can be exercised and interests served without participation (Friedland 1983). Systemic power reduces the need for and increases the efficacy of participation to achieve policies that benefit a particular actor or group.

Let me point out a number of potential problems in the analysis. First, the pro-growth coalitions seem to be dominated by businesses that were most dependent on the city and had least capacity for exit, precisely the actors that Molotch has specified as central to the "growth machine" (1976). For them, participation is not an indicator of influence, but of growth dependence (Friedland and Palmer 1984). It is also possible that centrality in local elite networks derives from that same growth dependence. It would be interesting to compare the involvement of those business elites who are growth-dependent and those who regulate the flow of capital into and out of the city. But to do so requires some description, which is absent, of the organizational structure of Lawrence's economy. The power of business in a community, and hence the extent to which its participation reveals its political power, is a function of its dominance of the local economy, its dependence upon that local economy, and its capacity for exit (Friedland and Palmer 1984).

Second, the outcomes were defined consensually, based upon the difference between participants on how successful the pro- and anti-growth forces appeared to be. There was no measure of what precisely was at stake and who actually benefited or was damaged in the process. Is there a relationship between perceived success and actual benefit? Or are outcomes defined based upon what is possible given the structure of power among contending forces? The pro-growth coalitions won eight out of 12 times. Do "private elites" have one of the lowest relationships between their preferences and outcomes because what is being decided is irrelevant to their interests, or because they did not have to participate to have their interests served and thus were not socialized into the consensus on who won and who lost? Is success measured relative to what individuals and groups want or what they thought they could get?

Third, the preferences of various groups must be seen in the same light. The authors treat them, as befits a pluralist analysis, as exogenous variables. But preferences need not reflect interests. Given the total dominance of business over policy initiation, the reactive nature of popular and official roles, and the relative success of growth proposals, it is equally reasonable to suggest that the pro-growth sentiment is indicative of the systemic power of business. Unfortunately, the authors have told us little about the economy of Lawrence and how its residents might be affected by the growth proposals so that we could establish the meaning of their preferences.

The relationship between participation and preference on the one hand and interest and power on the other remains to be specified. To do so, we need better information about the organizational structure of the business actors in a community, the interests they have at stake, and the nature of the growth programs—size, employment generation, revenue consequences, divisibility of benefit, and displacement. The present study is a step in the right direction. There is no reason that the next installment cannot tell us more about not only who thought they won most, but what was at stake in the conflict and who actually won and lost what. I look forward to reading it.

THE POLITICS OF POPULATION GROWTH

One of the factors that surely requires greater attention is the impact of capital migration on public policy, an impact that does not depend upon the participation of corporate elites. The first essay, "Community and Collective Goods," by Appleton and Williams, focuses on the corollary of capital migration—that of population—on policymaking in the cities of Florida. Appleton and Williams argue that communities that are overwhelmed by new immigrants will lack "community" because of the weakness of their social ties and the high probability that they will move on yet again. "Community" is a counterweight to the logic of the "market," and places lacking in community are more likely to be penetrated by the logic of the market, less likely to support the provision of collective goods. In their analysis of the cities of Florida between 1970 and 1983, they find that population growth—they don't measure in-migration directly—and median age—an indicator of the existence of ethnically homogenous "villages" of those whose only exit plans involve the next world—respectively diminish and augment the probability that communities will raise taxes. Political culture has no impact on tax policies.

It is not clear that the additive specification used is appropriate to the theory. Places with more attributes of a "community" per se need not have any a priori interests in more public goods. Rather, they are more likely to convert the needs of their constituents into collective goods. Similarly, if the authors wish to argue that "political cultures" operate as "transformation rules," then an interaction logic is more appropriate. As it is, the study directly contradicts the thesis put forward by Clark and Ferguson (1983) that social conservatism and fiscal conservativism are increasingly differentiated. In their additive analysis, they find that "social liberalism," and not "fiscal liberalism," of the mayors was the most important determinant of their willingness to engage in budgetary and functional cutbacks. Socially liberal mayors are more fiscally liberal in their behavior than are fiscal liberals! On the other hand, the fact that population characteristics have no impact on cutbacks of various sorts supports another part of the Clark and Ferguson theory, because these communities were rapidly growing and thus there was likely to be high uncertainty about voters' preferences and thus a greater space for the values of elected officials to play a directive role.

Finally, the authors provide evidence yet again that population growth is not an unequivocal boon. There is no relationship in Florida between population growth and the extent of impoverishment, the quality of the tax base, or a city's fiscal problems.

POLITICS AND GROWTH

These two essays both consider the local politics of growth. While one considers the conditions under which local coalitions support or oppose local growth policies, the other analyzes the impact of population growth on local budgetary behavior. Yet both shy away from analyzing the economic processes that generate the political phenomena they study. Growth policies are designed in response to the present or possible investments of capital. Population migrations respond to the movement of capital. Social institutions have either ended up in the error term of economists' equations, been assimilated as market phenomena, or, in the best of worlds, become exogenous variables. In analyzing the politics of growth, we must squarely confront the economic structure as it shapes the jobs, the population, the tax revenues, and the politics of the communities we study.

REFERENCES

Alford, Robert, and Roger Friedland. 1985. *Powers of Theory: The State, Capitalism and Democracy*. New York: Cambridge University Press.

Clark, Terry Nichols, and Lorna Crowley Ferguson. 1983. *City Money: Political Processes, Fiscal Strain, and Retrenchment*. New York: Columbia University Press.

Friedland, Roger. 1983. *Power and Crisis in the City*. New York: Shocken.

Friedland, Roger, and Donald Palmer. 1984. "Park Place and Main Street: Business and the Urban Power Structure." *Annual Review of Sociology* 10: 393–416.

Molotch, Harvey. 1976. "The City as a Growth Machine," *American Journal of Sociology* 82: 309–331.

Stone, Clarence N. 1976. *Economic Growth and Neighborhood Discontent: Systemic Bias in the Urban Renewal Program of Atlanta*. Chapel Hill: University of North Carolina Press.

PART II.

INTERGOVERNMENTAL FISCAL RELATIONS

FEDERAL GRANTS AND THE CITY OF LOS ANGELES:

IMPLEMENTING A MORE CENTRALIZED LOCAL POLITICAL SYSTEM

Alan L. Saltzstein, Raphe Sonenshein, and Irving Ostrow

ABSTRACT

This essay analyzes the effect of federal grants-in-aid on the political structure of a city. The acquisition and implementation of grants in Los Angeles has provided a vehicle for Mayor Bradley and the city council to overcome some of the inherently decentralizing features of the governmental structure. As a consequence, there is greater policy coordination today than previous writings about Los Angeles' policy process have led us to believe. This case illustrates that the implementation of federal urban policy ought to be examined not just from Washington's perspective, but from the city's viewpoint as well.

The research is based on elite interviews with city officials and participant observation.

Increases in aid to city governments have altered the nature of city politics. Aid to cities has risen from very small amounts just 25 years ago to over 12 percent of total revenue in the average city and as high as 40 percent in several of the larger, more deprived cities (U.S. Advisory Commission 1978: 120). Federal aid doubled every five years from 1960 to 1978 (U.S. Advisory Commission 1978: 121). If, as some have said, "power flows from

Research in Urban Policy, Vol. 2, pages 55–76.

ISBN: 0-89232-534-8

the purse strings," such changes in funding should result in significant alterations in power and influence within the federal system.

Most of those who have looked at the effect of federal grants-in-aid on city politics and policy have examined the operation of programs as they relate to legislative intent. The common perspective has been that of "implementation," defined most simply by Pressman and Wildavsky (1973: xv) as "a process of interaction between the setting of goals and actions geared to achieving them." Analysts have evaluated the goals of federal programs and traced the carrying out of these goals as administrators and state and local officials apply the policies (e.g., Derthick 1970, 1972; Frieden and Kaplan 1975; Bardach 1977).

These studies focused on the problems of implementing federal programs in an intergovernmental context. Most are pessimistic in tone. The subtitle of Pressman and Wildavsky's book, for example, is *How Great Expectations in Washington Are Dashed in Oakland, or Why It Is Amazing That Federal Programs Work at All, This Being the Saga of the Economic Development Administration as Told by Two Sympathetic Observers Who Seek to Build Morals on a Foundation of Ruined Hopes*. Bureaucratic infighting, intransigence, competing goals of various parties, and unrealistic expectations are frequently cited reasons for difficulties or failures in carrying out policy goals. Ripley and Franklin (1982: 9) summarize these concerns:

The best of the literature that includes some conceptual or theoretical discussion of implementation . . . strongly underscores several generalizations about implementation:

1. There are a large number of external factors that can influence implementation.
2. For implementation to go without major hitches, all or virtually all of these external factors must be operating in a supportive or at least benign direction. Any one or few operating in a non-supportive direction can derail the entire implementation process in a variety of ways.
3. There are a large number of factors internal to the implementation process—which are complex—that inevitably provide obstacles to smooth implementation.

The implementation literature thus begins from the perspective of Congress, by defining the purpose of federal aid as that defined in legislation. By contrast, we begin from the perspective of the aid recipient, in this case local governments. To the city, federal aid is money to be used for city purposes. From this perspective, the program succeeds or fails according to the city's goals.

We assume, following others, that local governments are major determinants of aid allocations and accomplishments (Browning, Marshall, and Tabb 1982; Porter, Warner, and Porter 1973; Saltzstein 1977; Stein 1979). Local governments receive aid because they seek it and are receptive to it. Over time, as major clients of the aid system, they act to alter the structure of the aid process (Stein 1983). We surmise that the dynamics of the aid process are triggered and even determined at the local level. Local decision makers seek and use federal aid for their own purposes.

We propose that federal aid is a way of securing local political goals. Los Angeles provides a particularly interesting case study of the relationship between federal aid and local political systems. Los Angeles was an unusually decentralized city before the influx of federal aid in the 1960s (Banfield 1965: 23). It was controlled by a weak mayor, a strong but amateur city council, and several appointed commissions with limited authority in the running of largely autonomous city departments. Thus, centralizing forces may have been weaker in Los Angeles than in most other cities. Federal aid might have played a unique role here.

In addition, the Los Angeles City Council plays an unusual role in local politics. City councils have declined in power; Los Angeles' has always been strong (Caraley 1977: 243) and today the council is stronger than ever. While federal aid may have led, in some cities, to alliances among mayors, bureaucrats, and business to the exclusion of other politicians, Los Angeles' use of federal grants has operated to *increase* the level of political influence (by both the mayor and the council) over the bureaucracy, while also bringing business into a governing coalition.

Despite these unusual features of historic decentralization and a strong city council (not to mention a popular black mayor in a city with an 18 percent black population), Los Angeles has not received much scholarly attention in recent years. As America's second largest city, Los Angeles' political behavior merits closer examination. We argue that in Los Angeles, federal aid provided the means by which a coalition of the mayor and members of the city council centralized authority and incorporated new clienteles into the decision-making process. This centralization was associated with an increased city involvement in providing social services. Consequently, Los Angeles is a different city politically than it was prior to the influx of aid in the early 1970s.

We examined the federal aid process in the City of Los Angeles from 1965 to the present, concentrating on the administration of Mayor Tom Bradley (1973 to present). The Bradley years are a logical focus for this inquiry because: (1) Significant changes in federal funding occurred. Block grants were developed and expanded considerably and Los Angeles was eligible to receive a larger share of these than previously. Substantial amounts of categorical funds were also made available through programs such as the Public Service Employment grants, the Anti-Cyclical Public Works grants, and the Urban Development Action grants (Ross 1981). Under Bradley, Los Angeles was a major participant in these and other federal programs. (2) A series of political and administrative changes in city government occurred during this same period. These included greater centralization of power in the hands of elected officials (mayor and council), a larger and more accountable professional bureaucracy, and an interacting mesh of interest groups politically and economically dependent on the grant process.

Our research suggests that these two events were related. The availability of grants coincided with the emergence of new political leadership that was able to forge a consensus within the city council and in the community. Thus, federal aid has not only distributed resources in Los Angeles; it has also provided the means for significant political and administrative changes.

The nature of intergovernmental policy can be revealed only by tracing interactions and perceptions of key actors over time (Stein 1983). Our method combined in-depth interviews, documentary analysis, and participant observation. City records, budgetary data, and newspapers were examined. Twenty key decision makers including members and staffs of the city council, the past and present city administrative officers, staffs of the mayor's office, the chief legislative analyst's office, and federal officials were interviewed. We particularly looked for informants who could discuss how the process had changed over time. Interviews were open-ended, lasting from three-quarters to two and one-half hours. Two of the authors were present at most interviews, permitting them to take more the form of conversations than formal interrogations.

Additionally, two of the authors have had significant working experience with the grants process in the Bradley years. One is a project manager of the grant-funded Community Development Department and formerly served on the mayor's Human Resources staff. The other was an intern in a grant-funded division of Mayor Bradley's office (1974) and was the city's first full-time grants deputy to a city council member (1975-76).

The essay is divided into three sections. The first will summarize the Los Angeles political system and the role of federal aid prior to the Bradley years. The second part chronicles the changes that were brought about during the Bradley years, both in the grants program and in the local political system. The final section discusses the implications of these changes.

LOS ANGELES' POLITICAL SYSTEM BEFORE BRADLEY

Before the increased availability of federal grants in 1965, the Los Angeles political system was remarkably decentralized, but with growing forces for change. The federal government was ready to send aid long before Los Angeles was ready to receive it.

Writing in 1963, Banfield and Wilson (p. 110) cited Los Angeles as an example of "extreme decentralization." They noted:

> The mayor shares the executive authority with a separately elected city attorney and a controller. Of the twenty-eight city departments, nineteen are run by independent boards and commissions whose members, although appointed by the mayor, are removable by him only in unusual circumstances. . . . The fifteen councilmen owe nothing to the mayor or to each other, and are therefore under no discipline.

Banfield and Wilson agreed that, except in the case of "ad hoc" or especially well-advertised measures, this decentralization was rarely overcome. As a result, "many things cannot be done because it is impossible to secure the collaboration of all those whose collaboration is needed" (p. 111).

Adrian examined the Los Angeles political system and found little evidence of centralizing electoral organizations. In his typology of nonpartisan electoral systems, Adrian placed Los Angeles in category III, where interest groups slate candidates, but where party or quasi-party organizations do not (1959).

Adrian's (1962) view was consistent with Banfield and Wilson's contention that a business community–*Los Angeles Times* alliance was the single most powerful force in local elections:

> In Los Angeles, the selection of a candidate to represent the important downtown business and commercial interests is made after a series of meetings in which are brought together the spokesmen of the metropolitan press, the larger manufacturing and utility companies, and the banks, department stores and other leading interests. The *Los Angeles Times* has often taken the lead in arranging such meetings. Campaign funds are raised almost entirely from corporate gifts by executives of large corporations. A public relations firm is hired to conduct the campaign. It is given a budget, told in a general way what issues are important, and left to manage the campaign as it thinks best.

Even this semi-centralizing private power alliance was overrated, according to Carney (1964). In Carney's view, challenger Sam Yorty's ability to defeat Mayor Norris Poulson in 1961 despite the "establishment's" backing of the incumbent helped indicate that "the *Times* and the business interests simply have not won often enough to let us say that they were the wheels of a machine which functioned behind the screen of non-partisanship" (p. 111). Carney noted that despite its historic decentralization, Los Angeles had enjoyed good government, but he wondered, presciently, whether this easy-going political system would be able to cope with emerging urban social issues.

The Office of the Mayor was weak by charter design and tradition. As

Banfield (1965: 83) noted, "The Mayor is not a party boss and he has no patronage to distribute; if he is to have his way, it must be by persuasion or force of personality."

The structure of government acted to discourage the growth of mayoral leadership. Crouch and Dinerman (1964: 173) stated:

> The . . . charter undoubtedly produced a system of government that depends upon maintaining a delicate balance between the mayor, the council and the commissions. The mayor appoints commissioners, proposes a budget that includes support for most departments other than the so-called proprietary departments of harbor, water and power and airport and may veto appropriations and ordinances approved by the council. The council adopts, modifies or rejects the mayor's proposals for ordinances or appropriations and exercises a check on his appointing powers. The commissions have responsibilities specifically assigned to them by the charter and, in performing those responsibilities, they find it is necessary to have continuing relations with both the mayor and the council. After the City Administrative Officer was injected into the structure, a fourth force was involved in the bargaining process that produces the city's policies and programs. Largely through his influence on the budgetary process the CAO makes a considerable impact on the whole system. Yet it cannot be said that the system of city government created by the charter provides strong executive leadership in the sense that the term has generally been used in American government and administration.

The city council had major charter powers, but its members tended to be conservative in their policy outlook. Even after the Watts riots in 1965, the majority showed little interest in social policymaking. Even if they had such interest, their staff resources were limited. In 1963, for instance, newly elected black Councilman Tom Bradley had budget authority for only one field deputy position (Sonenshein 1984: 68). The councilmen relied for staff support on the chief legislative analyst's (CLA) office, the research arm of the council, and the mayoral-oriented city administrative officer (CAO).

The relative weakness of the elected officials increased the power of the city bureaucracy, loosely controlled by city commissioners. General managers of departments could make numerous decisions on their own, subject to limited central authority.

On the other hand, some political actors were seeking to alter this decentralized political system even before 1965. Mayor Yorty, elected in 1961, sought to greatly augment the power of his office. He fought constantly with the city council to expand his prerogatives, sparking long-running political warfare among elected officials (Bollens and Geyer 1973: 110). In 1963 he tried to "purge" several council members who opposed his policies (Ainsworth 1966: 62). As a maverick conservative, however, Yorty did not have a social agenda setting out a program for using such increased power.

In the late 1950s and early 1960s, liberals and minority group members organized politically (and often separately) to gain council representation. One major vehicle for this change was the reformist California Democratic Club movement.

In 1963 three black city councilmen took office on the 15-member council. Along with liberal white members, the new black councilmen became a voice for changing the city's stance toward social problems and for attending to the needs of minority and low-income areas. Achieving these goals required changes in the role of the council, and ultimately the election of a new mayor.

The Federal Role before Bradley

Before Bradley's election in 1973, the city's political leaders were largely unresponsive to federal initiatives, despite increased availability of federal funds. The city's grants process prior to 1973 was highly decentralized, episodic, inefficient, and uncoordinated. Ted Rogers, a grants specialist for the CLA for the past 10 years, described the process as one in which individual departments became aware of grants, made their own contacts with federal agencies, and prepared their own proposals. The Office of the Mayor and the council were frequently unaware of grant applications and hence had little control over resulting programs. Many grants were not pursued, although the city was eligible for them (Rogers interview).

Federal officials tried unsuccessfully to give money to Los Angeles. Dr. Emma McFarlin, now coordinator of grants for the CLA, was sent by the U.S. Department of Housing and Urban Development to offer funds to Los Angeles after the Watts riots. She found little enthusiasm among local elected officials. Los Angeles had a poor reputation with federal officials in those years. The quality of the applications was uneven, and federal officials were uncertain whether the proposals bore significant support of elected officials or merely reflected departmental priorities (McFarlin interview).

Consequently, Los Angeles received less federal money than comparable cities. Greenstone and Peterson (1972: 276) claimed that Los Angeles lost millions of dollars as a result of conflicts among Yorty, community residents, and federal officials over the administration of War on Poverty funds in the late 1960s. The lack of mayoral influence, allegedly stemming from the weakness of the office, limited Yorty's ability to forge the necessary compromises.

The Watts riots of 1965 focused public attention on the social needs of the city and the lack of leadership emanating from the mayor. At the start of the riots, Yorty was out of town campaigning for higher office and saw no pressing need to return (Conot 1967: 202). Later his public feud with senators Robert Kennedy and Abraham Ribicoff during Senate hearings on the riots highlighted both his lack of concern for the poor and his perception that there was little he could do about the problems of the city (Bollens and Geyer 1973: 135).

Yorty's view of city government as a limited service provider probably coincided with the views of many Los Angeles city officials at the time. The following exchange below between the mayor and Ribicoff best describes this point of view:

SENATOR RIBICOFF. As I listen to your testimony, Mayor Yorty, I made some notes. This morning you have really waived authority and responsibility for the following areas: schools, welfare, transportation, employment, health, and housing, which leaves you as the head of a city basically with a ceremonial function, police and recreation.
MAYOR YORTY. And fire.
SENATOR RIBICOFF. And fire?
MAYOR YORTY. Yes.
SENATOR RIBICOFF. Collecting sewerage?
MAYOR YORTY. Sanitation. That's right.
SENATOR RIBICOFF. In other words, basically, you lack jurisdiction authority, responsibility for what makes a city move?
MAYOR YORTY. That is exactly it. (Ruchelman 1969: 314)

Yorty went on to point out that the city charter granted limited power to the mayor and considerable authority to the city council and the various commissions. Until the voters chose to change the charter, he assumed he had limited ability to act as mayor. (The voters had frequently turned down such charter amendments.)

Ribicoff argued that Yorty's testimony did not speak well for the city. He predicted that the federal government would provide significant funding for cities in the near future, but that Los Angeles would be ill-equipped to take advantage of it.

> I believe there will be federal programs initiated in the next two years that will really put America on the road to start doing something about the cities of America.
>
> That means the cities are going to have to be in a position to take advantage of these programs. I would say as I have listened to you, and if it is the Charter it is no reflection on you personally, that one city that won't be able to take advantage of these programs will be Los Angeles because you are not organized to do so. (Ruchelman 1969: 316).

Bradley and the liberals on the council saw Watts as an opportunity to forge a consensus for more direct intervention by the city in economic and social concerns. For the liberal faction on the council, federal grants represented a way to finance social programs without diverting basic funds from the city budget. Their increased availability became a major rhetorical argument in favor of social change.

Tom Bradley's election to the council in 1963 followed a career as a city police officer. He had "walked the beat" in south-central Los Angeles and was well aware of the social and economic needs of the city's poor. As a councilman during the 1960s, he became associated with the liberal wing of the Democratic Party.

His early career included close association with local Democratic Party activists. He was an important member of the Leimert Park Democratic Club which placed him in close contact with many of those who are now party leaders.

He also became active in the National League of Cities, in 1963 becoming the first nonmayor to be elected a vice president of that organization. All of these activities led him to view changes in the federal system as an opportunity to attack the problems of the city. He also quickly became a leader within the council. Long-time Councilman John Gibson, council president during most of the Yorty years, perceived Bradley's leadership ability from the start and placed him on important council committees (Gibson interview).

As chairman of the State, Federal, and County Affairs Committee of the council, Bradley became a leading advocate of an expanded city grants effort. He often challenged Yorty to be more aggressive in the search for federal and state funds, and through his leadership role in the National League of Cities, Bradley became an authority on the subject.

In 1971 the council set up the Board of Grants Administration (BGA) to coordinate the city's grantsmanship effort. Federal officials objected to the original format of the board, which excluded Mayor Yorty. Eventually, the board was set up (over Yorty's veto) with three council members, the mayor, and the CAO, who was budget adviser to the mayor.

The BGA acted as a significant centralizing force in city government. For the first time, city departments such as the Police and the Community Redevelopment Agency were required to pass through a review process led by elected officials and their staffs. This constituted a significant restraint on free wheeling by city bureaucrats (Bruce 1974). Further, it helped professionalize the city council by familiarizing at least some of its members with the nature of the grants process. The CLA was charged by the council to actively seek federal funds for the city and began to keep records of grants "victories" on a large board.

In his 1973 electoral rematch against Yorty, Bradley strongly emphasized his pledge to be a more aggressive grants seeker than the incumbent mayor. Bradley announced that he would frequently go to Washington, D.C., to seek federal funds to deal with city problems.

THE GRANT PROCESS IN THE BRADLEY YEARS

The Bradley years witnessed a radical increase in the receipt of federal funds by the City of Los Angeles. Federal support rose from under $100 million in 1972 to a high of $320 million in 1978-79.

Federal funds to the city tripled from 1971 to 1980. The increases are related to general enhancement of intergovernmental funding during these years, but they also reflect Bradley's aggressive grants seeking. The Community Development Block Grant program, CETA, and the 1977 Economic Stimulus Package provided the major sources of these increases. Funds were also obtained from the Economic Development Administration (EDA) and Urban Development Action grants.

Los Angeles was gaining relatively more than its expected share, contrary to the Ribicoff prediction. By 1980, total CETA funds obtained were second only to New York. Public works funding ranked third nationally and the total from the Economic Stimulus Package ranked fourth (Hale and Palley 1981: 5). This was a significant change in Los Angeles' standing relative to other cities.

Major uses of these funds included expansion of transportation, harbor, and airport facilities; the revitalization of business and commercial areas; and public housing, employment, and services for the handicapped, aged, youth, and women. Thus city functions expanded well beyond the limits of city government defined during the Yorty years.

While many federal dollars flowed to the city through formulas, others were obtained competitively. Once secured, distribution required greater organization to be utilized effectively.

Politically and administratively, the influx of grants provided the means to change decision making at City Hall. Throughout the Bradley years, the influx in grants has coincided with centralization of responsibility in both the mayor and the council, increased administrative capacity to handle the grants process, and improved political relations with Washington and community groups.

We will now examine Bradley's federal aid strategy and how that plan affected Los Angeles' government. As mayor, Bradley has moved to build federal grantsmanship into a "winning game" for as many players as possible. By his own grants-seeking strategy and by encouraging the city council to take advantage of federal grants, he has indirectly created forces for centralization in the city's political system. In effect, he has promoted joint mayor-council hegemony over city policy through the vehicle of federal grants.

When Bradley took office in 1973, no clear grants consensus existed within the city government. Dr. C. Erwin Piper, the CAO, had originally been appointed by Yorty and held abiding anti-grants opinions. While some council members favored active grantsmanship (particularly council President John S. Gibson, representing the development-starved harbor and the low-income Watts areas), others were apathetic on the subject and a conservative cadre still opposed the whole idea. Among some of the council members, there was the fear that grants would create an immense mayoral machine.

With careful attention to the council's views, Bradley began immediately to pursue federal grants from a wide variety of agencies. He built on a system of political and administrative links between himself and the federal government.

Bradley's narrow defeat by Yorty in a bitterly contested, racially oriented 1969 campaign generated considerable support for Bradley among national Democratic Party leaders. His election in 1973 was seen by many Democrats as a chance to implement liberal Democratic policy in a major city. This helped make Bradley, the first black mayor of a major American city, a visible national urban leader. Deputy Mayor Grace Davis, a former federal official, remembers being inundated with university volunteers and returned Peace Corps workers, anxious to serve the new Bradley administration. (Davis interview). Bradley also remained active in the National League of Cities, becoming its president in 1974.

Bradley was close to Jimmy Carter, both in campaigns and in government. Bradley's personal and political ties to Carter led to Los Angeles' becoming a showcase for federal urban efforts during the Carter presidency. Davis recalls getting several calls from Washington asking if Los Angeles would implement certain programs. "They were literally asking us to spend the money," she said. Ray Remy, until recently a deputy mayor, remembers frequent contacts between high-level Carter administration officials and the mayor's people, as well as occasional meetings between Bradley and the president (Remy interview).

While Bradley's influence with the White House was less extensive under Republican administrations, contacts within the Congress and the business community continued to keep the Washington link alive. According to Remy, Republican Senator Pete Wilson has helped Bradley frequently as a result of ties developed when Wilson was mayor of San Diego. Democrats in Congress have also been a source of support to Bradley.

Bradley built links to the city council by helping two black allies win council seats. In 1973, he endorsed David S. Cunningham for his own vacant Tenth District seat. Cunningham, an urban consultant, had long experience in grantsmanship and became the council's most active and sophisticated grants specialist. In 1974, Bradley helped elect Bob Farrell, a member of his staff, to a vacant seat representing the Eighth District. While Farrell lacked Cunningham's grants knowledge, he could be expected to understand and support the mayor's overall grants effort.

Cunningham has been deeply involved in the city's grants program through his friendships with numerous federal officials and his grantsmanship experience. He was the first council member to hire a full-time grants deputy (in 1975) and his current deputy, Dennis Nishikawa, is considered one of the most knowledgeable grantspeople in City Hall. As chairman of the Council Grants Committee, Cunningham makes frequent trips to Washington to secure expanded federal support (Cunningham interview).

Bradley's personal staff reflects his emphasis on building federal links. He hired several former federal officials onto his mayoral staff. One of his first deputy mayors, Manuel Aragon, was a former official with the U.S. Economic Development Administration. Almost immediately after Bradley took office in 1973, Aragon obtained for the city a large, unallocated grant from the Office of Economic Opportunity for planning human services. Remy came to the position of deputy mayor after serving as executive director of the Southern California Association of Governments, where he was in regular contact with federal officials and the private sector. McFarlin joined the mayor's staff after serving as an official in the regional office of the Department of Housing and Urban Development (HUD). These and other appointments of people with federal experience provided the mayor with a wide range of federal contacts and a thorough understanding of the federal grants process.

Reorganization and Expansion of the Grants Process

The influx of grants in the Bradley years expanded the size of the mayor's office from initially around 275 to over 600. Most new employees were hired on federal funds. While the expanded staff increased the influence of the mayor, it proved to be cumbersome to administer and involved the mayor personally in the details of grants administration. It further opened Bradley to charges that he was building a political machine.

For these reasons, Bradley initiated the creation of the Community Development Department (CDD) in 1976, following a major internal study of the organization of the mayor's office. The CDD consolidated the activities of human services planning, manpower, and the physical planning efforts of urban development and housing. All Housing and Community Development Block Grant applications are now processed by the CDD and must be approved by the agency before going to the city council. In many fields, it has become the central agency for grants-related contacts between federal and city officials.

The CDD has served to institutionalize the grants process and has taken much of the daily decision making out of the mayor's office (Porter interview). The CDD seeks grants, coordinates the application process, and recommends allocations to the mayor and council. Although the CDD's recommended priorities are often altered by the council, their opinions are weighed heavily by the council. While the CDD began as an outgrowth of the mayor's office, it still maintains a sort of neutrality between the mayor and the council (Ford interview). Federal officials are pleased with the concept because it provides them with a permanent, ongoing counterpart (Roberts interview). The CDD is currently headed by a career administrator, Douglas Ford, recruited from outside the Los Angeles area.

The CDD has expanded to become a major city department reaching over 600 employees at its peak, with an operating budget of nearly $20 million. Much of its original staff formerly worked for the mayor. Thus, the grants process has created a large agency with allegiance to the mayor and sensitivity to the council.

The CDD has become an important and ongoing part of the city bureaucracy. It has been one of the few departments to expand its budget and staff over the past 10 years. Its rate of growth was unaffected by the passage of Proposition 13 in 1978. Its expansion occurred during a time of significant retrenchment in city employment. The number of city budgeted positions declined from a high of 32,600 in 1977-78 to 26,700 in 1984-85, a loss of over 18 percent. In contrast, the CDD and the mayor's office combined have grown from fewer than 300 in 1972 to a high of 758 in 1980-81. Today, these departments combined total 717 employees. More employees work for the CDD than for the city council and the CAO combined.

The mayor has still retained the major leverage over the grants process. A budgetary change in 1984 placed federal funds from "stable" sources such as the Housing and Community Development Block Grant directly into the city budget process. Formerly such grant items were separated from the budget and enacted by the Council Grants Committee before being presented to the mayor. This change gives the mayor considerably more leverage since changes in these grant items now must be made by an override of the mayor's veto, requiring a two-thirds vote. Council acceptance of this procedure suggests that the federal grants process is no longer a matter of serious controversy.

The mayor's office retains control over some grants, generally those of broader economic concern to the city, a particular priority of Bradley. Thus the CDD has become a mechanism for divesting the mayor of grants in which he has limited interest, or whose distributional conflicts are so strong that he would prefer the council to have the responsibility. Those grants that are divisible by council district tend to be administered by the CDD.

With the creation of the CDD and the trend toward federal block grants, Bradley steadily turned the distributive function of grants over to the council. The council receives the recommendations of the mayor through the CDD but feels free to alter them. Council sessions have often been punctuated by the vocal lobbying of community-based organizations seeking federal funds.

Federal funds under the CETA program directly benefited council members by providing staff members. Council staffs rose in the mid-1970s due to CETA hiring, building another base of support for city grantsmanship.

Council members have been able to look for things to do for their constituents, either through the block grant or, for a time, through services provided by CETA workers. Cunningham used his CETA workers to set up a Community Service Center in his district; one of his CETA workers became the district's grantsperson.

Meanwhile, the mayor concentrated increasingly on "big-ticket" federally funded projects, largely in the area of economic development. The mayor aggressively sought funds from the EDA, HUD, and other federal agencies to create downtown and inner-city development projects, revitalize local industries, and bring businesses into low-income areas.

This division of labor offered benefits to both the mayor and astute council members. For the mayor, high-visibility projects brought favorable publicity and the valuable label of "job producer." The redevelopment program built links to the downtown business community, a major campaign funding source for Bradley. And Bradley has been able to stay largely above the distributive battles within the city over social service funds (although he is still involved).

For those council members who actively sought power through the grants process, this situation offered significant benefits. Cunningham, for instance, developed substantial influence over city bureaucrats due to his role in the grants process. Despite not representing the poorest district, he was able to obtain a good share of federal funds for his constituents. Gibson was able to locate substantial funding for his harbor area, in some cases through direct contact with U.S. Congressman Glenn Anderson (Gibson interview). While influence over social services funds could be divisive, a council member could gain active grass-roots support simply by fighting on behalf of district organizations.

Less-sophisticated council members were often annoyed at the activists' success. They would often ask, "Where's my grant?" The mayor made an effort early in his term to spread grant funds into areas outside the central city (Smith interview). As council members became aware of what grants could do, they more aggressively sought to become involved, by submitting proposals and requests for funds.

In 1977 the council removed the mayor and the CAO from the Board of Grants Administration and created the Council Grants Committee as a regular council committee. This reflected the council's increased interest in grants and its desire for a major role in the process. (Dr. Piper, the CAO, recalls that he felt relieved to be out of the line of fire from angry community groups.) In time, the council became so active in grants that today, virtually all have a full-time grants deputy, or a staff member who devotes significant time to grants. Even a council conservative such as Hal Bernson, after a brief term as chairman of the Grants Committee, became an advocate of grants (Smith interview).

Support of Community-Based Groups and Businesses

With increases in block grants, the role of nonprofit community-based organizations (CBO) as grant recipients increased as well. CBOs have developed into major providers of city services during the Bradley years. Currently, over 180 such organizations are receiving federal funds through the city.

Many of these organizations are large, diversified enterprises with deep roots in the various ethnic and racial communities of the city. They compete for grant contracts and are monitored and audited by city officials. As their funding has expanded, so has their political influence. Their presence has created a nongovernmental source of advocacy for expanded federal funds and a source of political support for the mayor and the council.

Downtown business has long favored an aggressive city policy of seeking federal funds, especially for redevelopment. Through the grants process, business has been included in the Bradley coalition, and has also offered significant donations to council members. Downtown redevelopment is widely considered to be one of Bradley's major accomplishments (Boyarsky 1980). The use of grants and redevelopment authority has served to attract major industries and commercial offices. Bradley's staff has worked closely with the business community and shielded major city-business interactions from the interplay of interests on the council.

Finally, turnover in city staff has helped build links for grantsmanship. As noted above, CAO Piper was distinctly unfavorable toward grants. A conservative man with limited city experience prior to his appointment by Yorty, Piper saw grant programs as "welfare," feeling that they had very limited positive impact on the city (Piper interview). Bradley retained Piper because the CAO handled the budgetary function honestly and carefully and he represented an aura of fiscal integrity. Upon Piper's retirement, however, Bradley secured a new CAO, Keith Comrie, who views the grants process very positively. In Comrie's job interview, Bradley specifically asked the CAO candidate for his views of grantsmanship (Comrie interview).

Bradley's Leadership Style

The leadership style of Mayor Bradley has been a critical factor in this evolving system of support for city grantsmanship. While the presence of federal grants has certainly strengthened the authority of the mayor's office, considerable power still rests with the council. Where Yorty fought this division, Bradley has worked with and around it.

Yorty saw the policy process as a continuing war between mayor and council. Bradley's style is best described as cooperative and noncombative (Remy, Gibson, Calleia interviews). His 10 years on the council provided an apprenticeship unlike that of any recent mayor; thus, Bradley can think and act like a council member. Former Deputy Mayor Remy adds, "He treats them with respect and is willing to share honors and rewards with them."

Blunt conflicts between mayor and council certainly occur. Council members have, on occasion, accused the mayor of building a political machine; they have attacked his policies and said terrible things about the quality of his staff and appointments. Overall, however, the council members refrain from attacking the mayor, and those battles that do arise seem not to leave lasting scars. Most council members, whether or not allied with Bradley, see him as cooperative; he further appears to be detached from the details of council decision making. Over time, mayor and council have divided responsibility and generally respected the limits of each other's turfs.

Conclusion

Federal funds have made possible increased social service and development expenditures for the City of Los Angeles. Consequently, the city has expanded its service delivery capacity and has been able to serve new groups and interests. The mayor and council have expanded their offices to provide a greater administrative capacity to determine needs and attract outside funding. The network of interests served by the city thus is much greater than in the Yorty years.

Politically, a consensus on the value of federal grants has emerged. City council members, once apathetic or even hostile to grants, are now largely favorable to their pursuit. Several anti-grant members left the council, to be replaced by more accepting ones. Even some of the most conservative members have grown to like grants. New distributional formulas have expanded the number of council districts eligible for funding. CBOs and businesses have provided major nongovernmental constituencies for federal grantsmanship, in ways that affect both the mayor and the council.

Thus, the Bradley years have witnessed the expansion of the functions of government in Los Angeles from minimal service provision and low visibility to higher service delivery and more widespread political visibility. Conflict over service delivery and the merits of federal aid during the Yorty years has been replaced by a consensus on the pursuit of aid and a mutual sharing of aid decisions.

The influx of federal funds to Los Angeles has altered the management of the city in several ways. Aid has been significantly increased and fewer restrictions are placed on its use. A broad array of services have been provided. The bulk of the aid, according to Ross (1982: 12), has been used for social services and economic development. By Ross's estimates, the aid has had a redistributive effect, providing increased services and funds to low-income and minority groups.

City officials have tried to limit the extent to which federal funds are used for traditional city functions. This adds emphasis to the notion that the city's leaders want to control the use of federal funds. General revenue sharing is incorporated directly into the budgetary process, but most other funds are used for services that are outside the housekeeping functions of government.

The official explanation for this kind of distribution is avoidance of dependence on federal funding. A specific strategy of concentrating federal funds into one-time capital expenditures as opposed to labor costs has helped to minimize city dependence on these funds (Calleia interview). The city has indeed been able to separate some grant-funded and locally funded activities. Declines in federal support in recent years were implemented by limiting support to outside agencies. Likewise, grant-funded services increased following the passage of Proposition 13, while city housekeeping functions were cut.

In some ways the city is economically dependent on federal grants; in other ways it may be politically dependent. Federal aid has been a vehicle for centralizing authority in the mayor and city council, in a coalition of elected officials. (The mayor, of course, is by far the leading single actor in the coalition.) Aid has been used to build political coalitions for elected officials, to provide services in council districts, to aid ailing businesses, and to expand the economic base of the central city.

All of these things can take place, including the coalition-building process drawing on businesses and CBOs, because grants are an outside resource added to the existing pile. It adds to overall resources, or appears to, rather than being the basis for a battle over scarce, limited resources. Mayor and council seek federal funds to do the things they have promised, thereby satisfying their supporters in the community and avoiding acrimonious infighting among elected officials over resources.

The glue for this cooperation between mayor and council is the ability of grants to satisfy their different goals. The mayor represents the city as a whole and must satisfy city-wide interests. The structure of the American system dictates that the economic welfare of the city must dominate mayoral decisions. As Peterson (1981:29) states:

> Cities like private firms compete with one another so as to maximize their economic position. To achieve this objective, the City must use the resources its land area

> provides by attracting as much capital and as high a quality labor force as is possible. Like a private firm, the City must entice labor and capital resources by offering appropriate inducements.

Those interests that benefit from the overall economic health of the city will be the natural constituency of the mayor. Thus, Bradley has concentrated on economically oriented grants: downtown renewal, harbor and airport renovations, mass transit, and economic development. Many of these grant programs remain lodged in the mayor's office.

City council members are dominated by district concerns. The lack of local party organizations and the independence of the council position limits their concern for city-wide policies. Council members build their own candidate organizations in their districts. The impact of an economic development project is not clearly related to the welfare of a council member's constituency, even though it may be placed in the district. A new factory supported by city funds, for instance, may not necessarily hire people from the district and may create problems for nearby residents.

Aid to social service agencies may, however, directly benefit constituents. An employment training program, a senior citizens' center, or a day-care center will directly link the council member with his or her constituents. Thus the council member will be more concerned with the use of grant funds to enhance district services.

The mayor limits his intervention in council determinations on allocations of health and social welfare funds. In return, the council allows the mayor to take the lead in transportation and economic development programs. There is overlap; both bodies are involved in all decisions, but our interviews suggest the differing political interests of the mayor and the council.

The long-run consequence of the grants system in Los Angeles may be a mayor's office with expanded formal and informal powers working with a council that is stronger and more professional than ever before. Bradley in 1984 proposed a measure that, had it been implemented, would have significantly increased the power of elected officials. He offered a charter amendment to give the mayor and the council the right to fire major city bureaucrats. (The voters, ever wary of politicization of government, voted it down in the November 1984 general election.) Without the leverage given him by the grants process, we doubt the mayor could have proposed this significant extension of formal authority.

The city is not as decentralized today as it once was. We need to revise some of our views of Los Angeles in this light. A major vehicle for this change has been the city's involvement in the federal grants process. These trends toward centralization have involved both the mayor and the council.

However, it is not yet clear if these changes are permanent. Since Reagan's election in 1980, federal aid to cities has declined. Bradley will someday no longer be mayor. How will such changes affect the centralization brought about as a result of Bradley's grants stategy?

Even without major federal grants, Bradley has continued to pursue the strategy of bringing new resources into the city, rather than dividing existing ones. An example are the Olympic Games held in Los Angeles in 1984. Bradley's efforts were the key to bringing the games there—and they certainly represent a new resource obtained through linkages outside Los Angeles. Thus, as long as Bradley is mayor, Los Angeles' political system will tend to be focused on what comes in from the outside as well as what is already there.

If a new mayor is elected who confronts the city council without bringing in new resources, bureaucratic power and fragmentation could reemerge as private actors play elected officials against each other. It is unlikely, however, that the next mayor would select the Yorty model to follow as a guide to running the city. Further, most of the mayoral contenders who would succeed Bradley are council members, with a strong sense of the respect due to the council.

It is most unlikely that the role of the council will revert to what it was in the late 1950s and early 1960s. Expectations have been raised that council members will have professional staffs and will help deliver services to their constituents. They will expect to be fully involved in the formation of city policy. Elected officials will continue to step on bureaucratic turf.

As former Councilman Gibson noted, "When I started in the Council we didn't have all these staff people going out looking for problems to solve." Ambitious council people and shrewd mayors will continue to expand their influence over city policy, bringing more of the city's efforts within the boundaries of the electoral process.

IMPLICATIONS

"Implementation" to Los Angeles officials means securing federal funds to further a coalition offering expanded city services. Funds are scarce; they will be used to most effectively accomplish this goal. This notion of effectiveness, however, may be at variance with that seen from the perspective of Congress or the federal bureaucracy. To the Los Angeles City Council members, effectiveness may mean distributing the funds to several districts with varying degrees of actual need (or, in the case of public housing funds, keeping them out of certain districts though the need may exist). It may also mean "cutting in" certain community-based organizations that politically support the coalition. Some of these CBOs may misuse the funds, though this is relatively rare.

The mayor's office may accept the guidance of key business leaders in determining the use of urban redevelopment funds, and these leaders will personally gain. Yet all of these occurrences may aid in centralizing authority—an objective often sought by federal officials.

In the implementation process, delays may occur; some groups in need may not be reached; the application of federal legislation may be at variance with the lawmakers' intent. Without the creation of the coalition, however, Los Angeles would have received little aid, and the aid that was received would be dispensed as it was prior to Bradley: disjointedly and haphazardly. By providing the political prerequisites of a more centralized system, federal aid has created the means for a more coordinated approach to service delivery and to the indigenous solution to the problems of Los Angeles.

INTERVIEWS

Harreld Adams, assistant general manager, Community Development Department
Gil Archuletta, former assistant chief legislative analyst
Thomas Bradshaw, city administrative officer's staff member
Edna Bruce, former grants specialist, CLA
Anton Calleia, executive assistant to the mayor
Keith Comrie, CAO
David S. Cunningham, city council member, Tenth District
Grace Davis, deputy mayor
Douglas Ford, general manager, CDD
John Gibson, former city council member, Fifteenth District, and former Council President
Carlos Jackson, former grants assistant, mayor's office
Dr. Emma McFarlin, coordinator of grants, CLA
Dennis Nishikawa, grants deputy, Councilman Cunningham
Dr. C. Erwin Piper, former CAO
Steven Porter, assistant general manager, CDD
Ray Remy, former deputy mayor
Herbert Roberts, Los Angeles representative, U.S. Department of Housing and Urban Development
Ted Rogers, staff member, CLA
Diane Sallee, chief deputy, city council member Joan Milke Flores, Fifteenth District
Grieg Smith, chief deputy, city council member Hal Bernson, Twelfth District

REFERENCES

Adrian, Charles R. 1959. "A Typology for Nonpartisan Elections," *Western Political Quarterly* 12 (June): 449–458.

Ainsworth, Ed. 1966. *Maverick Mayor: A Biography of Sam Yorty of Los Angeles*. Garden City, N.Y.: Doubleday and Co.

Banfield, Edward. 1965. *Big City Politics*. New York: Random House.

Banfield, Edward, and James Q. Wilson. 1963. *City Politics*. Cambridge, Mass.: Harvard University Press.

Bardach, Eugene. 1977. *The Implementation Game: What Happens after a Bill Becomes a Law*. Cambridge, Mass.: MIT Press.

Bollens, John C., and Grant B. Geyer. 1973. *Yorty: Politics of a Constant Candidate*. Pacific Palisades, Calif.: Palisades Publishers.

Boyarsky, Bill. 1980. "Bradley Has Done Much Despite Shortcomings," *Los Angeles Times* (September 9).

Browning, Rufus, Dale Rogers Marshall, and David H. Tabb. 1981. "Implementation and Political Change: Sources of Local Variation." In Daniel Mazmanian and Paul Sabatier, eds., *Effective Policy Implementation*. Lexington, Mass.: Lexington.

Bruce, Edna. 1974. "The Grantsmanship Game in Los Angeles," *Nation's Cities* (September): 15–16.

Caraley, Demetrios. 1977. *City Governments and Urban Problems*. Prentice-Hall.

Carney, Francis M. 1964. "The Decentralized Politics of Los Angeles," *The Annals of the American Academy of Political and Social Science* 353 (May): 107–121.

Conot, Robert. 1967. *Rivers of Blood, Years of Darkness*. New York: Bantam Books.

Crouch, Winston, and Beatrice Dinerman. 1964. *Southern California Metropolis: A Study in Development of Government for a Metropolitan Area*. Berkeley: University of California Press.

Derthick, Martha. 1970. *The Influence of Federal Grants: Public Assistance in Massachusetts*. Cambridge, Mass.: Harvard University Press.

———. 1972. *New Towns In-Town*. Washington, D.C.: Urban Institute.

Frieden, Bernard J., and Marshall Kaplan. 1975. *The Politics of Neglect*. Cambridge, Mass.: MIT Press.

Greenstone, David J., and Paul Peterson. 1972. *Race and Authority in Urban Politics: Community Participation and the War on Poverty*. New York: Russell Sage.

Hale, George E., and Marian Lief Palley. 1981. *The Politics of Federal Grants*. Washington, D.C.: Congressional Quarterly Press.

Harrigan, John J. 1981. *Political Change in the Metropolis*. Boston: Little-Brown.

Peterson, Paul E. 1981. *City Limits*. Chicago: University of Chicago Press.

Porter, David, David Warner, and Teddie Porter. 1973. *The Politics of Federal Aid: Resource Mobilization in Local School Districts*. Beverly Hills, Calif.: Sage Publications.

Pressman, Jeffrey L., and Aaron B. Wildavsky. 1973. *Implementation*. Berkeley, Calif.: University of California Press

Rasmussen, E. 1979. "The Allocative Effects of Grants in Aid: Some Extensions and Qualifications," *National Tax Journal* 29: 211–219.

Ripley, Randall B., and Grace A. Franklin. 1982. *Bureaucracy and Policy Implementation*. Homewood, Ill.: Parsley.

Ross, Ruth. 1981. *Case Studies of the Impact of Federal Aid on Major Cities: City of Los Angeles*. Washington, D.C.: U.S. Department of Commerce, National Technical Information Service.

Ruchelman, Leonard. 1969. *Big City Mayors: The Crisis in Urban Politics*. Bloomington: Indiana University Press.

Saltzstein, Alan. 1977. "Federal Categorical Aid to Cities: Who Needs It versus Who Wants It," *Western Political Quarterly* 30: 377–383.

Sonenshein, Raphael. 1984. "Bradley's People: Functions of the Candidate Organization." Ph.D. diss., Yale University.

Stein, Robert M. 1979. "Federal Categorical Aid: Equalization and the Application Process," *Western Political Quarterly* 32: 397–408.

Stein, Robert M. (1983). "Policy Implementation in the Federal System: An Evolutationary Explanation of Growth and Change." American Political Science Association, Chicago, Ill. Unpublished.

Stenberg, Carl W. 1984. "Beyond the Days of Wine and Roses: Intergovernmental Management in a Cutback Environment." In Harlan Hahn and Charles Levine, eds., *Readings in Urban Politics*. New York: Longman.

Thomas, Robert P. 1984. "Implementing Federal Programs at the Local Level." In Harlan Hahn and Charles Levine, eds., *Readings in Urban Politics*. New York: Longman.

———. "Policy Implementation in a Federal System: The Case of Grant Compliance." In Robert Eyestone and George Edwards III, eds., *Public Policy Formation and Implementation*. Greenwich, Conn.: JAI Press (forthcoming).

U.S. Advisory Commission on Intergovernmental Relations. 1978. "Federal Initiatives and Impacts," *Intergovernmental Perspectives* 4: 8–10.

MASTER PLAN AND SYSTEMS EFFECTS:
IMPLEMENTING DECENTRALIZATION IN FRANCE

Jean-Claude Thoenig

ABSTRACT

What is the direction of decentralization in France? What are the dynamics of current changes and continuities?

Concepts from sociology and political science are useful to understand what is taking place. Three concepts are especially used here: systems analysis, the public policy approach, and the paradigm of action by system-induced results. They are applied to data collected by surveys of subnational civil servants and elected officials (1981–1984).

The attitudes and behaviors of local decision makers indicate the significance of current decentralization policy. This is clear in a 1984 survey by Francois Dupuy of 1,090 local higher civil servants:

> The policy of decentralization aims to replace the supervisory role of the administration over local governments with an advisory role. Will this development have concrete consequences for you?

This article owes a great deal to work conducted jointly with Francois Dupuy (CNRS); I am grateful to him for his comments. English translation by Kevin Byrnes.

Research in Urban Policy, Vol. 2, pages 77–87.

ISBN: 0-89232-534-8

Yes:	69.1%
No:	28.4%
No opinion:	2.5%

That a change in administrative practices is under way seems relatively accepted. Yet the precise impact of this change remains unclear.

While we lack the time perspective for definitive evaluation, some concrete observations are already available (Dupuy-Thomas 1984; Dupuy and Thoenig 1983, 1985; Mabileau 1983, 1984; Meny 1983c; Merrill 1984). We will attempt to make sense of such observations less to develop a general theory of decentralization than to clarify actions of practicing administrators.

The law of March 2, 1982, on "the rights and liberties of communes, departments, and regions" is considered a milestone. In two years, 15 laws and 133 appropriation orders have been signed by the government, and the list still grows. Many proposals have yet to be resolved (local fiscal policy, rules concerning local elected officials, cumulation of powers, etc.). This production of texts by the national government drives the reform process (Ashford 1983; Keating 1983; Kesselmann 1982).

Yet it is worth asking whether the redefinition of relations between the State and local governments follows from a master plan of some sort. This is unclear due to the mixed responsibilities between the administration and the National Assembly. One perspective is that since there is action by public authorities, there is change. At the other extreme is the voluntary decision by some ideologically conscious actor at a given point in time. Certainly the 1981–1982 orientation toward local government is a change. From the mid–1950s until the early 1970s, three approaches characterized policy in this area: (1) functional regionalism, (2) intercommunal cooperation, and (3) reform of State administrations through decentralization as well as by efforts to control rampant urbanization. Problems were engaged peripherally rather than head-on. From the early 1970s until 1981, the State aimed to limit its weaknesses through modernization of communal administration. In contrast, the strategy since 1981 attempts a global redefinition of relations between the State and local governments (Meny 1983a, 1983b; Thoenig 1983).

The perception of change must not, however, obscure continuity among certain policies. For example, no provision was made for geographically remapping local governments. Today, France still has more basic local democratic entities (including 36,000 communes) than all of the EEC countries combined. Similarly, municipal councils and general councils in the departments still are elected by the people. The mayor or president in turn is elected by his fellow council members, and he directs the local administration essentially following the laws of 1871 and 1884—the foundation of centralized leadership in local government. Finally, intermediary level (regional) governments have no more control over the communes. Thus silence (if not consensus) postpones discussion of such issues as the size of communes, relationship between the people and political authority, and connections between subnational governments.

We might summarize the actions since 1981 as follows: Leading regional and departmental participants ("les grands notables") as well as the political parties were strengthened; the lesser participants acted to safeguard the essentials of their positions; and the people continued their traditional relationship with municipalities and departments, a mixture of universal suffrage and individual dependence.

Decision-making analysis has a drawback: The act of decision and the role of decision maker can be accorded too much importance. The decision of March 2, 1982, and the rapid appearance of measures conforming to the new law suggest the actions of a single actor and his immediate circle. (It is no accident that the laws came to be known as "la reforme Defferre" after the mayor of Marseilles.)

This event-centered account of decentralization is insufficient, even if it does uncover the more-or-less visible hand of a dominant actor. There are two special dangers.

One is banal. Most choices do not mechanically reflect the influence of decision makers; many actors participate, and the list of interest groups is long. Another dynamic is based on the structural interdependence and interchange of actors. There is an entire system involving the various national and local participants in reform—a system that dates not from 1981 but from before. From this systems perspective three issues are particularly significant: (1) the transfer of powers from the state to the departments, (2) the regulation of local civil servants, and (3) the debate over the accumulation of positions ("le cumul"), that is, the traditional right to hold simultaneously more than one position, like mayor and minister.

The second danger is overvaluing the act of decision itself. The text of the law may be seen as a relatively empty frame; the subsequent decrees, orders, and circulars have greater meaning since they determine how the law is expressed. They can even empty a formal decision of its content, deflecting its original intent. Realizing this, many actors seek to promote their particular interests by acting discreetly at the outset and concentrating their efforts on the less-visible but more important administrative phase. For example, the local agents of the state civil service corps see their position endangered by new regulations, but they see the use of temporary decrees as a safeguard of their power. Other actors manipulate the calendars of reform to postpone measures intended to reverse the accumulation of positions or reorganize State and local fiscal policies.

The effective program of texts promulgated and measures enacted since

May-June 1981 reinforces the feeling that the government's primary concern was a grand gesture and that the affected participants all did whatever was easiest and most acceptable. The leading participants have received the power they wished for and often exercised before 1981, while the civil servants have been rewarded for their support with special attention paid to their status or, like the prefectorial corps, have received substantial consolation prizes (career advantages, improved life-style). Ironically, the reformer of 1982 echoed his counterpart of 1884 in declaring that reform must be progressive, irreversible, yet gradual, and that time would be the final judge.

A deep-seated way of thinking sees a single, all-encompassing problematic behind decentralization. It sees reform as just a necessary and inevitable result of common sense, simply a matter of time. Yet this does not explain why or how reform happens, and the origins of reform do not predict the results of implementation (Bourricaud 1982). After the presidential election of 1981, decentralization became a problem in itself, with its own particular stakes. Each actor has his own stakes, which not only fluctuate but contradict those of others.

What rationale guides the political entrepreneur? The government, promoting its options, avoids too-precise criteria, time limits, or quantitative results. It pursues several avenues simultaneously, facing different publics and various eventualities. It wishes to show that it is the first in a century to "do something" about decentralization. Yet it keeps a free hand once implementation begins, to gain advantage no matter what occurs. Its rationale is ex post, not ex ante.

It is not clear that the problems announced are the ones treated. For example, it is widely held that France is too centralized, yet studies show that the State is not all-powerful. There is much power at the local level. Whatever centralization exists in France is as much a result of local strategies as of actions from Paris (Trosa 1983; Ashford and Thoenig 1981). Decentralization is not only a historical process but a system of action in which government policy structures policy in general. A public policy approach may be substituted for the decision-making approach (Jones 1970).

Decentralization will be whatever local officials make of it. The law of July 16, 1971, on the merging of communes, was followed in three years by only a 3% reduction in the total number of communes (De Kervasdoué et al. 1976). The decrees of March 14, 1964, intended to reinforce local institutions, were undercut by a coalition of State-elected officials and civil servants (Gremion 1976, 1979). As further implementation occurs, the extent of resistance to "la reforme Defferre" will become clearer. Any attempt to determine success or failure at this point is premature.

Focusing observations solely upon what happens at the subnational level, after the national authorities have made a decision, is also dangerous. There is not really a national sphere distinct from the local; they interpenetrate structurally. Many actors operate on both levels. Nor should we distinguish pre- and postdecisional eras; by considering them together we gain perspective. *Analysis must take an organizational and policy-oriented consideration of strategies and relations among actors and local administrations. An initial synthesis suggests the following tendencies:*

While the legal texts suggest a vertical transfer of powers from the State to the local governments, practice indicates horizontal movement at each level between local commissaries and their local elected counterparts. The complex ensemble of relations between elected officials and State agents, while less decisive than formerly, still functions. The interdependence of local elected officials and State civil servants sometimes becomes attenuated or even inverted. Increasingly, each local situation is becoming a special case.

The reform measures directly affect the communes weakly, the regions moderately, and the departments most of all. Seemingly destined to disappear, the departments remain vital. Heterogeneity of local administration continues to grow. The relation between the State and the general populace seems hardly changed since 1981, remaining highly differentiated from one area to the next (Peyrefitte et al. 1976).

Let us now examine each level, beginning with *the department.* Executive powers were transferred from the State representative (prefect) to the departmental regional representative (president of the general council) rapidly and without major problems. This changes the fundamental (legal) control from the top down to the bottom up. This important transfer has already given the general councils a strong, regular influence with the State and its agents (Dupuy and Thoenig 1983). Along with increased powers, the president of the general council has increased responsibilities for hiring personnel and directing various services. The prefect, on the other hand, has lost many of his powers to the department. Theoretically, the prefect has received added authority over the increased number of local officials involved in departmental administration. In practice, his ability to coordinate the various ministries in his department is weak. Each ministry seeks to preserve its sphere of influence by transferring decisions to Paris; in the meantime, the prefect must waver between his conflicting bureaucratic roles on behalf of State and department. The local agencies of State ministries are mostly concerned with charting a successful course through the transition period.

A new departmental administration has been established, amalgamating services and staff from many sources. The departments vary considerably in the quality, organization, and influence of these services. Some departments have developed organizational machines rivaling the national administration, while others remain organizationally and fiscally conservative. The director of this administration often becomes an important departmental actor, linked to the president of the general council much as the secretary-general of a town is linked to its mayor.

The relationship between the general council president and the council members varies with local circumstances, but it tends to fall between two extremes: centralization under the president, who becomes the council's regulator and lays down its agenda, and collegialism, where the council is primary. Empirical indicators like budgetary revisions show a tendency toward tempered presidentialism counterbalanced by the fact that the president of the council is usually not supported by the same electoral base as the council members.

The pairing of general council president-prefect, formerly the keystone of departmental power, is still essential, although some aspects have changed. Each partner depends on the goodwill of the other to succeed. This interdependence limits how far each partner can go. Models of partnership range from symbiotic collusion to overt conflict. Elected officials have been willing to express such conflicts publicly, while prefects have shown more reserve. The prefect must adapt to the new state of things, retrenching behind the bureaucracy, agreeing with the desires of the elected officials, seeking support from the central administration, or resigning.

Relations between departmental elected officials and State managers of local service bureaus have become more volatile and complex. Departmentally administered services are power resources for the elected officials and a constraint upon State agents. State service agencies must also contend with the local prefect; they can no longer collaborate with the general council in containing the influence of the prefect.

Paradoxically, relations with Paris have become important for departmental actors. The prefect and local State agencies exercise their channels of influence in Paris to strengthen themselves against their respective local partners. The government, through the prime minister, must regularly instruct the prefects to limit and control relations between the local State service agencies and the general councils. Legally, the general council and its executive have the right to control State services that deal with departmental matters, but the directives of Matignon prevent the council president from effectively intervening. Thus Paris becomes more important than ever to the departments, even though decentralization is officially a disengaging of the State from local public affairs.

In summary, the management of public affairs at the departmental level includes the following:

1. Change in the decision-making rules of the game
2. Increased power around the president of the general council

3. Emergence of new decision-making channels next to the traditional politico-administrative ones
4. Increased political differentiation between departmental elected officials and others, especially municipal elected officials.

Turning to the level of the commune, we note that some 800 communes have populations over 10,000 and are largely self-sufficient and solidly organized, while the other 26,000 have populations under 700 and are far from self-sufficient. The law of March 2, 1982, provided for an end to legal control of communes from above and authorized local economic interventions by the commune. This has made little difference in actual practice. As previously, the prefect counts for little, the mayor goes to the minister for help, and the communal budget gives limited financial help to local enterprises in need. Especially for the small communes, autonomy remains largely theoretical.

The communes have received basic operational independence in administering urban responsibilities (Denis 1983). But before 1983 the larger towns could already, for example, grant construction permits, although few actually did. For the small communes, the transfer has become an embarrassment. Nearly 90% of the mayors interviewed by the *Gazette des Communes* in 1983 want to receive instruction from the Bureau of Civil Engineering (Equipement) concerning construction permits in their jurisdictions. Without a technical agent behind whose expertise he might hide, the mayor must shoulder all responsibility for granting—and refusing—construction permits.

Such prerogatives as the right of approval over municipal personnel and the recruitment of cabinet members confirm the mayor's role as an employer or patron. Protection offered by Parliament to lower-level communal employees becomes rather meaningless since, for budgetary reasons, such supplementary personnel often cannot be hired.

Some fiscal measures in 1984 favored the smaller communes, and the ministers have increased the number of specific subventions for communes. Yet a fundamental, overall fiscal reform has not taken place.

The situation in the *regions* is more open (Chevallier et al. 1984; Gremion 1983). The region represents an area of few preestablished constraints. Its budget, while reduced, is freer to reallocate funds from year to year. On the other hand, there is less administrative guidance from State services. Political power, as in the department, tends toward a tempered presidentialism.

SYSTEM-INDUCED RESULTS

The "master plan" interpretation sees the 1981–1982 decentralization as a conscious action by the French government. By seeking to preprogram a sequence of actions and events, a redefinition of relations between the State and local governments is its eventual goal (Padioleau 1981). This theory does not stand up to analysis. There are too many uncertainties: The term for implementation is too long, the objective is vague, unexpected obstacles can arise, and autonomous actors can intervene at any point.

By contrast, systems analysis of this process does not seek to reconstitute some causal chain of events between the initial policy decision and final results, or look for a collective intentionality guiding decisions or events. Rather, the process is structured around a system of actions in which events intervene to alter not only basic rules of the system but also strategies of leading actors (March and Olsen 1976). Specific results flow not from intended actions, but from the workings of the system. The significance of events for the actors must be identified. Actors have disparate goals and analyses of the situation. The analyst registers how the system's actions are affected by particular strategies, unanticipated events, or outright dysfunctions. The aggregate of these actions produces collective effects, which differ from effects at the level of the individual actor. Collective effects are beyond the capacity of any one actor or group of actors to change (Stout 1980). Intentionality is therefore not a key variable; meaning is derived from the actions themselves. The process produces its own content.

Taking everything into account, the communes gain relatively little from decentralization. The existence of State service agencies is actually an advantage to mayors, who can draw on them for resources. Still, the State measures have had important indirect consequences. The power of the departments has grown substantially, to a point where municipal officials feel it is a serious problem. The law of March 2, 1982, forbids any form of supervision by one local government over another, but in practice, the departmental general councils have many powerful advantages—in planning, contracting, and financing. From these often follow allocation of funds to local governments within the department. Some rural mayors have simply been taken over by the presidents of their general councils and have no recourse to a third party for help. The decentralization of the State may lead to a new centralization at a level nearer and more burdensome to the commune.

This issue also arises between communes. The larger towns convert their urbanism agencies into economic development agencies, both to increase influence over smaller towns and to counter departmental influence. But these small communes enjoy relative overrepresentation in the general council of the department and can attempt thereby to counterbalance the influence of larger, central towns. In general, the large towns do better in this competition, and such events have important long-term consequences.

A possible scenario in terms of system-induced effects concerns the national economic and budgetary crisis. Does management of this crisis overcome decentralization policy? The search for solutions to recession has undercut the State's attempt to redefine its relations with local governments. This has sometimes caused the State to abandon its old role of economic interventionist. Decentralization by the State can become Machiavellian: While granting more local autonomy, the State abandons any problems that cannot be solved in the context of recession. The policy of Defferre clearly reflects this ambivalence. Budgetary cutbacks in 1983 and 1984 and the failure to construct an overall fiscal reform have led the fiscal means for implementation to dwindle steadily at both State and local levels.

Another chain of events involves local administrative and technical services. Here again strategies do not turn on the redefinition of State-local relations. Rather, each party involved has its own problems, whose articulation explains the dynamics of the process. Local communal officials jealously guard their autonomy in hiring higher-level municipal staff. In their eyes, he who appoints the staff controls the service. A favored strategy is hiring from outside the commune to keep a free hand, and the availability of talented State civil servants thus becomes a valuable resource. This bridge between State and local administrations, some fear, may lead to a flood of State agents into local management positions (Thoenig 1982).

The State administration also confronts unexpected problems. Consider the Bureau of Civil Engineering (Equipement). If the transfer of powers to the localities has not ended its powerful service network, its future is called into question. It seeks to survive, therefore, in small- and medium-sized communes, offering an alternative to the services of the region, department, and private sector. Its agents, especially the large number who work on contract, have been granted (by the law concerning public service) the status of civil servants. This same law stipulates that henceforth noncivil servants may not be employed. Such an arrangement may appear innocuous (it has received union approval) but could bring decisive consequences.

The great strength of the Equipement, its advantage over local administrations that led to its quasi-monopoly over public civil engineering, is its capacity to supplement its own force of 45,000 State civil servants with over 70,000 contractual agents. Offering salaries above civil service levels, the Equipement could attract truly talented staff. But it risks losing this margin of superiority. By converting all its agents into civil servants, uniformly subject to the State civil service system, it becomes subject to budgetary restraints. It could too soon become another rigid bureaucracy, hardly able to compete with private enterprise. All of this is done in the name of equality, but should reform mean pulling the State out of local government and bureaucratizing more of its own administration? Local governments that demand high-quality work may contract more with private firms.

Could system-induced effects prevail over the master plan of decentralization? This question should be considered seriously by anyone skeptical of a merely symbolic decentralization, administered by decree from on high. In the meantime, scientific research, if it wishes to take part in this discussion, should apply its best analytical tools to the complexities of decentralization.

REFERENCES

Allison, G. 1971. *Essence of Decision*. Boston: Little, Brown.

Ashford, D. 1983. "The Socialist Reorganization of French Local Government: Another Jacobin Reform?" *Environment and Planning: Government and Policy*, vol. 1.

Ashford, D., and J. C. Thoenig. 1981. *Les aides financières de l'Etat aux collectivités locales en France et à l'étranger*. Paris: LITEC.

Becquart-Leclerq, J. 1976. *Paradoxes du pouvoir local*. Paris: Presses de la Fondation Nationale des Sciences Politiques.

Bourricaud, F. 1982. "L'envers du décor," *Le Figaro* (July 25): 5.

Centre de Recherche sur la Décentralisation Territoriale. 1983. *Décentralisation et fonction publique local*. Reims: Faculté de Droit, Cahier de l'Administration territoriale, no. 5.

Chevallier, J., et al. 1984. *L'institution régionale*. Paris: PUF.

De Kervasdoué, J., et al. 1976. "La loi sur les fusions et regroupements de communes," *Revue Française de Sociologie* (July-September): 423–450.

Denis, A. 1983. "Le transfert de l'urbanisme: un droit ou un privilège," *Intervention*, no. 3 (March-April): 13–17.

Dupuy, F., and J. C. Thoenig. 1983a. *Sociologie de l'Administration française*. Paris: Colin.

———. 1983b. "La loi du 2 mars 1982 sur la décentralisation. De l'analyse des textes à l'observation des premiers pas," *Revue Française de Science Politique* 33, no. 6 (December): 962–986.

———. 1985. *L'Administration en miettes*. Paris: Fayard.

Dupuy-Thomas, D. 1984. "Le social au quotidien: l'enjeu municipal dans la décentralisation." Congrès de l'Association Française de Science Politique, Grenoble, January 25–28. Mimeographed.

Gremion, C. 1979. *Profession: décideurs. Pouvoir des hauts fonctionnaires et réforme d l'Etat*. Paris: Gauthier-Villars.

Gremion, P. 1976. *Le pouvoir périphérique. Bureaucrates et notables dans le système politique française*. Paris: Le Seuil.

———. 1983. "Région ou département: les raisons d'un nonchoix," *Intervention*, no. 3 (March-April): 18–25.

Jones, C. 1970. *An Introduction to the Study of Public Policy*. Belmont, Calif.: Duxbury Press.

Keating, M. 1983. "Decentralization in Mitterand's France," *Public Administration* 61 (Autumn).

Kesselmann, M. 1982. "The Tranquil Revolution at Clochemerle: Decentralization in France and the Crisis of Capitalism." Conference: Local Institutions in National Development, Bellagio, Rockefeller Foundation, March 15–19. Mimeographed.

Mabilcau, A. 1984. "Décentralisation et processus décisionnels." Colloquium: La libre administration des collectivités locales. Besançon, April 19–20. Mimeographed.

———, ed. 1983. *Les pouvoirs locaux à l'épreuve de la décentralisation*. Paris: Pédone.

March, J., and J. Olsen. 1976. *Ambiguity and Choice in Organization*. Bergen, Norvège: Presses universitaires.

Meny, Y. 1983a. "La politique de décentralisation: réforme de société ou réforme pour les élites?" Florence: Institut Universitaire Européen. Mimeographed.

———. 1983b. "Pouvoir administratif d'Etat et collectivités territoriales." Pp. 113–126 in A. Mabileu, ed., *Les pouvoirs locaux à l'épreuve de la décentralisation*. Paris: Pédonne.

———. 1983c. "La politique de décentralisation du gouvernement Mauroy: légitimation, intégration et bureaucratisation." Florence: Institut Universitaire Européen. Mimeographed.

Merrill, R. 1984. "La décentralisation au niveau départemental en France: trois études de cas." Congrès de l'Association Française de Science Politique, Grenoble, France, January 25–28. Mimeographed.

Padioleau, J. 1981. *Quand la France s'enferre*. Paris: PUF.

Peyrefitte, A., et al. 1976. *Décentraliser les responsabilités*. Paris: Livre de Poche.

Projet. 1984. "Décentraliser vraiment?" Special no. 185–186 (May-June). Paris.

Stout, R. 1980. *Management or Control*? London: Indiana University Press.

Thoenig, J. C. 1975. "La relation entre le centre et la périphérie en France. Une analyse systémique," *Bulletin de l'Institut International d'Administration Publique* (October-December): 77–124.

———. 1982. "La politique de l'Etat à l'égard du personnel des communes," *Revue Française d'Administration Publique* (July-September): 57–88.

———. 1983. "Les politiques de réforme des collectivités locales en France." Pp. 83–108 in J. Lagroye and V. Wright, eds., *Les structures locales en Grande Bretagne et en France*. Paris: Documentation Française.

Trosa, S. 1983. "L'avenir de la démocratie locale: scénarios pour la décentralisation." *Annuaire des Collectivités locales*. Paris: LITEC-GRAL, pp. 1–19.

Worms, J. P. 1966. "Le préfet et ses notables," *Sociologie du Travail* (July-September): 249–275.

COMMENTARY: YES, WE DO SEE LOCAL AUTONOMY

Stephen L. Schechter

"Intergovernmental revenues help cities do more, but," suggests Terry Nichols Clark, "cities seek out grants consistent with local preferences."[1] This premise and its localistic perspective provide the basis for the article in this section and, hence, for my commentary on it.

Many years ago, Morton Grodzins argued for the need to study the American system of government as viewed from the community. In fact, this local orientation was one of the hallmarks of the Grodzins approach. But he also argued that the local view was necessary not because modern times had isolated local governments for separate action but because the American federal system was, in his words, "telescoped" on the community.[2] The system may have developed a case of federal-local cleavage since Grodzins made his observations, but we will not know until surveys studies sensitive to this issue are conducted on all planes of government.

In "Federal Grants and the City of Los Angeles: Implementing a More Centralized Local Political System," by Alan L. Saltzstein, Raphe Sonenshein, and Irving Ostrow, the authors examine federal aid as a means of securing local political goals. Their subject is the city government of Los

Research in Urban Policy, Vol. 2, pages 89–91.

ISBN: 0-89232-534-8

Angeles from the mid–1960s to the mid–1980s, concentrating on the administration of Mayor Tom Bradley (1973 to the present).

This article or a version of it will undoubtedly become part of most reading lists on Cities of the West, if for no other reason than it ably and succinctly chronicles the demise of "extreme decentralization" in Los Angeles city government. This article will be of wider appeal to those interested in the study of city politics qua politics, because it shows how a coalition of local elected officials led by Mayor Bradley was able to use federal funds as an outside (i.e., "free") resource to consolidate and share power. However, the authors err in their opening argument:

> Until recently, studies of federal aid to cities have viewed the process from Washington's perspective. Observers have analyzed patterns of aid distribution, examining the extent to which recipients are congruent with legislative goals. . . . This perspective assumes that actions at the federal level are the major determinants of aid allocation. Local governments are classified as similar whether or not they apply for aid, or seek to influence the allocation process.
>
> Our study follows on the heels of those who assume that local government is itself a major determinant of aid allocations. . . . Local governments receive aid because they seek it and are receptive to it.

First, the historiography of federal aid studies is incorrect. There have long been and will long be studies of federal aid from Washington's perspective. At the same time, there have been and will continue to be federal aid studies from a local perspective. Over 10 years ago, I was slogging around in Pueblo, Colorado, discovering many of the same local political uses of federal aid in that city of the West as the authors find in Los Angeles, California.[3] Ten years before that, the students of Edward C. Banfield and Morton Grodzins, and others were making their discoveries about the local ends served by federal aid. And so on. Care is needed not to reinvent the wheel.

Second, there seems a tendency here to eschew the national perspective, even when it seems congruent with their findings. Local governments receive aid not only because they see it and are receptive to it, but also because it is granted to them. As the authors suggest, Bradley's Los Angeles became a prime recipient of federal aid not only because it served Bradley's goals but because he played the grants game so well, and because he found so willing a federal player. And it is this coincidence of local and national goals that makes this case so important.

NOTES

1. Terry Nichols Clark and Lorna Crowley Ferguson, *City Money: Political Processes, Fiscal Strain, and Retrenchment* (New York: Columbia University Press, 1983), p. 243.

2. Morton Grodzins, *The American System: A New View of Government in the United States,* ed. Daniel J. Elazar (Chicago: Rand McNally, 1966), p. 211.
3. Stephen L. Schechter, "From Industrial City to Metropolitan Civil Community: The Politics of Constitutional Change in Pueblo, Colorado," prepared for delivery at the 1977 Annual Meeting of the American Political Science Association, Washington, D.C., September 1–4, 1977.

COMMENTARY: THE DIFFICULTIES OF "DEFEDERALIZING"

Barry G. Rabe

Disposal of the Old Federalism in favor of a decentralized New Federalism may be easier said than done. Political and economic decentralization may indeed be a "megatrend" for the remaining years of the twentieth century, but a variety of factors have continued to slow the transfer of political authority and resources from federal to state and local levels. In fact, the issue of decentralization in numerous areas of domestic policy has steadily dropped on the agenda of the administration that has so staunchly supported the concept.

Much of the delay in implementing this widely appealing elevation of the role of subnational units of government can be attributed to apprehension among the very state and local government officials who stand to gain new stature. Although "fed bashing" has become a way of life for many subnational officials, as well as policy analysts, these officials are far more chary about cutting themselves off from federal funding and, in areas such as environmental protection and occupational safety, federal assumption of regulatory authority.

The Los Angeles case, as presented by Saltzstein, Sonenshein, and Os-

Research in Urban Policy, Vol. 2, pages 93–94.

ISBN: 0-89232-534-8

trow, provides additional explanation of why the New Federalism arguments may be rhetorically appealing but politically unworkable. Federal funding was used by the Bradley administration to help underwrite the transformation of the city's political system. Far more than merely supplement or supplant the delivery of basic services, federal funding was used as a major source of stimulating economic development. It became politically—not just economically—internalized. Although the authors note that Los Angeles may be somewhat exceptional in this regard, a number of other cities, with Mayor Schaefer's Baltimore perhaps the most obvious example, may have followed a similar pattern. Rather than simply pare back certain services, a fully implemented defederalization might threaten the basic system of local governance.

The difficulty of achieving, rather than just discussing, decentralization in domestic policy may not be confined to the United States and its conservative national government. Even in Socialist France, a comparable commitment to transferring authority to local governments has stalled. Thoenig suggests that both a "master plan" and the funding necessary to secure the reshaping are lacking. As recession and substantial cutbacks in federal domestic spending have dampened state and local interest in assuming new responsibilities in the United States, recession has undercut France's attempt to "redefine its relations with local governments."

Neither of these articles suggests that decentralization is impossible, but each helps explain why popular ideas often unravel in the stages of either policy formation or policy implementation. Attempting to do less at the national level, therefore, may not differ all that much from attempting to do more. Only the nature of the complaints of the subnational officials may change, from too much national interference to too little national support.

PART III.

POLITICAL LEADERSHIP: NEW STRATEGIES FOR ASSESSING THE OPTIONS

FEDERAL AID AND MOBILIZATION OF BLACK POLITICAL INFLUENCE

Robert M. Stein and Keith E. Hamm

ABSTRACT

Though many researchers have argued persuasively for a link between federal anti-poverty programs and black political behavior, the empirical support for this relationship has not been forthcoming. An examination of local implementation of these anti-poverty programs, however, suggests that different styles of local administration may account for the linkage between federal anti-poverty programs, black political behavior, and the impact of increased black political mobilization.

The influence of Great Society federal aid programs (1964–1970) on black political behavior has been studied from a number of perspectives, including black candidate recruitment (Welch and Karnig 1980; Moynihan 1969; Greenstone and Peterson 1973; Kramer 1969), black political organizations (Pressman 1975; Bachrach and Baratz 1970), and the election of blacks to public office (Hamilton 1979; Browning and Marshall 1969; Eisinger 1975; Welch and Karnig 1980). Recently Welch and Karnig (1980) and Clark and Ferguson (1983) have sought to determine the impact that both federal

Research in Urban Policy, Vol. 2, pages 97–115.

ISBN: 0-89232-534-8

aid and black political behavior have on municipal expenditures, thus extending inquiry in this field to the policy effects of black political behavior.

Empirical research in this field has considerably outpaced its theoretical development. This condition has produced ambiguous findings that fail to conclusively test the federal aid–black political behavior relationship. The purpose of this paper is address the theoretical gaps in this literature and to provide an alternative conceptualization for evaluating federal influence on black political mobilization and its electoral and policy effects. Finally, we examine some preliminary data relevant to this alternative conceptualization.

Though many researchers have argued persuasively for a link between federal anti-poverty programs and black political behavior, the empirical support for this relationship has not been forthcoming. At best, researchers have identified a modest relationship between federal aid to cities and various aggregate measures of black political behavior (Eisinger 1975). Even these modest relationships diminish to insignificance when other factors (e.g., size of the black population, black socioeconomic status, and governmental structure) are included in the same analysis (Karnig and Welch 1980; Clark and Ferguson, 1983). Moreover, it is not altogether clear whether federal aid programs have had a positive or negative influence on black political behavior and politics. Moynihan (1969) and Hamilton (1976) argue that the Community Action Program (CAP) and Model Cities—major federal anti-poverty programs—were mismanaged and of little use in either the fight against poverty or the political mobilization of black Americans. At least one author (Hamilton 1969) has shown that federal assistance actually retarded the development of black political interests by pitting poor blacks against upper-middle-class blacks generating "intracommunity struggles over the use and distribution of federal monies" (Hamilton 1969:21). Finally, Piven and Cloward's (1972) analysis of federal anti-poverty programs argues that these programs were intended and succeeded in politically pacifying blacks and retarding their political development.

THE FEDERAL AID–BLACK POLITICAL BEHAVIOR THESIS

The general thesis underlying an intergovernmental aid explanation of black political behavior centers on the costs associated with political participation and how federal assistance defrayed some of these costs for urban blacks. Requirements established under Title II-A of the 1964 Economic Opportunity Act (EOA) ensured "maximum feasible participation" of blacks and poor persons in the implementation of the EOA. The authors of this section of the EOA sought to address the problem of poverty through a direct involvement of the poor in the implementation of federal poverty programs. Based on an alternative theory of poverty which stressed the poor's lack of means and opportunity to influence the distribution of government resources, some drafters sought to make the poor politically active and effective actors in city politics. Exactly how neighborhood associations and its poor residents would achieve these goals remained elusive, even for authors of this section of the law. Minimally, there was agreement among drafters that the poor should be involved in the implementation of any anti-poverty program. (See Sundquist 1969; Matusow 1984; Cloward and Ohlin 1960; Moynihan 1969.)

The controversial character of this section of EOA and its intrusion upon local politics prompted Congress (at the urging of city mayors) to amend the Economic Opportunity Act in 1967, deleting the "maximum feasible feasible participation" clause and effectively restoring control over federal anti-poverty programs to City Hall (Levitan 1969:14). Interestingly, only 3.2 percent of the affected cities chose to exercise their newly acquired power, choosing instead to maintain a decentralized, neighborhood-controlled administration of federal anti-poverty programs (Levitan 1969:116). A possible explanation for this unexpected decision may rest with the political power and credibility neighborhood associations have acquired under the provisions of the EOA. Voter registration drives, candidate recruitment, and training may have established these community-based associations as a potent political force. City officials were not eager to antagonize a new mobilized electorate with which their own political fortunes were so closely tied. Rather, they found it politically expedient to allow the newly forged relationship between the federal government and neighborhood associations to remain intact. It is the response of municipal governments to the 1967 amendments that has prompted many researchers to assign a significant political impact to the EOA (Levitan 1969; Greenstone and Peterson 1973; Orden 1973). Empirical tests of this thesis, however, raise a number of problems and unresolved issues that provide a basis for our development of an alternative explanation of this relationship.

A REASSESSMENT OF PAST EMPIRICAL RESEARCH

The weak or nonexistent relationship between federal aid programs and measures of black political behavior and representation may be a function of a number of remedial problems, including (1) a failure to differentiate between participation in federal poverty programs and the implementation of these programs in individual cities, (2) an ambiguous conceptualization of the relationship between federal poverty programs and black political behavior, (3) the limited time frame in which this potential relationship has been studied, (4) the omission of important nonfiscal federal influences on black political behavior (i.e., Voting and Civil Rights acts), and (5) a reliance on the size (or proportion) of black population as a main determinant of successful black electoral behavior.

Most researchers have assumed that either participation in federal anti-poverty programs or the level of participation (i.e., funding level) would be sufficient to influence the level and nature of black political participation. Unfortunately, neither the presence of a federal anti-poverty program nor the level of funding tells us anything about how the program operated within a given city. Matusow's (1984:255) assessment of "maximum feasible participation" rests largely with local implementation rather than with direct federal influences:

> The fate of maximum feasible participation, in fact, came to hinge less on OEO than on widely varying local circumstances. Power elites had firm control in some cities, a feeble grip in others; some CAAs serviced established institutions, others fomented class and racial strife. And between these poles an array of other possibilities played themselves out. Since remarkably little is known about CAAs in the great majority of communities no final judgment on CAP will be possible until an army of local historians recovers the program's lost fragments.

Knowing how the poverty program was implemented and specifically the extent to which blacks were involved in the implementation of the program may be a better indicator of federal influence than just the presence or level of federal funding. Federal aid programs are likely to have a strong and positive influence on black politics and individual behavior in cities where responsibility for the implementation and administration of federal poverty programs was vested with neighborhood associations rather than with city officials (Peterson 1969; Greenstone and Peterson 1974). Thus, information on the nature of program implementation within each city is essential for assessing the influence federal anti-poverty programs had on black politics.

Vanecko's (1969) and Jacobs' (1970) studies of CAPs in 100 U.S. cities examines the question of program implementation and its independent effect on the political behavior of neighborhood residents. Vanecko identified two different methods for implementing CAPs and other related poverty programs—community mobilization/organization and community service. Consistent with the Cloward and Ohlin (1960) thesis, community mobilization was aimed at organizing and turning out the poor, or more precisely the residents of the poor neighborhood, for political action. Community service was aimed at reforming institutions servicing the poor rather than seizing control of these governments and agencies.

The legislation creating CAP and other related anti-poverty programs was flexible enough to allow participating cities and neighborhoods to choose between either of these two strategies. Based on survey data collected from the principal CAP actors in each city (i.e., CAP executive directors), Vanecko identified a strong relationship between the way CAP programs were implemented and perceived institutional and political changes. CAPs with a political emphasis achieved a greater degree of institutional change, particularly in terms of service levels and responsiveness to citizen demands, than service-oriented CAPs. Interestingly, a mobilization orientation was negatively associated with increased levels of electoral participation but positively related to "increased presentation of demands to public bodies by residents of the targeted neighborhoods" (Vanecko 1969:615). When the CAP orientation favored political mobilization, its impact on political behavior was directed at lobbying activities for particular benefits (e.g., welfare check issuance) rather than electoral activities. Vanecko's findings show that CAPs adopting a political orientation were successful at developing politically effective attitudes among residents of the CAP area. These attitudes, reinforced by significant service gains and institutional reforms, laid the foundation for future electoral activity which was necessary to protect and expand upon programmatic achievements. This suggests that even under the most favorable conditions CAPs initially had only a modest and indirect effect on mobilizing black voters.

Researchers studying the influence of federal aid on black political behavior have assumed that this relationship is direct and unimpeded by intervening factors. Moreover, these same researchers have assumed that the aid–black political behavior relationship is uniform for a number of dependent measures including registration, turnout, the election of black candidates, and policy outputs responsive to black preferences. This conceptualization of the research question has prevailed in spite of evidence that has shown little support for a direct and linear relationship (Brouthers 1983). An alternative conceptualization might distinguish between black political mobilization (i.e., voter registration and turnout) and the effects of mobilization on electoral and policy outcomes (e.g., the number of black elected officials and black public employment). For example, one might hypothesize that anti-poverty programs have an immediate and positive effect on the level of black voter registration and turnout. This condition would seem to be necessary (though not sufficient) for the electoral success of black candidates. Thus, the effect of federal anti-poverty programs on electoral success and policy outputs is indirect, mediated by the level of black voter registration and turnout established at some earlier point in time.

This latter use raises another problem: the appropriate time span in which to study the federal aid and black political behavior relationship.

The cross-sectional and contemporary (circa 1964–1968) character of many studies implies that federal aid effects are not only direct but immediate. Given the complexity of federal anti-poverty programs and the difficulty of mobilizing black political action, it is reasonable to expect that federal anti-poverty programs have a lagged effect on black political behavior. The time needed for developing black leadership and for registering and turning out newly registered black voters is longer than even the life of many of the federal government's anti-poverty programs. A more realistic time span would be one in which the effects of anti-poverty programs were identified with a time period well after initial delivery and program implementation. This extended time frame allows for an examination of changes in a number of black behavioral measures.

The most important federal influence on black politics in the last 20 years is the 1965 Voting Rights Act which established the federal government as a monitor and promoter of black voter registration and turnout. There is little doubt that these laws had a significant effect on the level of black voter registration and turnout in and outside the South (CQA 1965, 1970, 1972; Scher and Button 1984). Though state and local coverage was extensive in six southern states, a significant number of nonsouthern states and cities were also covered by the requirements of the 1965 Voting Rights Act. Amendments to the 1965 Act in 1975 extended coverage to an even larger number of nonsouthern states and cities. The consequences of these federal laws are obvious for voter registration, yet their effect is more ambiguous for black voter turnout, the election of black candidates, and implementation of black policy preferences.

Researchers have correctly suggested that the electoral success of black candidates may be a function of the proportion of blacks residing in the city. Controls for the percentage of black population define the upper boundary of black political mobilization and thus the potential for achieving desired electoral and policy outcomes. Without a significant proportion of a city's electorate black (e.g., 50.1 percent), black voters cannot expect to translate even a 100 percent rate of black voter registration or turnout into electoral or policy successes (Brouthers 1983).[1] Two problems occur, however, with the use of black population as a control variable. First, this measure does not distinguish between blacks of voting and nonvoting age. Hadden and Borgatta (1965:118) have shown that there is a negative relationship between the proportion of a city's population that is black and the median age of the black population. Cities with large black populations often comprise a disproportionately larger number of non-voting-age black persons. Moreover, the percentage of black population is sensitive to outmigration of whites who, unlike the remaining black population, can afford to leave deteriorating urban conditions for the surrounding suburbs. Controls for black population must take into consideration both the relevant black population (i.e., those over 18 years of age) and the source of black dominance. This latter condition, which can result from out-migration of whites, may explain an interesting anomaly in the empirical literature. Karnig and Welch (1980:126–129) found a weak and sometimes negative relationship between the number of black elected officials and policies (e.g., social welfare spending) of interest to black constituencies. This finding can be explained in terms of recent urban economic history and its effect on white mobility. The out-migration of whites to the suburbs not only was a boost to black political dominance, it also depleted the city of its tax and revenue base. Many newly elected black mayors (e.g., Harold Washington of Chicago) inherited city administrations fiscally strained and close to bankruptcy. Under these conditions black mayors were constrained in their ability to increase spending and extend services to their black or white constituencies. If black mobilization achieved a critical threshold before the city's economic downturn, we would expect to observe a positive relationship between the number of black elected officials and spending policies favorable to black preferences. Eisinger (1982) and Clark and Ferguson (1983) offer evidence to support this proposition.

AN EXPLANATION OF BLACK POLITICAL BEHAVIOR AND ITS CONSEQUENCES FOR URBAN POLICY

Our study examines four dependent measures of black political behavior and their policy consequences: black voter registration, black voter turnout, black elected officials, and black public employment. The first three measures are conventional indices of black political behavior and have been widely studied in the literature. Black public employment measures a possible consequence of black political mobilization. Consistent with theories of urban political machines (Wolfinger 1974; Lowi 1964), public employment is a vehicle for maintaining the loyalty of electoral constituencies to the incumbent regime. Unlike outlays for goods and services (e.g., social welfare spending), individual benefits from public employment are not trivialized since a public job is not shared like many municipal spending programs. The political advantage of this trait of public employment is not lost on incumbent officeholders. Public employees have significantly higher rates of voter turnout and support for incumbents and their policy positions (Courant, Gramlich, and Rubinfeld 1979; Eisinger 1982; Gramlich and Rubinfeld 1982). Consequently, public employment is not only a private benefit to be extracted from government by influential constituents, but is also an effective mechanism with which incumbents can maintain the support of their electoral constituencies.

As noted earlier, the impact of black political mobilization is significantly influenced by two contextual factors: black voters as a proportion of the entire electorate and municipal fiscal conditions. The relationship between black voter registration and turnout and the number of black elected officials is likely to be stronger in cities where black voters approach or exceed 50.1 percent of the entire electorate. Similarly, the electoral success of black candidates will be positively related to higher levels of black public employment when the fiscal conditions can sustain an expansion of the public work force. These two contextual factors operate as controls for our explanation of black political behavior and its policy consequences. The models for black elected officials and black public employment are estimated with and without the control variables for municipal fiscal stress and the proportion of the black electorate.

OPERATIONAL MEASURES, DATA, AND HYPOTHESES

Mobilization measures: Yearly data since 1968 on black voter registration (BLKREG), turnout (BLKTURN), and the black proportion of the electorate (BLKMAJ) for states and some cities are available in the U.S. Bureau of the Census, *Voting and Registration in the Elections of November 1968–82*. These data are collected as part of the current population survey and are based on interviews with a sample population (N=61,500). As part of a special analysis, the census provides data on black registration and turnout for the largest standard metropolitan statistical areas (SMSAs).[2] We are able to use the SMSA data as a best estimate of city-level black electoral behavior since an overwhelming majority of blacks in each SMSA reside in the largest (central) city in SMSA.[3] At present these data are only available to us in published form for 1982, limiting our analysis to the 31 central cities included in that publication. Future access to the Census Bureau's original data will allow us to generate survey-based measures of black electoral behavior for a much larger sample of cities. In spite of these data limitations the census data remain the most extensive and reliable source for municipal level data on black electoral behavior. Our analysis of these 31 cities is intended to be illustrative of what might be done with a more extensive data base. BLKREG and BLKTURN are expressed as percentages of total eligible (over 18 years of age) black voters and registered black voters. The proportion of the city's electorate that is black (BLKMAJ) is dichotomized—cities where blacks equal or exceed 50.1 percent of registered voters and cities where blacks represent less than 50.1 percent of registered voters.

CAP orientation and level of participation: A number of researchers have studied CAPs in individual cities during their initial period of program implementation (Vanecko 1969; Austin 1972; Jacobs 1970. The National Opinion Research Center (NORC) survey of CAP officials in 100 U.S. cities (Vanecko 1969; Jacobs 1970) covered all 31 cities included in our study and was used to measure how each city implemented its CAP (CAPORIENT). The NORC survey was administered to the CAP executive directors in 1966. Each respondent was asked to identify from among nine possible goals "the goal most developed in terms of the programs aimed at its achievement" (Jacobs 1970). The choices included:

1. Organizing the poor in order to increase their potential power
2. Helping the poor to participate effectively in the decision-making process of the community
3. Creating economic pressures to increase the employment opportunities for the relatively unskilled poor
4. Providing education, job training, and counseling services for poor adults
5. Supplementing the education, social experiences, and job training for poor adolescents
6. Improvements in the education and social experiences of young children in the poor community
7. Obtaining decent housing and recreation areas for poor people
8. Improving public services in poor areas
9. Improving the quality of consumer goods and services in poor neighborhoods

Analysis of responses for both the 100-city sample and our 31-city sample identified four dimensions of CAP goals: mobilization (items 1 and 2): job opportunities (items 3 and 4), education (items 5 and 6), and general social services (items 7, 8, and 9). CAPORIENT was defined as mobilization-oriented if either item 1 or 2 was identified by the city's CAP executive director as the most developed CAP goal. A service orientation was assigned if any other goal was chosen (items 3–9).

Matusow's (1984) analysis of CAPs in six cities draws from a unique data source—internal Office of Economic Opportunity (OEO) memoranda. Between 1964 and 1967 internal agency reviews were conducted by the OEO in selected cities that received EOA funding. These memoranda, made available to the authors by Professor Matuso, provide a candid and detailed description of program implementation during the early days of the War on Poverty. Memoranda for nine cities (three more than reported in Matusow 1984) are available from Matusow's collection, and with survey data from other sources (Vanecko 1969; Jacobs 1970), provide an effective cross-validation for our measure of CAPORIENT. In addition to Matusow's records for nine CAPs, case studies for other cities (Austin 1972; Greenstone and Peterson 1973; Kramer 1969; Jacobs 1970) netted additional information on the implementation of CAPs in 18 of the 31 cities in our sample. A comparison of survey and case study measures of CAPORIENT indicates a strong correlation between the two operational measures. There was clear agreement between the two classifications for 13 of the 18 cities. We could not conclusively determine CAPORIENT from the case reports of the five remaining cities, accounting for the lack of congruence with the survey measure of CAPORIENT.

Since CAPORIENT captures the nature of program participation, an additional measure was sought that would provide a quantitative measure of municipal participation in the federal government's anti-poverty program. The average per capita EOA aid allocation to each city (PCCAP) between 1964 and 1968 provides a measure of each city's level of participation in the federal government's anti-poverty program.

Fiscal stress: Five 1980-level macro socioeconomic conditions define fiscal stress (STRESS): change in population size (1970–1980), unemployment, dependent population (percentage of population below 18 and above 65 years of age), per capita personal income, and median owner-occupied home value. Each indicator was standardized and summed for each city. As noted earlier, stress operates as a control variable and cities were grouped for analysis purposes by rankings on the standardized stress score. The sample was divided at the median into stressed and less-stressed cities. A wide range of stress measures have been advanced in the literature. (See Ross and Winters 1981.) Our goal was to operationalize stress in such a way as to (1) distinguish it from the effects of stress (e.g., diminished expenditures and public employment) and (2) to draw on the widest interpretation of the concept. Our own conceptualization is closest to Nathan and Adams' (1982) hardship index which defines stress in terms of declining population and its consequent effects on resident population. We recognize that others might refer to these measures as socioeconomic rather than fiscal stress.

Voting Rights Act coverage: Coverage by the 1965 Voting Rights Act and its 1975 amendments (VOTEACT) is defined in terms of the length of a city's coverage by the Act's (and its amendments') provisions. Cities were divided into three groups: (1) those cities never covered by the 1965 Act or its amendments, (2) cities covered only since 1975, and (3) cities covered since the 1965 Act. Presumably the longer a city has been under the provisions of the Voting Rights Act the stronger its influence on black political behavior and the policy consequences of increased black voter participation (Bullock et al. 1984).

An important determinant of black political mobilization and its effect on the electoral success of black candidates and public policies is the size of the black population. As noted earlier, however, the operationalization of this concept must measure the size of the potential black electorate (i.e., those eligible to vote) and not all black residents. The percentage of total population that is black and over the age of 18 (BLKOV18) is included in our analysis of black political behavior as an indicator of the maximum level of black political mobilization possible in a city.

Black elected officials and public employees: The number of black elected officials (BLKOFF) was obtained from the *National Roster of Black Elected Officials* for the years 1974–1982. There is some debate over the appropriate method for measuring this variable. Most research has compared the proportion of city council that is black with the proportion of city population that is black (subtracting one from the other). Bullock and Dennis (1984) and Engstrom and McDonald (1981) note that there are a number of methodological problems with this measurement strategy including (1) the problem of including the main independent variable (percentage black population, or blacks over 18) in the measure of the dependent variable, (2) treating all cities with no black officials equally when the percentage of population that is black varies, (3) treating all deviations between council representation and percentage black population the same. To avoid these problems we have chosen to use black elected officials as a percentage of total elected officials in the city rather than the percentage difference figure. This allows us to still include the percentage of population that is black and over 18 as an independent variable.

Our measure of the policy consequences of black political mobilization is the percentage of total full-time municipal labor force that is black (BLKEMP). Data for this measure are taken from Eisinger's (1982) study of black public employment. Our choice of this policy measure is based on a simple political observation. As blacks achieve a greater level of mobilization and political influence, they should be able to direct a significant portion of the city's largess to their own constituency.

A longitudinal design is the most appropriate means for investigating the effects of federal anti-poverty programs on black political behavior. Due, however, to the limitations of the data and the difficulty in obtaining even partial data for a relatively large sample of cities, we are forced to limit our empirical investigation to a cross-sectional design. Specifically, we attempt to explain 1982 levels of black political behavior and urban policy in terms of historically antecedent conditions in each city (i.e., CAPORIENT, PCCAP, and VOTEACT). Though a weaker design than repeated observations over time, the assumptions of our explanation are not violated with the use of this design. The delayed, or lagged, effects of federal actions (CAPORIENT, PCCAP, and VOTEACT) on black political behavior are still operative with a cross-sectional design. Threats to the validity of our findings, particularly historical artifacts, are prominent, and we must caution against generalizing too widely from these empirical investigations. Three hypotheses are to be tested:

Hypothesis 1: Levels of black mobilization (i.e., turnout and voter registration) will be positively related to CAP funding, CAP orientation (i.e. mobilization), and coverage by the provisions of the 1965 Voting Rights Act and its 1975 amendments.

Hypothesis 2: CAP funding, CAP orientation, and Voting Rights Act coverage will be positively related to the percentage of black elected officials in cities that have attained the necessary threshold of political mobilization (i.e., BLKREG > 50.1 percent of the electorate).

Hypothesis 3: CAP funding, CAP orientation, and Voting Rights Act coverage will be positively related to the proportion of the public work force that is black in cities with a strong fiscal base.

The use of STRESS and BLKMAJ as control variables poses a methodological problem. Partitioning our sample (n=31), even with a dichotomous control variable, would produce too small an *n* for any meaningful analysis. An alternative strategy is to include each control variable in the regression analysis as a dummy variable, switching the values of 0 and 1 in separate analysis. This produces two regression models per control variable and allows us to compare the coefficients for both values of the dummy/control without depleting degrees of freedom.

FINDINGS

Bivariate relationships between our independent variables and measures of mobilization and its electoral effects partially confirm our original hypotheses. PCCAP and CAPORIENT are significantly related to black registration and turnout in 1982. This latter finding is particularly significant given the large number of contextual factors that often influence voter turnout and performance in a specific election. As expected, neither PCCAP nor CAPORIENT is significantly related to the percentage of black elected officials or the size (percentage) of the black municipal work force. Any effect PCCAP and CAPORIENT have on the electoral and policy effects of mobilization is mediated by an intervening variable(s) or relationship. Coverage by the 1965 Voting Rights Act and its subsequent amendments has a strong and positive relationship with three of the four

Table 1. Correlation between Measures of Black Political Behavior and Selected Independent Variables: 1982

	BLKREG	*BLKTURN*	*BLKOFF*	*BLKEMP*
PCCAP	.341*	.401*	.128	.115
CAPORIENT	.380*	.348*	.081	.135
VOTEACT	.280*	.317*	.374*	.020

*p < .05

dependent variables. The strongest relationship is observed among VOTEACT, BLKOFF, and BLKEMP. Cities with the longest period of coverage have a significantly larger percentage of black elected officials.

In spite of these strong bivariate relationships, the multivariate model (Ordinary Least Squares) for black voter registration and turnout does not show a strong independent effect for the measures of federal influence. In each of the regression models BLKOV18 is the single best predictor of BLKREG and BLKTURN. Moreover, VOTEACT and CAPORIENT have significant independent effects on only black registration and turnout. Federal programs (PCCAP and CAPORIENT) and public laws (VOTEACT) have no significant and independent effect on either the percentage of black elected officials or black public employment. In the case of BKLOFF and BLKEMP the size of the adult black population is the only significant variable in the regression model.

These findings are consistent with earlier hypotheses. Federal anti-poverty programs and the Voting Rights Acts have a significant and independent stimulative effect on black political behavior. The success of black candidates and the size of the black public work force is uneffected, at least in an independent manner, by these federally initiated policies and programs. These findings, however, leave open the possibility that federal influence on these political and policy consequences of black political behavior are masked by other factors.

MOBILIZATION EFFECTS ON ELECTORAL AND POLICY OUTCOMES

Table 3 reports the regression estimates for the percentage of black elected officials and black public employment when we include the dummy variable for the proportion of the electorate that is black (BLKMAJ). Consistent with earlier hypotheses, federal actions have their greatest impact on the electoral success of black candidates when blacks are at least 50.1 percent of the total electorate (BLKMAJ > 50.1). In this model, the size of the black population over 18 is not significantly related to the success of black

Table 2. Regression Estimates for Measures of Black Political Behavior, Public Employment, and Black Elected Officials: 1982 (t-value)

	Dependent Variable			
Independent Variable	*BLKREG*	*BLKTURN*	*BLKOFF*	*BLKEMP*
PCCAP	.563	.530*	.083	.154
	(1.28)	(1.45)	(.134)	(.430)
CAPORIENT	6.26*	3.12*	.129	.112
	(2.83)	(2.92)	(.080)	(.821)
VOTEACT	4.43*	3.65*	1.06	.724
	(2.10)	(3.01)	(.818)	(.950)
BLKOV18	.096*	.128*	.321*	.870*
	(3.97)	(4.12)	(3.20)	(4.49)
N	31	31	31	31
f-ratio	12.1	14.2	17.9	28.5
R^2	.345	.564	.526	.649
R^{*2}	.272	.517	.473	.610

*p < .05

Table 3. Regression Estimates for Black Elected Officials and Black Public Employment with Size of Black Electorate: 1982

	BLKOFF		*BLKEMP*	
Variable	*BLKMAJ > 50.1*	*BLKMAJ < 50.1*	*BLKMAJ > 50.1*	*BLKMAJ < 50.1*
Intercept	−24.18	1.79	1.56	−1.21
BLKOV18	.097	.166*	.154	.266*
	(1.08)	(4.34)	(.674)	(2.86)
PCCAP	.258*	.063	.241	.002
	(2.45)	(.260)	(1.10)	(.928)
CAPORIENT	1.67*	1.59	1.09	1.14
	(2.96)	(1.60)	(.740)	(1.11)
VOTEACT	4.09*	.380	3.83	2.12
	(4.39)	(.560)	(.431)	(.625)
BLKTURN	.494*	.061	.521	.049
	(4.18)	(1.09)	(.222)	(.423)
BLKMAJ	7.58*	−5.21*	.117	.312
	(11.2)	(9.58)	(.523)	(.975)
N	31	31	31	31
f-ratio	75.4*	82.3*	11.1	9.3
R^2	.886	.783	.228	.112
R^{*2}	.864	.740	.074	.065

*p < .05

candidates. In these cities the potential size of the black electorate is likely to have approached its maximum level, producing an invariant measure for this subsample of cities and its insignificant BLKOV18 coefficient. Most importantly, the coefficient for BLKMAJ (i.e., when BLKMAJ > 50.1) is significant and positive. Moreover, its t-value indicates that it alone accounts for the largest portion of explained variation in BLKOFF.[4]

When we turn our attention to cities where blacks represent less than 50.1 percent of the electorate (BLKMAJ < 50.1) the estimates for BLKOFF change drastically. For this equation, only the coefficient for BLKOV18 is significant. No other variable in the model has a significant effect on the percentage of elected officials that are black. Interestingly, BLKTURN is not related to the success of black candidates when blacks are in the electoral minority. This finding is not altogether surprising and may reflect the political reality confronting black candidates in multiracial cities.[5] Blacks standing for office in racially diverse cities must broaden their electoral constituency beyond black voters if they expect to win office.

The findings for our model of black public employment are far less conclusive. The estimates for both models do not vary significantly. Moreover, the f-ratios for both models is statistically insignificant. Only the size of the potential black electorate (BLKOV18) has a significant coefficient in the model for cities where black voters dominate the electorate. Though this relationship was expected, its magnitude is not sufficient to produce a statistically significant f-ratio for the regression model. Individual federal policies have no appreciable effect on the level of black public employment. The size of the potential black electorate is unrelated to the level of black public employment when black voters represent less than 50.1 percent of the registered vote. This finding is particularly significant, since others studying public employment (Eisinger 1982) have found that the size of the black population is the single strongest predictor of black public employment. The poor performance of the black public employment model may reflect the influence of prevailing economic conditions.

CAP EFFECTS ON BLACK PUBLIC EMPLOYMENT BY FISCAL STRESS

As noted earlier, the accession of a black electorate in many cities coincided with a decline in municipal economic conditions. Declining economic conditions may have operated as a severe constraint on the expenditure decisions of city governments, independent of the electoral success of black candidates. Table 4 reports the regression coefficients for BLKEMP with the inclusion of the dummy variable STESS. Significant federal level effects

Table 4. Regression Estimates for Black Public Employment with Level of Fiscal Stress: 1982

	Black Public Employment (%)	
Variable	*STRESS = High*	*STRESS = Low*
Intercept	−2.40	1.85
BLKOV18	.216*	.101
	(3.74)	(.785)
PCCAP	−.015	.213*
	(−.100)	(2.45)
CAPORIENT	3.11	3.45*
	(1.71)	(2.85)
VOTEACT	.382	1.84*
	(.400)	(2.16)
BLKTURN	.067	.067
	(1.30)	(1.22)
STRESS	−2.74*	7.92*
	(7.52)	(8.92)
f-ratio	129.1	145.4
R^2	.398	.419
R^{*2}	.278	.303

*$p < .05$

are observed when urban fiscal conditions are free of excessive strain. In this equation PCCAP and CAPORIENT account for 42 percent of the variation in the percentage of black public employment. Moreover, the coefficients for BLKOV18 and BLKTURN are insignificant.

The same model for fiscally stressed cities produced radically different results. In this model, only the coefficient for the percentage of population that are black adults is statistically significant and accounts for almost all of the model's explanatory power ($R^2 = .398$). The coefficients for CAPORIENT, PCCAP, VOTEACT, and BLKTURN are statistically insignificant. Fiscal stress appears to drain cities of the resources needed to expand the black labor force, independent of the political penetration of a black electorate.

DISCUSSION

The growth of black political influence is neither simple in its origins nor direct in its impact on urban politics and policies. Our analysis has shown that federal aid programs, particularly in terms of their local implementation, can have a significant and positive effect on the level of black electoral mobilization. Moreover, this federal influence on black political behavior operates within some important urban constraints. Local support for a politically oriented anti-poverty program is a necessary (but not always sufficient) condition for higher levels of black voter registration and turnout.

The impact of federal anti-poverty programs on the electoral and policy consequences of black political mobilization is mediated by two contextual factors: the size of the black electorate and the fiscal health of the city. The creation of a black electoral majority in some cities may have occurred as a consequence of white out-migration, a condition brought on by the pressures of a declining urban economy. Out-migration of white middle- and upper-middle-class residents could have raised the black proportion of the electorate above 50.1 percent without any appreciable change in the level of either BLKTURN or BLKREG. This particular road to black electoral influence is not associated with the political spoils of previous urban administrations. On the contrary, since 1975 many newly elected black mayors have been forced to cut rather than expand the size of municipal government in response to declining urban economic conditions.

This reasoning is largely speculative, as we only have circumstantial data to link fiscal decline with black electoral majorities and the legacy of the federal anti-poverty program. Future research needs to examine the city-level relationship between black electoral behavior and its political consequences, controlling for specific changes in the size and composition of the city's population. Moreover, it is unclear that elected officials in fiscally stressed cities lack the resources to provide their electoral constituency with significant policy benefits. The use of part-time employment is an effective means with which to gain and maintain support without the fiscal burdens of permanent wage increases or costly pensions and benefit packages. An examination of part-time employment before and after municipal elections, especially in fiscally stressed cities, should provide a more exact test of this thesis.

NOTES

1. This does not preclude the possibility of the election of black candidates through the efforts of a multiracial electoral coalition.

2. The cities included Baltimore, Buffalo, Boston, Cincinnati, Chicago, Cleveland, Denver, Detroit, Indianapolis, Kansas City, Minneapolis, New Orleans, New York, Philadelphia, Milwaukee, Seattle, Tucson, Dallas, San Antonio, Houston, Atlanta, San Diego, Los Angeles, Long Beach, St. Louis, Miami, Tampa, Newark, Pittsburgh, San Francisco, and Columbus.

3. Analysis of the percentage of black population in each SMSA shows that in each SMSA 90 percent of the black population reside within the largest central city.

4. This judgment may be premature. A number of interactive terms may have significant

coefficients. Unfortunately, our sample size does not permit us to extensively investigate these possibilities as it would rapidly exhaust the model's degree of freedom. The R^2 for each regression model has been corrected for small sample size using the following formula: corrected $R^2 = 1 - (1-R^2)\ N-1/N-k$, where N = number of cases and k = number of variables. For a further discussion of this technique see Pinduck and Rubinfeld (1976:59)

5. Ideally we would need to examine the number of candidates running for each position before we can be certain that this explanation is valid. At present this information is not readily available.

REFERENCES

Austin, David. 1972. "Resident Participation: Political Mobilization or Organizational Cooptation," *Public Administration Review* 32: 409–420.

Bachrach, Peter, and Morton Baratz. *Power and Poverty: Theory and Practice*. New York: Oxford University Press.

Brouthers, Lance Eliot. 1983. "The Cube Law and Black Representation on American City Councils," *Political Methodology* 9: 147–158.

Browning, Rufus, and Dale Rogers Marshall. 1976. "Implementation of Model Cities and Revenue Sharing in Ten Bay Area Cities: Design and First Findings." In C. O Jones and R. Thomas, ed., *Public Policy Making in a Federal System*. Beverly Hills: Sage.

Bullock, Charles, James Anderson, David Brady, and Joseph Stewart. 1984. *Public Policy and Politics in America*. Belmont: Brooks-Cole.

Bullock, Charles, and Christopher Dennis. 1984. "Conditions Affecting the Election of Blacks on Southern Counties." Paper presented at the annual meeting of the Southwestern Political Science Association, Fort Worth, Texas.

Clark, Terry Nichols, and Lorna Crowley Ferguson. 1983. *City Money: Political Processes, Fiscal Strain, and Retrenchment*. New York: Columbia University Press.

Cloward, Richard, and Lloyd Ohlin. 1960. *Delinquency and Opportunity: A Theory of Delinquent Gangs*. New York: Free Press.

Congressional Quarterly Almanac. 1965. "The Voting Rights Act of 1965," *Congressional Quarterly Almanac* 21: 533–571.

———. 1970. "Congress Lowers the Voting Age, Extends Voting Rights Act," *Congressional Quarterly Almanac* 26: 192–199.

———. 1972. "Voting Rights Enforcement," *Congressional Quarterly Almanac* 28: 258.

Courant, Paul, Edward Gramlich, and Daniel L. Rubinfeld. 1979. "Public Employee Market Power and the Level of Government Spending," *American Economic Review* 69: 806–817.

Eisinger, Peter. 1975. "The Community Action Program and the Development of Black Political Leadership." Paper presented at the annual meeting of the American Political Science Association, New York.

———. 1982. "The Economic Conditions of Black Employment in Municipal Bureaucracies," *American Journal of Political Science* 26: 754–771.

Engstrom, Ronald, and Michael MacDonald. 1981. "The Election of Blacks to City Councils: Clarifying the Impact of Electoral Arrangements on the Seats/Population Relationship," *American Political Science Review* 75: 344–354.

Gramlich, Edward, and Daniel L. Rubinfeld. 1982. "Micro Estimates of Public Spending Demand," *Journal of Political Economy* 90: 536–560.

Greenstone, David, and Paul Peterson. 1973. *Race and Authority in Urban Politics: Community Participation and the War on Poverty*. New York: Russell Sage Foundation.

Hadden, John, and Richard Borgatta. 1965. *American Cities*. New York: Rand McNally.

Hamilton, Charles. 1976. *The Struggle for Political Equality*. New York: National Urban League.

———. 1979. "The Patron-Recipient Relationship and Minority Politics," *Political Science Quarterly* 95: 211–228.

Jacobs, Bruce. 1970. *Community Action and Urban Institutional Change*. Boston: Barss, Reitzel and Assoc., Inc.

Karnig, Albert, and Susan Welch. 1980. *Black Representation and Urban Policy*. Chicago: University of Chicago Press.

Kramer, Ralph. 1969. *Participation of the Poor*. Englewood: Prentice-Hall.

Levitan, Sar. 1969. *The Great Society's Poor Law: A New Approach to Poverty*. Baltimore: Johns Hopkins Press.

Lowi, Theodore. 1964. *At the Pleasure of the Mayor: Patronage and Power in New York City, 1898–1958*. New York: Free Press.

Matusow, Allen. 1984. *The Unraveling of America*. New York: Harper and Row.

Moynihan, Daniel. 1969. *Maximum Feasible Misunderstanding: Community Action in the War on Poverty*. New York: Free Press.

Nathan, Richard, and Charles Adams. 1976. "Understanding Central City Hardship," *Political Science Quarterly* 91: 47–62.

Orden, Susan, 1973. "The Impact of CAP on Social Service Agencies," *Social Problems* 23: 18–32.

Peterson, Paul. 1969. "The Federal Community Action Program: Implementation in Five Cities," *American Political Science Review* 63: 141–167.

Pindyck, Robert, and Daniel L. Rubinfeld. 1976. *Econometric Models and Economic Forecasts*. New York: McGraw Hill.

Piven, Frances, and Richard Cloward. 1972. *Regulating the Poor: The Function of Public Welfare*. New York: Vintage Press.

Pressman, Jeffrey. 1975. *Federal Programs and City Politics*. Berkeley: University of California Press.

Scher, M., and A. Button. 1984. "Voting Rights Act: Implementation and Impact." In Charles S. Bullock and Charles S. Lamb, eds., *Implementation of Civil Rights Policy*. Monterey: Brooks-Cole, pp. 20–54.

Sundquist, James. 1969. "Origins of the War on Poverty." In James Sundquist, ed., *On Fighting Poverty*. New York: Basic Books.

U.S. Office of Economic Opportunity. 1965. *Community Action Workbook*. Washington: U.S. Government Printing Office.

Wolfinger, Raymond. 1974. *The Politics of Progress*. Englewood Cliffs: Prentice-Hall.

Vanecko, James. 1969. "Community Mobilization and Institutional Change: The Influence of Community Action Program in Large Cities," *Social Science Quarterly* 53: 608–630.

HOW (SOME) COMMUNITY ORGANIZATIONS ADAPT TO FISCAL STRAIN

Brett W. Hawkins, Mary Ann E. Steger, and Jean Trimble

ABSTRACT

Although studies of fiscal strain have proliferated in recent years, few, if any, have systematically examined the question of what kind of community organizations cope with strain. The data in this study characterize 57 community organizations and their activities in the face of reduced funding. Our purpose is to identify organizational characteristics that are associated with successful adaptation to the current environment of scarcity. The evidence is that organizations having more specialists (such as attorneys and computer specialists), those engaging in more fund raising of their own, and those using more volunteers are more adaptive.

In recent years many publications have appeared on the subject of fiscal strain. Nearly all of them have focused on governmental jurisdictions or agencies, but a few descriptive studies have also appeared concerning community organizations.[1] Our study is of 57 such organizations and uses correlational methods to try to advance the knowledge base supporting fiscal management of community organizations. In the tradition of theories of organizational decline and resource dependency, we assume that non-

Research in Urban Policy, Vol. 2, pages 117–125.

ISBN: 0-89232-534-8

profit community organizations must make choices about adapting to their environments.[2] Nonprofits in general, and especially those that provide services, face an erosion of their environment's ability or willingness to support previous levels of activity. Our research purpose is to identify organizational characteristics that are associated with successful adaptation to the current environment of scarcity.

We address two statistical questions: (1) What characteristics of community organizations are associated with the use of specific strategies for adapting to fiscal strain? (2) What characteristics of community organizations are associated with effectiveness in adapting to fiscal strain?

Neither governmental agencies nor the private sector, community nonprofits constitute a galaxy of ethnic, cultural, charitable, educational, service, and advocacy groups. One estimate of the size of this third sector puts its 1981 total income at $192 billion, including some $64.5 billion worth of time contributed by corporate executives and other volunteers.[3] Government (federal, state, and local) is by far the largest source of revenue for these organizations. The second largest source is composed of dues, fees, and charges assessed by the organizations themselves.[4]

In the past few years inflation and a shift in governmental priorities—state as well as federal—have put community organizations under serious financial pressure. According to one survey, over half of the nation's nonprofits receiving governmental support experienced reductions in that support, and another 35 percent received the same amount in the face of inflation.[5] In Michigan, state government cuts and policy decisions adversely affected about half of the 285 organizations surveyed under sponsorship of the Michigan League for Human Services.[6]

SAMPLE AND INDEPENDENT VARIABLES

In drawing our sample of community organizations, we were interested in organizations having the following traits: nonprofit status, a minimum of one paid staff member and one outside funding source, a history of service provision (as opposed to advocacy work alone), and at least two years' longevity. Our purpose in being selective was simply that we wished to examine adaptation to fiscal strain among established service organizations that are not wholly self-supporting. These are the organizations in the nonprofit sector that are likely to be influenced by cuts in government funding and yet still be in existence with a reasonable chance of survival.

Although it is sometimes difficult to obtain lists of community organizations, United Way of Greater Milwaukee prepares a resource directory on organizations in this area.[7] In the spring of 1983 we used this directory and sent questionnaires to 141 service organizations that appeared to fit our requirements, and a cover letter expressly asked respondents if their organizations had all of the characteristics listed above. Eleven organizations reported that they did not have the required characteristics, and another eight had ceased to exist. Of the remaining 122, 57 completed and returned questionnaires, for a response rate of 47 percent.

We are fully aware that our sample is not a probability sample and may be subject to nonresponse bias. Although the final response rate is respectable for studies of community organizations[8] (which are often short-lived and part of a shifting population that is difficult to demarcate reliably), we tried to compensate for nonresponse by including groups that varied on the independent variables important to our conceptual scheme. Through follow-up phone calls and a second mailing, we obtained an analytically useful sample, the units of which do vary widely on the key organizational variables.

Theories pertinent to the success of organizations in adapting to environmental change suggest that adaptation depends in part on the attributes of the organization itself. For example, interest group theory suggests that organizational size, quality of leadership, human resources, and financial resources are important.[9] Administrative theory also points to size and leadership qualities, as well as to expertise, productivity, and client mobilization.[10] In addition, the resource dependency model calls attention to the interorganizational dimension of organizational resources, that is, to the fact that support may be obtained from other organizations.[11]

Guided by these theoretical considerations and by the experience of the authors with community organizations, we selected as independent variables eight indicators of organizational attributes likely to be conducive to successful adaptation to scarcity. As shown in Table 1, these are total staff (an indicator of organizational size), specialists used (an indicator of expertise), staff with private-sector management experience (also an indicator of expertise), volunteer help (an indicator of client mobilization), budget size (an indicator of financial resources), percentage of budget raised by own efforts (an indicator of productivity), number of members (a general indicator of human resources), and whether the organization is sponsored by or affiliated with another organization (an indicator of interorganizational ties).

Our sample organizations vary widely on these indicators. Illustratively, 25 percent of them have annual budgets of less than $100,000, but 17 percent have budgets of more than $1 million. Total paid staff of sample organizations varies from one to 369. Ninety percent of the groups use specialists such as lawyers, accountants, and computer experts. The average group uses four, but many use more. One uses 17. Volunteers vary from two to over 400.

Besides using specialists and volunteers, many groups (45) also have

Table 1. Characteristics of Community Organizations Associated with Adapting to Fiscal Strain and Effectiveness in Managing Strain: Bivariate and Multivariate Associations

	Total Paid Staff (1)	*Number of Specialists Used (2)*	*Total Staff/ Board with Private-Sector Management Experience (3)*	*Total Volunteer Help (4)*	*Total Current Budget (5)*	*Percentage Budget from Own Fund Raising (6)*	*Number of Members (7)*	*Organization Sponsored or Affiliated (8)*
Adaptive Strategies:								
Use new funding source (1)	(.38)	(.64)*	(.40)	(.69)*	(.46)	(.49)	.04	−.21
Use for-profit activities (2)	−.36	(.50)*	−.07	.06	−.29	−.17	(.52)*	(.56)*
Effectiveness:								
Old funding sources cut but budget level maintained (3)	−.21	.28	.01	.24	.14	(.62)*	.08	.06

( )Boxed coefficients represent positive gammas of .30 or larger. These are emphasized in the text.

*Asterisked coefficients represent independent statistical relationships when the others in that row that showed a noteworthy bivariate gamma (see the boxed coefficients) are controlled using partial-correlation analysis. With "effectiveness," the second factor in the multivariate equation is number of specialists used. Asterisked coefficients are also emphasized in the text.

people on their staffs or boards of directors with management experience in the private sector. Since a good number of nonprofits operate as small businesses in their economic development or housing rehabilitation activities, management skills of this sort are often useful. Sample organizations have one to 51 persons with management experience in the private sector.

Nonprofit organizations need not rely solely on their own resources if they are affiliated with or sponsored by another organization (or part of a coalition). In our sample, 58 percent of the groups are affiliated with other organizations, are part of a coalition of groups, or are sponsored by other organizations.

We assume that all these factors can be manipulated by those who manage community organizations, some more easily than others. Perhaps the factors most easily changed by the organization itself involve the recruitment and use of specialists and volunteers; experts, clients, and friends can often be persuaded to help. Almost any organization, in addition, can raise some money through its own efforts. Getting people to join the organization as members, affiliating with other organizations, and getting staff with private-sector management experience are more difficult, although well within the realm of possibility for many nonprofits. Even budget and staff can be increased as a result of altering the more changeable factors.

FISCAL STRAIN AND DEPENDENT VARIABLES

The great majority of our community organizations have experienced fiscal strain. For example, more than 80 percent have had their funding from primary sources cut. Because of these cuts, sample groups reduced services (47 percent) or postponed capital improvements (37 percent).

In spite of cuts from their primary sources, 22 groups were able to maintain budget levels. This shows that some nonprofits are successfully adapting to fiscal strain. The most common adaptive strategy was seeking and getting new outside funding sources. Forty-one of our 57 groups succeeded in getting new outside funding, especially from foundations and churches; and more than half developed new ways of raising their own money. The latter included auctions, bake sales, bingo, letters soliciting contributions, charging for some services, and operating for-profit activities. Ten of our 57 "nonprofits" turned to for-profit ventures.

In this study we employ indicators of adaptation to an environment of scarcity as dependent variables. Three are used: (1) securing a new source of funding, (2) initiating for-profit activities, and (3) maintaining a budget level even though primary funding sources reduced their support. We refer to the third indicator as "effectiveness" because such groups had outside funding cut but were able to replace the lost money with other monies (externally generated or from their own sources) and hence maintain budget levels.

ANALYSIS OF ADAPTATION TO FISCAL STRAIN

In Table 1, eight characteristics of our 57 organizations are correlated with two strategies that the organizations have used to cope with fiscal strain and with one indicator of effectiveness in coping. We find that the first six organizational attributes all correlate with using a new funding source. (A noteworthy correlation is taken here to mean a positive gamma of at least .30. All variables are ordinal; some are ordered dichotomies.) According to coefficient size, these attributes are having more volunteers and specialists, raising more funds on their own, having a larger budget, having more staff or board members with private-sector management experience, and having more staff.

When initiating for-profit activities is the adaptive strategy, moderately large correlations appear between this strategy and being affiliated with another organization, number of members, and using more specialists. The only organizational attribute associated with effectiveness in adapting to fiscal strain is own-effort fund raising. However, number of specialists comes close to our standard (gamma = .28).

It may be noted that each of our eight independent variables has a gamma of .30 or larger with at least one other independent variable. Seven of them intercorrelate with two or more. Partial correlation analysis enables one to ascertain the effect of each variable characteristic while controlling for the effect of the other characteristics. Our procedures for this multivariate analysis are straightforward.[12] (Here coefficients of .20 or above are considered worthy of note.) Although this standard is not strict, we reason that with survey data and independent variables, all of which correlate with the dependent variable under analysis, an independent association of this magnitude is a reasonable basis for discriminating further among variable characteristics in their linkage to organizational adaptation and may point to an important adjustment to fiscal strain.

When getting a new source of funding is the adaptive strategy, we seek to identify the independent effect of each of six characteristics while controlling for the other five that also correlate with this adaptive strategy. When these partials are computed, only number of volunteers and number of specialists retain noteworthy associations. When for-profit activities is the adaptive strategy, all three characteristics with noteworthy bivariate correlations also display independent relationships. Finally, when the dependent variable is our indicator of effectiveness and two characteristics are used to assess independent effects (including the one with the .28 gamma), only own-effort fund raising displays an independent effect.

CONCLUSIONS

Our analysis does identify particular organizational characteristics that are linked to successful adaptation to resource scarcity by community organizations. Indeed, all eight organizational indicators used as independent variables correlate at the bivariate level with at least one adaptive strategy.

However, two or three characteristics suggest themselves more strongly than the others. Number of specialists, an indicator of organizational expertise, correlates at a moderately high bivariate level with both adaptive strategies and also displays an independent association with both strategies when other correlates are partialed out. In addition, it comes close to our bivariate standard with the indicator of effectiveness. Own-effort fund raising correlates at a moderately high level with one adaptive strategy and with effectiveness. No other organizational characteristic produces as many as two correlations with a dependent variable. Volunteer help, however, does produce the largest single gamma with any dependent variable.

As noted earlier, specialists, own-effort fund raising, and volunteers are factors that nonprofit service organizations can change relatively easily. Most organizations can persuade specialists to help them and save some money by calling upon volunteers to perform work normally done by the paid staff. All community organizations would like to be independent of outside funding and can benefit from raising funds on their own.

A reasonable question about this analysis is whether any change or action designed to cope with fiscal strain might be easier for an organization already possessing more resources, financial and human. It seems likely that larger, better-off, and better-staffed organizations of any type—nonprofit, for-profit, or governmental—will tend to be more adaptive to environmental challenge, as indeed theory suggests. Obviously, one result of our study of community organizations facing environmental change is further support, albeit in a little-researched context, of existing theory. Successful adaptation is associated with organizational expertise, productivity, and client mobilization.

However, our evidence does not support the proposition that adaptation is a simple function of current size or existing financial differences among organizations. Staff size does not correlate consistently with adaptation indicators, and those organizations with more money do not necessarily adapt better. Size of budget does not correlate with our effectiveness measure or with adaptation when for-profit activity is used as an indicator of adaptation. In addition, when partials are computed using all eight independent variables (we used six, three, and two earlier), budget size has no independent association with any of the dependent variables.

We would not argue, however, that financially better-off community organizations are no likelier to withstand resource scarcity than those on the edge of insolvency, all other things being equal. The point is rather that community organizations need not believe that, unless they are large and well off, they are simply doomed when cuts are made in outside funding sources. Our evidence offers encouragement to all community organizations to secure specialist and volunteer help and to raise money on their own.

That is the principal message of the Milwaukee study to the financial managers of community organizations. It is clear that the environment to which community organizations must adapt will continue to be one of reduced assistance from government. The incentive is strong for nonprofits to consider very carefully any organizational modifications that hold out the prospect of successful adaptation. Among the modifications that merit consideration are those suggested here.

NOTES

1. Empirical studies of fiscal strain among nonprofit community organizations include Urban Institute, "Serving Community Needs: The Nonprofit Sector in an Era of Governmental Retrenchment" (Washington, D.C.: The Institute, September 1983), and Michigan League for Human Services, "Private, Nonprofit Agency Survey on Economic and Social Distress in Michigan" (Lansing, Mich.: The League, 1983). The Urban Institute study is a progress report from their large Nonprofit Sector Project.

Studies of governmental jurisdictions and agencies include Joan K. Martin, *Urban Financial Distress: Why Cities Go Broke* (Boston: Auburn House, 1982); Irene Rubin, *Running in the Red: The Political Dynamics of Urban Fiscal Stress* (Albany: State University of New York Press, 1982); and Terry Nichols Clark and Lorna Ferguson, *City Money: Political Processes, Fiscal Strain, and Retrenchment* (New York: Columbia University Press, 1983).

2. Richard H. Hall, *Organizations: Structure and Process* (Englewood Cliffs, N.J.: Prentice Hall, 1982), pp. 317–320.

3. Rushworth M. Kidder, "Public, Private, Nonprofit: Balancing the Fat Boy in the Canoe," *Christian Science Monitor* (February 6, 1984).

4. Urban Institute, "Serving Community Needs," p. 3

5. Ibid.

6. Michigan League, "Private, Nonprofit Agency Survey," p. 3.

7. United Way of Greater Milwaukee Inc., "Human Services Resource Directory for the Greater Milwaukee Area, 1980 Edition" (Milwaukee, Wis.: United Way, 1980).

8. The response rate for the Urban Institute study was 50 percent. The response rate for the Michigan League study was 54 percent.

9. See David B. Truman, *The Governmental Process* (New York: Alfred A. Knopf, Inc., 1951).

10. Charles H. Levine, "Organizational Decline and Cutback Management," *Public Administration Review* 38 (July/August 1978): pp. 316–325.

11. Hall, *Organizations*, pp. 317–318.

12. We did not use regression because of the level at which the variables were measured. One could use partial gammas with ordinal variables. We did not do so because we did not have enough cases for the literal holding constant required through cross-tabulation. Kendall's tau may also be used with ordinal scales and are considered to give correlations that are "somewhat analogous to product-moment correlations" (Hubert M. Blalock, *Social Statistics*, McGraw Hill, 1960, p. 317).

We proceeded as follows. We computed bivariate taus and used them as input for conventional partial correlation analysis. We then computed partials by the standard method. Of course, one might also input bivariate gammas. Our reason for not doing so was that the statistical package we used, the second edition of SPSS, allows the user to output a matrix of taus but not of gammas (for later input). Taus are, therefore, more convenient, and they are more analogous to the product-moment approach.

It may be noted that the bivariate taus support the same inferences as the bivariate gammas.

MEASURING MAYORAL POWER:
COMPARING FORMAL AUTHORITY WITH REPUTED POWER

John Allen Williams and Robert Y. Shapiro

ABSTRACT

In this article we construct a simple index to measure the formal authority of mayors. We compare executive power at the state and local levels, and more importantly, we seek to find an alternative and supplement to reputational measures of power, which can only be obtained from costly surveys of local informants. Our analysis suggests a modest similarity between state and local executives, and a revised version of our index is a reasonably good indicator of the way in which mayoral power will be estimated by community influentials. The modest strength of this relationship suggests that researchers can construct an index of structural authority that can be used as a measure of power in comparative analysis.

The concept of power is important for the study of policy formation, and it provides a way to compare political systems. Unfortunately, this concept has been difficult to measure for use in applied policy research. This measurement problem has made it hard to compare the policy-making processes of different levels of government, and it has particularly hampered comparative urban research, in which "reputational" measures of mayoral power have been examined for relatively small numbers of cities. These measures are estimates of a mayor's power obtained from local influentials

Research in Urban Policy, Vol. 2, pages 127–135.

ISBN: 0-89232-534-8

(informants), and they are usually not available because they require costly survey methods. For this reason, it is necessary to examine alternate measures of power.

Several years ago, Nelson C. Dometrius[1] used a revised version of Joseph A. Schlesinger's index of formal power to predict state administrators' perceptions of gubernatorial power.[2] In this paper we use a similar index to predict the power attributed to city mayors. Based on Dometrius's work, we construct a simple index and examine how well it corresponds to a reputational measure of mayoral power. We then revise the index to improve its predictive ability, since it is the strength of this correlation that reveals how well our measure of formal authority gauges reputational power.

We are concerned throughout this work with mayoral power as the mayor's "potential ability . . . to bring about changes in the system,"[3] and e briefly examine mayoral influence—the exercising of power on policy decisions. Although cities frequently have a professional administrator in addition to their chief elected official, we have limited our study to mayors. We focus on the chief elected official of cities in order to compare our results with Dometrius's research on state governors, and earlier studies suggest that a mayor is still quite powerful even in the presence of a city manager.[4]

THE MAYORAL AUTHORITY INDEX

The revised Schlesinger index used by Dometrius combined three elements of gubernatorial administrative power: appointment power, scored from 0 to 10; budget power, scored 0 or 1; and veto power, scored 0 or 1.[5] The combined index, a sum of the three components, was therefore weighted heavily in favor of appointment power. We attempted to replicate this index as closely as possible, using data collected for the 51 U.S. cities making up the National Opinion Research Center's Permanent Community Sample. These cities have been studied extensively by Terry Nichols Clark and others,[6] and our study contributes to this ongoing research on local communities.

We were only partially successful in constructing an index completely comparable with the gubernatorial index. We were able to measure its most important component, appointment power, as well as veto power. We were unable to construct a measure of budget power analogous to Dometrius's, and the alternate one we developed did not perform very impressively in an analysis similar to the one described below.[7] As a result, our measure of formal authority consists of appointment power and veto power.

Using responses to a 1974 survey by the International City Management Association (ICMA),[8] we constructed our index as follows:

1. *Mayoral appointment power.* Each city's score on this component was determined by the way in which 18 officials were appointed.[9] For each of the 18 positions the city received a score of 4 for a mayoral appointment, 3 for a mayoral appointment with council approval, 2 for joint mayor and council appointment, 1 for a civil service commission or board or council appointment, and 0 for a direct election by the people. A ratio was then computed, with the sum of scores for as many as 18 positions divided by the total possible score (that is, a maximum of $18 \times 4 = 72$). To parallel Dometrius's index, this ratio was recoded so that scores of 0 to .10 = 1, above .10 to .20 = 2, . . . , and above .90 to 1.00 = 10.
2. *Mayoral veto power.* Respondents were asked in the 1974 survey to indicate in what cases the mayor could exercise veto power and what majority of the council was required to override the veto. Only two respondents indicated that the mayor could exercise an item veto for ordinance or appropriations, so we scored a city 1 if the mayor had any veto power and all other cities 0. Except in one case, we did not use the council overriding majority as part of the index due to missing data in 29 out of 51 cases. The exception was a city whose response made us suspect that mayoral vetoes could be overriden easily, and was therefore scored 0.

Our initial mayoral authority index was then created by summing the scores on mayoral appointment and veto power to produce a scale from 0 to 11.

PERCEPTIONS OF MAYORAL POWER

Dometrius used as his measure of gubernatorial power, to be predicted by his revised Schlesinger index, the perceptions of state administrators concerning the relative influence of the governor and the legislature over their agencies, based on three surveys by Deil S. Wright.[10] This measure was intended to measure gubernatorial administrative power, and no claim was made that his revised index would predict overall gubernatorial power.[11] With respect to city mayors, however, the index we developed gauges more than purely administrative power.

Our measure of perceived power assessed the potential ability of the mayors to influence policy in five issue areas (school board election, municipal bond issue, urban renewal, air pollution control, and a mayoral election) as reported in 1967 by seven informants in each of the 51 cities of the Permanent Community Sample.[12] We noted the time lag between this survey and the objective data making up the formal authority index, but a check of the *Municipal Yearbooks* for 1966 and 1974 showed mayoral veto to have changed in only seven cities during the period.[13] These cities were dropped from the analysis since it seemed probable that they had undergone other structural changes as well. This could not be directly assessed for our appointment measure, since that information was available in only the 1974 survey. Additionally, our best formal authority index (to be presented below) correlated .65 with a 1967 mayoral authority index of Clark's. We have chosen to use our own index in order to make comparisons with the state-level work, and we have used the best data available to us.

ANALYSIS

We first tested our index of formal authority to see how well it predicted the power attributed to mayors. Equation 1A of Table 1 shows the results when the appointment and veto components were entered separately into a regression equation. The equation explains about 36% of the variance in mayoral power. The index formed by combining both elements, shown in equation 1B, did not do as well, explaining only 22% of the variance. In this index the highly predictive veto power was combined with the very heavily weighted appointment power. Weighting the latter 10 times as much as veto power seemed clearly inappropriate, and we adjusted our index accordingly.

Appointment power as originally computed was the sum of the scores for all 18 positions divided by the total possible score of 72 if the mayor was maximally powerful on every appointment, then recoded to extend the scale from 1 to 10. We revised the index by using the original ratio, without recoding it. As a result of this, appointment power became a continuous variable from 0 to 1, reflecting finer differences among the communities, and it was less subject to distortions introduced by recoding. Veto power remained a dichotomous measure, scored 0 or 1.

Equations 2A and 2B of Table 1 give the results of this effort. The untransformed appointment power and veto power components, when entered separately into the equation predicting mayoral power, explained about 36% of the variance. When combined into our second mayoral power index, they accounted for about 34% of the variance. This is a dramatic improvement in the performance of the index, one that is virtually all duc to the contribution of the mayor's veto power.

To further examine the validity of our final index, we correlated it with perceived mayoral *influence*, as measured by Clark's "ersatz decisional"

Table 1. Summary of Regression Analyses Predicting Mayoral Power[a]

Equation	*Constant*		*Veto*	*Appointment*	*Summary*	R^2
1A: Components of MAI – I	1427.308	b	3.078	–.003	—	.359
		se	.952	.265	—	
		beta	.600	.00	—	
		F	10.45*	.00	—	
1B: Mayoral Authority Index – I	242.732	b	—	—	.560	.223
		se	—	—	.177	
		beta	—	—	.472	
		F	—	—	10.02*	
2A: Components of MAI – II	1376.595	b	3.032	.158	—	.359
		se	.951	2.596	—	
		beta	.591	.011	—	
		F	10.16*	.00	—	
2B: Mayoral Authority Index – II	856.866	b	—	—	2.360	.344
		se	—	—	.550	
		beta	—	—	.587	
		F	—	—	18.38*	

[a]N = 37.
*p < .01.

method.[14] Until now we have been addressing mayoral *power*, conceptualized as the potential ability of the mayor to effect system changes. The influence measure taps actual participation in specific decisions. We find that the correlation of our formal authority measure with both perceived mayoral power and influence increases when we examine the revised index. As shown in Table 2, the correlations between mayoral power and the two indices increase from .47 to .59, and between perceived influence and the two measures, from .25 (not significant) to .38. These results suggest that this type of measure of formal authority—or in fact veto power alone, should its strong role hold for additional cities—may be a useful surrogate for perceived power and perhaps actual past mayoral influence as well. Although we have not emphasized a specific causal connection among formal mayoral authority, perceived mayoral power, and actual influence on particular issues, such a relationship is quite likely. The perception of mayoral power among informants may be affected directly by knowledge of both the mayor's formal authority and his or her past influence attempts. Formal authority could also affect the mayor's perceived power indirectly through its effect on actual influence. Our finding of correlations among separately measured indicators of formal authority, perceived power, and actual influence are consistent with this, and the tendency of these variables to covary is empirically useful.

Table 2. Product-Moment Correlation Coefficients among Indicators of Mayoral Power[a]

	1.	*2.*	*3.*	*4.*	*5.*	*6.*
1. Veto power	1.00					
2. Appointment power	.67[c]	1.00				
3. Mayoral Authority Index – I	.79[c]	.99[c]	1.00			
4. Mayoral Authority Index – II (Final Index)	.98[c]	.81[c]	.90[c]	1.00		
5. Mayoral Power ("Issue-Specific Reputational")	.59[c]	.41[c]	.47[c]	.59[c]	1.00	
6. Mayoral Influence ("Ersatz Decisional")	.46[c]	.18	.25	.38[b]	.43[c]	1.00

[a]N ranges from 34 to 44.
[b]$p < .05$.
[c]$p < .01$.

DISCUSSION

Two results emerge from this study. First, the relationship between certain structural indicators of power and perceived power suggests some modest likenesses at the state and local levels. Certainly these levels are not identical, as was shown by the need to revise our original index. But some basic similarities appear to exist, and comparative studies exploring relationships among variables at different levels of analysis might uncover more of them.[15] Our confidence in generalizing about a relationship is increased when it is observed in a variety of settings, for it is then more likely to be a regular phenomenon than an idiosyncratic variation.[16]

Second, and more importantly, although our method of measuring formal authority is relatively simple and far from definitive, it can be used with some success to predict reputed power. Refinements in measurement can no doubt be made with additional data and empirical analysis.[17] An index of the type we have described should be particularly useful in studies that compare policies (usually spending, using cross-sectional or panel data) for large numbers of cities.[18] Measures of reputational power are not likely to be available, and analysts seeking to contrast strong versus weak mayors (either as independent variables or interacting with other variables) can examine legally defined responsibilities that make some mayors more powerful than others. The data required to do this are less expensive and easier to obtain than judgments from credible informants. In addition, empirical studies that examine reputational power in a smaller number of cities might also make use of a measure of more formal, structural power. To the extent that formal authority and reputed power are not correlated, researchers will gain new information about potential sources of mayoral power—the resources that mayors have that do not contribute to perceived power, but that nonetheless may allow them to shape policies in their cities.

ACKNOWLEDGMENTS

Coauthorship is equal. We wish to thank Terry Nichols Clark and the anonymous reviewers for their helpful comments and suggestions; the responsibility for analysis and interpretation is our own.

NOTES

1. Nelson C. Dometrius, "Measuring Gubernatorial Power," *The Journal of Politics* 41 (May 1979): 589–610.

2. Joseph A. Schlesinger, "The Politics of the Executive," in Herbert Jacob and Kenneth N. Vines, eds., *Politics in the American States*, 1st ed., (Boston: Little, Brown, 1965), pp. 207–233. Cited in Dometrius, "Measuring Gubernatorial Power," p. 589.

3. Terry Nichols Clark, "The Concept of Power," in Terry Nichols Clark, ed., *Community Structure and Decision-Making: Comparative Analyses* (Scranton: Chandler Publishing Company, 1968), pp. 46–47.

4. Terry Nichols Clark, "Cities Differ—But How and Why? Inputs to National Urban Policy from Research on Decision-Making in 51 American Municipalities." Report to Office of Policy Development and Research, U.S. Department of Housing and Urban Development, September 1975. Report #HUD/RES 1310; NTIS Accession #PB278980/AS; available from National Technical Information Service, 5285 Port Royal Road, Springfield, VA 22161. Paperback code: A07 ($7.25); microfiche code: A01 ($3.00); 141 pp. Twenty of our 51 cities had a city manager and four were commission cities. Clark's study shows that for these same 51 cities, the mayor in a mayor-council city was more powerful than the manager in a council-manager city. Indeed, in three of the council-manager cities, the mayor was rated more powerful than the manager. Clark's experiment with a "chief executive" index showed it to be "almost identical to the mayor index."

5. Dometrius, "Measuring Gubernatorial Power," p. 609.

6. See, for example, Terry Nichols Clark, "Community Structure, Decision-Making, Budget Expenditures, and Urban Renewal in 51 American Communities," *American Sociological Review* 33 (August 1968): 576–593. The Permanent Community Sample and the results of numerous previous studies using it are discussed in Clark, "Cities Differ," *passim*.

7. We were not able to locate a measure of budget power equivalent to the measure used by Dometrius; however, an approximation was made. Respondents in the ICMA survey were asked to indicate the amount of time the city council spent on each of several functions, among them preparing, reviewing, and adopting the annual budget. (The entire list of functions considered was reviewing administration of city functions; initiating new proposals of the council; preparing, reviewing, and adopting the annual budget; zoning and planning; considering proposals of the executive branch; individual constituent requests; appointment and personnel decisions; and other.) We thought it reasonable that the more time a council spent on the budget, the less was the power of the mayor over the budget. The respondents ranked the four functions on which the council spent the most time. We coded 1 for those

cities in which the budget function was *not* among the top four functions taking up the council's time. The remaining cities, in which the budget function was not ranked, were scored 0. This was not an entirely adequate or comparable measure of mayoral budget authority. It did not perform well in the empirical analysis, correlating hardly at all with the measure of power attributed to the mayor.

8. We are grateful to Terry Nichols Clark for making these data available to us.

9. The 18 officials were the following: auditor or board of auditors, controller, treasurer, city assessor or board of assessors, city clerk or secretary, street superintendent, public works director, planning director, city engineer, police chief, fire chief, public safety director, city attorney, health officer, chief personnel officer, director of recreation, librarian, and superintendent of schools.

10. Deil S. Wright, "Executive Leadership in State Administration: Interplay of Gubernatorial, Legislative, and Administrative Power," *Midwest Journal of Political Science* 11 (February 1967): 1–26. Cited in Dometrius, "Measuring Gubernatorial Power," p. 593.

11. Dometrius, "Measuring Gubernatorial Power," p. 597.

12. Clark, "Cities Differ," p. 21. The informants were the chamber of commerce president, Democratic Party chairman, Republican Party chairman, president of the largest bank, a labor leader, newspaper editor, and president of the bar association. No assertion is made that these were the most powerful members of the community, but that they were in a position to know who, if anyone, was powerful. See also the National Opinion Research Center, "Interview Schedule for Panel of Community Leaders," NORC 505, January 1967, for the exact wording of the questions. Respondents were asked, "Is there any single person whose opposition would be almost impossible to overcome or whose support would be essential for . . . ," followed by the mention of a specific issue area. The mayoral power score for a city was the percentage of mentions of the mayor in the five issue areas multiplied by 1,000.

13. International City Managers' Association, *The Municipal Yearbook*, 1966, 1974.

14. For construction of the "ersatz decisional" mayoral influence scores, see Clark, "Cities Differ," pp. 19–24. The questions probed actual participation in decisions relating to air pollution control, poverty programs, urban renewal, and selecting the mayor.

15. For a nonquantitative example of a study of comparative executive behavior in influencing the federal government, see Donald H. Haider, *When Governments Come to Washington: Governors, Mayors, and Intergovernmental Lobbying* (New York: The Free Press, 1974). He notes that "the comparative study of governors, mayors, and county officials . . . in the execution of their multiple responsibilities as chief executive officers of general-purpose units of government remains one of the least explored areas of political inquiry" (p. xi).

16. For an extended discussion of the utility of the "most different systems" as opposed to "most similar systems" research designs, see Adam Przeworski and Henry Teune, *The Logic of Comparative Social Inquiry* (New York: Wiley Interscience, 1970), chapter 2.

17. Further refinements should be made to the index by examining other formal mayoral powers and other structural features of local governments. These might include a good indicator of the mayor's budgetary power, the independence of the school system, the degree of unionization of city employees, and the number and authority of independent boards and commissions. For studying particular policies, the ability of the mayor to appoint the relevant key officials may assume special significance.

Additional analysis should examine directly whether formal authority is largely a surrogate for reputed power or whether it is in part analytically distinct. If an index of formal authority may be readily substituted for reputed power, it should be related to a variety of independent and dependent variables (city characteristics and urban policy outputs and outcomes) in essentially the same way. The magnitudes of the correlations that we have reported do not necessarily assure this, strictly speaking. These relationships with other variables should be taken into account in developing better measures. See John Piazza, "The Analysis of Attitude Items," *American Journal of Sociology* 86 (November 1980): 584–603.

18. For a recent study in this tradition, see Terry Nichols Clark and Lorna Crowley Ferguson, *City Money: Political Processes, Fiscal Strain, and Retrenchment* (New York: Columbia University Press, 1983).

NO ONE WANTS TO SAY NO: BUDGETARY DISCIPLINE IN URBAN GOVERNMENT

Harald Baldersheim

ABSTRACT

City governments are complex organizations, composed of on the one hand a large number of service departments, and on the other hand a small number of managerial officers responsible for the overall financial well-being of a city government. To what extent do the financial officers succeed in imposing some measure of financial discipline on service departments that are always hungry for a larger slice of the budget pie. Under what conditions do they maintain budgetary discipline, and when do they fail?

The material collected for this paper indicates that managerial strategies matter more than organizational set-ups. In situations of administrative conflicts discipline is most heavily influenced by type of service technology, while in situations in which political conflicts occur the maintenance of discipline depends on the ideology of the political majority.

INTRODUCTION

In this paper, the maintenance of budgetary discipline is studied as a dependent variable. By "maintenance of budgetary discipline" we mean the

Research in Urban Policy, Vol. 2, pages 137–144.

ISBN: 0-89232-534-8

Figure 1. Decision Making on Supplementary Appropriations

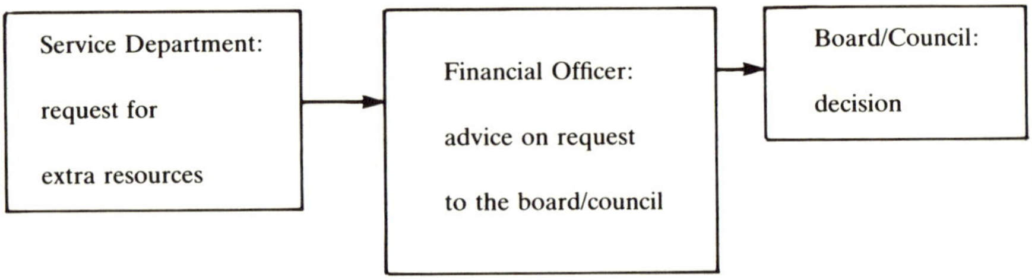

efforts local authorities make to enforce the spending limits they impose on service departments in their annual budgets. Studies of local budgeting usually see a department's share of an annual budget as the final outcome of a game. The measure of the department's success in the game is the size of its slice of the budget pie[1]. However, the game is not over with the passing of the yearly budget. Departments frequently apply for supplementary appropriations throughout the fiscal year. The spending limits will be broken to the extent that departments succeed with their requests. The budget is a set of political priorities established by the elected council at the beginning of the fiscal year. As a result of extra appropriations, at the end of the day the political outcome may be quite different from the original one. Decisions concerning supplementary appropriations are surrounded by some characteristic conflicts. Our aim is to describe these conflicts and explain their outcomes.

Here, the process of decision making is simplified into a three-party game. The actors are (1) the politicians, whose overriding concern is assumed to be votes, seats on the city council, and positions in committees under the council, (2) the service departments, interested in expansion of their domains, and (3) the financial officer or management,* whose job is to make ends meet by proposing a balanced budget and, preferably, setting a little aside against unforeseen contingencies. In short, we assume that the processes of decision making are structured by three competing goals: the politicians' maximizing votes, the departments' maximizing budget shares, and the financial management's maximizing budget surpluses.

The relationship among these three parties is an institutionalized game in which the politicians and the service departments represent pressures making for higher spending, while the financial officer's role is to hold back. When and to what extent do the financial officers succeed in holding back? One would expect natural coalitions to arise between service departments

*In the following, the words *financial officer*, *manager*, and *management* are used interchangeably.

and politicians, since politicians gain votes and seats precisely by satisfying consumer demands for services, which is an outcome that also satisfies the service departments. The fact that so many local authorities are facing financial difficulties now[2] may indicate that the financial officers have had a relatively weak position in this game despite an ability to win some of the battles. The frequency of officers' "victories" and "losses" in the game is used as an operationalization of our dependent variable (the maintenance of budgetary discipline): the more losses, the less budgetary discipline.

What are the factors that influence the officers' success in the game? In order to answer the question we have to look at situations in which a conflict exists between two or three parties and see what patterns of alignment arise. Such conflicts occur when a service department requests resources and the financial officer is unwilling to recommend that the request be granted. The politicians, who make the final decision, may then support the officers' view, and the department has lost; or they may support the department's claim, and the officers have lost. However, the political decisions are not always unanimous, and so the officers' successes or failures are a function of the political coalitions that emerge in each case: Is it one supporting the management, or one supporting the department?

The Data

The material we have collected to study these processes concerns supplementary allocations of resources to service departments ("extra appropriations") made by the executive board of the city councils of three Norwegian cities (Bergen, Trondheim, and Stavanger)[3]. These extra appropriations come as supplements to a department's ordinary budget, with which the department is expected to manage. In fact, departments are discouraged from making requests for extra resources above what they get through the annual budget since the allocation of supplements is thought to erode political priorities and financial control with service provision. However, for a number of reasons departments persist with such requests throughout the financial year. The greater number of requests are granted by the board of the city council, but in a number of cases they are granted against the recommendations of the financial management.

Our material covers all extra appropriations made in the years 1976 and 1979 in these cities. Altogether 1,016 decisions of this nature were uncovered and traced through the machinery of decision making. The material was collected from archives in the respective cities. The interpretation of the material on appropriations and other relevant organizational procedures was aided by interviews with informants in each municipality.

EXPLANATIONS OF BUDGETARY DISCIPLINE

Managerial control varies from city to city and from one department to another, and it varies over time. Five different explanations of managerial control cum budgetary discipline will be tested.

Weak Management and Ill-Chosen Organizational Structures

This explanation emphasises that financial advisers and controllers often have a peripheral position in the processes of decision making in local authorities.[4] They are brought into the process at a late stage when political commitments have already been made; furthermore, their organizational location away from the centers of spending makes financial control into an after-the-fact affair.

The cities in our sample have two types of management: unitary and collegial. In the unitary type, the financial officers is the sole intermediary between the departments and the board. In the collegial type, the financial officer has to share access to the board with the heads of the various departments. In the latter case, he is therefore not so much at the hub of the lines of communication and is expected to have less control over outcomes.

Bad Habits of a Period of Financial Abundance: Levels of Slack

This explanation attributes a lack of financial discipline to habits acquired in a period when means were less scarce. In situations of economic and fiscal growth there will be more emphasis on satisfying consumer demands then on economy and husbandry in local government. Therefore, departments will be rewarded for sparing the politicians from grievances from voters rather than for making economies. Local authorities need time to adjust to more straitened financial circumstances. But those authorities that have experienced the sharpest financial decline will probably also be those with the best budgetary discipline.

Technologies of Service Provision

Technologies may be divided into personal and nonpersonal.[5] Examples of the former kind are teaching and nursing, where service provision requires a close personal interaction between clients and professionals. Examples of thc latter type are those that rely on machines and technical equipment to provide a service, such as departments for works, sports facilities, parks, and other civic amenities.

Politicians may find it difficult to reject requests for supplementary appropriations when they come from departments that rely on personal technologies since the victims of the cuts are more easily identifiable. The political consequences of cuts in personal services may have to be faced more immediately than when cuts are made in nonpersonal services. This may make politicians reluctant to accept advice to reject requests for supplements from departments employing highly personal technologies. Consequently, managerial control may be highest with regard to requests from technical service departments.

Political Ideologies, and Life in the Political Marketplace

Political parties with socialist ideologies are often thought of as mostly oriented toward satisfying consumers and clients of public services, while nonsocialist (e.g., conservative) parties are more oriented toward the taxpayer and more interested in economies in public services. Consequently, boards with a socialist majority may be expected to be less inclined to accept advice from managers to reject giving supplements to a department, while nonsocialist majorities may be inclined to support managers in this respect.

In a political marketplace model it is assumed that political parties compete for the largest possible share of a fleeting mass of voters with unstable party preferences.[6] Rejecting departmental claims for extra resources may offend crucial segments of the electorate, and the politicians may therefore be unwilling to do so. The harder the political competition, the less inclined politicians may be to reject such departmental claims. We may assume that competition among parties increases when an election is approaching. Competition is probably more intense in an election year than in a year without an election. Politicians may, therefore, be less inclined to support managerial views in an election year than they are in nonelection years.

Strategies

The budgetary process is an institutionalized game that is repeated over and over again with the same actors in the same roles year after year. The actors gradually learn what to expect from each other. Strategies are formed on the basis of anticipated reactions. If, for example, the departments know that the manager always makes a cut in their requests, they will probably tend to ask for more—to be on the safe side—than if they know that cuts are an exception. Therefore, the greater the tendency of the manager to cut down requests, the more necessary it will become for such cuts to be made.

A manager's tendency to cut requests may also have further repercussions in the process of decision making. If the manager knows that the board, as a rule, restores the cuts they are asked to make, the manager may be inclined to make large cuts, just to be on the safe side and to achieve *some* reduction in the supplementary allocations. If the board gets used to recommendations that imply larger cuts than are necessary to balance the books at the end of the year, they may feel tempted to make large restorations. Consequently, a tendency for managers to disagree with their departments may increase the likelihood of disagreement between managers and boards and thus reduce managerial control and budgetary discipline.

RESULTS

The basic pattern of the game emerges quite clearly in Table 1. The table shows that the financial management on average cuts down the requests to 79% of the original demands, while the board on average raises the sum to 87% of the original. There are variations between cities as to the size of cuts and restorations. In the end, the departments get between 85 and 89% of what they ask for. These are city averages, however. Variations between what departments get, can be much larger.

Table 1. Managers' Recommendations and Boards' Decisions Expressed as a Proportion of the Department's Requests for Extra Appropriations (averages)
(Departmental requests = 100*; by city and overall)

	Overall	*Bergen*	*Trondheim*	*Stavanger*
Department's request	100	100	100	100
Manager's recommendation	79	81	84	73
Board's decision	87	89	89	85

*Calculations based on the monetary sums requested.

Table 1 is based on the monetary sums requested and granted. Table 2 depicts the frequency with which supplementary allocations are requested, and the frequency of conflict in the various stages of the processing of the requests.

The table shows, first, that there is agreement in the greater number of cases both between manager and board and between manager and departments. Disagreements are, however, more frequent between manager and departments than between manager and board.

Our operationalization of "budgetary discipline" means that discipline equals managerial control over outcomes. Managerial control is measured in three different ways:

Table 2. Frequency of Agreement/Disagreement between Board-Manager, Manager-Department, and Board-Department in the Three Cities Combined (percent)

	Agreement	*Disagreement*	*(N*)*
Manager-Board	90	10	(818)
Manager-Department	72	28	(573)
Department-Board	78	22	(587)

*N varies because of missing data.

- The board's *overall* acceptance rate of managerial advice on requests for supplementary appropriations; i.e. the proportion of *all* outcomes which are consonant with the manager's advice; the board accepts his advice in 90% of the cases.
- The board's acceptance of managerial advice in *conflict situations*; i.e. on those issues where the manager goes *against* the department's request; in such conflict situations, the rate of acceptance is reduced to 67%.
- The *depth* of the board's acceptance of managerial advice, i.e. the proportion of managerial recommendations which are passed *unanimously* by the board; the board reflects the party political composition of the council; still, 83% of all recommendations are passed without any dissent.

Table 3 reports the results of our tests of the five explanations of variations in budgetary discipline. To test these explanations dependent and independent variables were dichotomised and epsilons used as measures of association.

Variations in overall managerial control is best explained by "strategy", while managerial control in conflict situations is best explained by type of service technology. The depth of the manager's influence on the board (managerial control III) is best accounted for by political variables (the ideology of the majority of the board), but administrative structure and strategic choices are also of some significance.

Of the five explanations suggested, political ideology and strategic choices seem most promising. The latter yields the best single result (i.e., with regard to explaining overall managerial control). The level of economic slack only influences the depth of managerial control, but not very much. (A reduction of slack leads to an increasing number of dissenters on the board.)

Table 3. Variations in Budgetary Discipline (epsilons)

	Managerial Control I: Overall Control	*Managerial Control II: Control When in Conflict with Department*	*Managerial Control III: Political Conflict over Manager's Recommendation*
Explanations:			
1. Administrative structure: unitary/nonunitary	3	5	17
2. Slack: increase/decrease	3	10	13
3. Services: nonpersonal/personal	4	13	5
4a. Socialist/nonsocialist	2	7	24
4b. Political competition: election year/nonelection year	3	2	2
5. Strategy: Managerial conflict with department: yes/no	30	—	14

ACKNOWLEDGMENT

Paper presented to Workshop on *Fiscal Austerity and Urban Innovation*, Conference on Mise en question de l'État providence et l'émergence de la Cité, Paris, October 10–12, 1983.

NOTES

1. Aaron Wildavsky, *The Politics of the Budgetary Process* (Boston: Little, Brown, 1964); K. E. Brofoss and A. T. Cowart. *Decisions, Politics and Change: A Study of Norwegian Urban Budgeting* (Oslo: Universitetsforlaget, 1979).

2. K. Newton, *Balancing the Books* (London: Sage, 1980): L. J. Sharpe, *The Local Fiscal Crisis in Western Europe* (London: Sage, 1981).

3. For a detailed explanation of what we have classified as "extra appropriations" see D. Vestrheim, *Organisasjon, økonomi og styring i bykommunar*, Working Paper No. 11 from the Research Program on Cities, Subprogram on Government, Bergen 1981.

4. M. Meyer, *Change in Public Bureaucracies* (Cambridge: Cambridge University Press., 1979).

5. Charles Perry, "Hospitals: Technology, Structure and Goals," in J. G. March, ed., *Handbook of Organizations* (Chicago: Rand McNally, 1965), pp. 910–971.

6. Anthony Downs, *An Economic Theory of Democracy* (New York: Harper and Brothers, 1957).

DID PROPOSITION 13 CHANGE SPENDING PREFERENCES?

Alan L. Saltzstein

ABSTRACT

The passage of Proposition 13 in California forced cities to make budgetary decisions with changed resources and uncertainty about future funds. This uncertainty may have forced city officials to alter spending priorities. This hypothesis is examined by evaluating expenditure patterns before and after its passage in 25 large California cities. Overall spending increased from 1978–79 to 1981–82. There was considerable variance in the rate of change and priorities did appear to have changed. Mean Police expenditures increased significantly, Parks and Recreation declined considerably. Public Works and Police and Fire changes were negatively correlated. Public Works spending was also related to city votes for liberal candidates. The most significant effects of the Proposition, thus were spending changes rather than reductions. City officials most likely perceived the "crisis" of the post Proposition 13 period as an opportunity to redefine priorities.

California voters altered more than local government finance when they passed Proposition 13 ("13") in June 1978. Local government's use of a large source of income, the property tax, was severely limited. The state

Research in Urban Policy, Vol. 2, pages 145–157.

ISBN: 0-89232-534-8

legislature provided additional funds to local governments and attached strings to this aid, thereby intermeshing state and local government as never before. Several court decisions followed that changed the meaning of parts of the initiative and brought the judiciary into government finance questions more directly than in the past. Decision makers often assumed that austerity was desired by the voters and thus became concerned with "cutback management" and "privatization," two newly defined terms in the Public Administration Dictionary.

Analysts of the meaning of Proposition 13 for governmental policymaking have concentrated on the effect of these events on service outputs and impacts. There appears to be little agreement as to the effect that these events have had.

Some have argued that service cutbacks and a diminished public sector have occurred. A series of articles in the *Los Angeles Times* now expanded into book form surveyed a large number of local governments and found significant service reductions in many cities, particularly older cities which had been most heavily dependent on the property tax (Schwadron, Richter, and Citrin 1984). Schwadron and his colleagues argue that cutbacks have been widespread and particularly burdensome for the poor (p. 118). Case studies of selected cities support this conclusion though they tend to be based on cities that suffered the greatest revenue reduction (Levine, Rubin, and Wologan 1982; May and Meltsner 1981).

Others, however, looked at increased state funding of local services, the rise of user fee income, and judicial rulings that have altered the impact of the initiative and concluded that declines in services were in fact illusory or limited to atypical cities (Rabushka and Ryan 1982: 94). These authors also maintain that impacts, measured by indices such as crime rates and student achievement scores, were unchanged.

A third author argues that the initiative signaled a dramatic redefinition of politics in California, reestablishing the relevance of grass-roots participation and shifting the focus of political discussion from service to fiscal issues (Kirlin 1982: 10). Kirlin maintains that the substance of political discussion changed. Proposition 13 was a revolt against the increased complexity of mid-twentieth-century government which had created a political system with little citizen control. The initiative then cut through this complex system, reestablishing citizen control.

These analyses of the effects of "13" are tentative and speculative. The events are too close at hand and are still unraveling. Changes in economic growth, inflation, and other sources of government income have altered the immediate effects to the point where may cities today seem to be generating significant surpluses again. The initial cuts in services, then, may have little long-run significance in many cities. The link among budgeted amounts, service levels, and economic and social impacts is always difficult to determine (Nachmias 1979: 3). Relating such changes to "13" then requires a longer time span and more precise measurement than appears in these studies.

A more approachable focus for examining effects of "13" on public policy is the budgetary process and changes in budget shares. Discussions with city officials, a review of budget documents following the passage of "13" and newspaper accounts suggest that budgetary decisions were made differently in the summer 1978 than in previous years. It was mid-spring 1978 before most decision makers perceived that "13" might pass. The vote took place in June; most city budgets are adopted in the summer. It was not known until late in the summer if the state would supply additional funds to the city, and the allocation of those funds was the subject of intense negotiations. While some city officials exhibited considerable farsight and began preparing for reductions prior to that summer (Kemp 1984), many did not and even those who did had no way of predicting the amount of changes needed. Basic questions of priorities and service levels were raised in most cities, then, as they were forced to prepare budgets with significantly less revenue. The process had to be done quickly and before the public's eye.

The state bail-out also contained several restrictions on the use of the money that, if enforced, directly impacted budget decisions. A "maintenance of effort" in public safety funding was required that was interpreted as a prohibition on declines in public safety funding. Enforcing this provision thus mandated that other services be cut if total expenditures were reduced. Analysts of the city budgetary process argue that decisions on operating budgets are usually incremental adjustments from the previous year (Crecine 1969). Maintaining the normal incremental decision process in 1978 was very difficult to do. The months following the passage of "13" may have forced city officials to alter their priorities, establishing a new base for future adjustments.

This study is the beginning of an attempt to determine if in fact spending patterns in cities changed following passage of "13." Shares of the total expenditures devoted to the major functions of government before and after passage are examined. City budget data for 25 cities are used to lend insight into these queries.

1. Did spending priorities for cities change after the passage of "13"?
2. What accounts for these changes? A preliminary assessment is carried out evaluating the influence of user fee income, population growth, previous spending levels, and several political indicators.
3. Did the mandating of police and fire service levels of the political climate favoring the expenditures have an effect on budget outcomes?

RESEARCH DESIGN

The analysis is based on expenditure and revenue data for California's 25 largest cities. This includes all cities larger than 100,000 in population in 1982. Excluded are San Francisco, a city-county and thus not comparable with the others, and Los Angeles, whose budget is 10 times the size of the next largest city in the group. The cities were chosen because they collectively represent a comparable group with similar functions.

Data were obtained for the fiscal years 1978–79 and 1981–82. These years were used because the former is the year immediately prior to the passage of "13" and the latter is the most recent for which verifiable figures are available. The data are published by the State Controller's Office, State of California. The information is supplied by the cities and audited carefully by the controller's office.

Expenditure comparisons are made for the common functions of local government only. These are defined as police, fire, libraries, public works, and parks and recreation. These functions are the focus of analysis because they are common to all cities in this classification. They also constitute about two-thirds of the average city budget. The major exclusion is public utilities, which are normally established on a different financial base and vary considerably from city to city. Fees and service charges also exclude those associated with utilities, thus permitting comparison on a similar base. Thus, for each city, expenditures for major functions are totaled and the proportion each function represents of this total is calculated. The analysis focuses on changes in expenditures and changes in these proportions from 1978 to 1982. It is assumed that significant changes in these proportions represent changes in budget priorities (Natchez and Bupp, 1973: 959).

ANALYSIS

Expenditure Totals of California Cities Since Proposition 13

Spending has increased significantly in the years since the passage of "13." Total spending has increased an average of 50.3 percent in these cities. Per capita spending has gained nearly 40 percent. Both of these figures surpass the increase in the consumer price index (CPI) during this period (38.6) (Schwadron, Richter, and Citrin 1984: 3).

This increase, however, has not occurred uniformly. Eleven of the cities have experienced some form of cutback management. Their rate of spending increase per capita was less than the rate of inflation. Three cities

Table 1. Changes in Total Spending and per Capita Spending, 1979–1982

		Mean (000)	*Mean per Capita*
Total	1979	45,761	226.3
	1982	64,572	303.1
% Change	1979–1982	50.3	39.6
Police	1979	12,694	60.9
	1982	21,450	94.4
% Change	1979–1982	73.5	55.7
Fire	1979	8,040	36.9
	1982	12,035	53.1
% Change	1979–1982	42.2	25.4
Public Works	1979	15,823	81.9
	1982	20,909	107.7
% Change	1979–1982	61.4	31.5
Library	1979	1,738	8.8
	1982	2,506	12.1
% Change	1979–1982	51.2	37.5
Parks & Recreation	1979	7,420	35.0
	1982	7,671	35.8
% Change	1979–1982	18.0	2.2

doubled their budgets during this period and two doubled per capita spending.

The rate of increase varied by function. (See Table 1.) Police expenditures increased by over 73 percent in total and over 55 percent per capita. Park and recreation expenditures, however, are far below the CPI at 18 percent total and 2.2 percent per capita. Public works, libraries, and fire departments experienced intermediate levels of increase in that order. Again, considerable variation among cities is present.

Table 2 analyzes patterns of changes in the percentage of the total budget for these functions. Changes reflect the relative growth or decline of each function. Significant changes in spending priorities appear to have taken place. The average police share of the budget has increased from 27.3 percent to 31.9. Parks and recreation budgets, on the other hand, decreased from 16.0 percent to 11.9 percent. Other functions have maintained approximately the same share of the total.

Standard deviations reflect the variation in the cities' proportion of the total among themselves. A higher standard deviation indicates greater differences within the group. The increase in the standard deviation for police departments implies greater diversity among cities. The opposite is the case for park and recreation departments. Most such departments, in other words, were similarly cut back.

Large standard deviations in several functions imply that the differences

Table 2. Percentage of Total Budget, 1979–1982

	1979		*1982*		
	Mean	*Standard Deviation*	*Mean*	*Standard Deviation*	*T Test*
Police	.273	.053	.319	.067	.01
Fire	.176	.052	.176	.051	WS
Public Works	.353	.090	.350	.095	NS
Library	.038	.027	.037	.027	NS
Parks & Recreation	.160	.059	.119	.032	.01

in budget shares were by no means consistent from one city to the next. The public works expenditure shares, for example, varied from approximately 19 to 52 percent of the total in 1982; police department shares ranged from 16 to 44 percent. Are variations in expenditure shares a reflection of different policy choices that may have been brought on by Proposition 13? Some indication of such trends is revealed in Table 3. Changes in the proportion of the expenditure total for the years in question are correlated with one another.

Significant correlations imply common spending patterns in the cities. Police and fire department increases and decreases appear to be interrelated; cities that increase one are likely to have increased the other. Public works expenditures, however, increase when police expenditures decrease. Two clusters of city patterns are suggested. Police and fire expenditures increase in some cities while public works expenditures decrease relatively. In other cities the opposite occurs.

A closer look at public works and police expenditure patterns indicates that very precise policy changes have taken place in at least one-fourth of the cities in the survey. Five cities (Concord, Stockton, Sunnyvale, Berkeley, and Oxnard) decreased the police expenditure share significantly from

Table 3. Changes in the Percentage of the Budget Total, 1979–1982

	Police	*Fire*	*Public Works*	*Library*
Police				
Fire	.692**			
Public Works	−.874**	−.781**		
Library	.266	.036	−.307	
Parks & Recreation	.301	.120	−.473*	.249

*Significant at .01.
**Significant at .001.

1978 to 1982. Four cities (Bakersfield, Fullerton, Garden Grove, and Glendale) increased the police expenditure share by more than 10 percent. Four cities (Bakersfield, Fullerton, Glendale, and San Jose) decreased the public works budget by 10 percent or better. (The latter two experienced a decrease of greater than 20 percent.) Five cities (Berkeley, Concord, Oxnard, Sunnyvale, and Stockton) increased the public works budget by better than 10 percent. The increases and decreases are clearly related; eight of the 10 cities reporting large increases or decreases in one of these functions record the opposite in the other. (The social and economic characteristics of the cities reveal little similarity between these two groups.)

The analysis suggests that distinct policy choices were made in these cities. Some chose to increase public works functions at the expense of police and fire growth; others chose the opposite.

Thus spending in California cities has increased in the years following the passage of "13" and it has increased in ways that seem to depart from past patterns. The relative emphasis on particular services has been altered.

Revenue Changes: Their Influence on Changes in Expenditure Patterns

Increases in service charges are frequently cited as a significant product of the tax revolt. In California the fee for service has become a major source of income. Its proportion of revenue has changed from 6.5 percent in 1978 to 8.3 percent in 1982 (Caltax 1983: 1). Fees were given increasing legitimacy in 1979 with the passage of an expenditure limitation initiative, Proposition 4. The proposition specifically exempted user fees that cover the cost of service from the limitation. Thus city officials had an added incentive to search for additional fee revenue.

The press has documented increases in fees for numerous services. These include new sources such as charges for better jail accommodations, paramedic service fees, and the rental of videotapes (Schwadron, Richter and Citrin 1984: 74). Builders have been known to pay more than $3,000 per house to cover increased services associated with each unit. Developers have "donated" facilities such as standing sculptures, parks, and a new city hall to secure the right to build new subdivisions (Kirlin and Kirlin 1982).

The cities in this survey increased fee revenue 72 percent during the years in question. Fees increased from 12.5 to 15 percent of total revenue. The 1982 proportion of fees to expenditures for major functions ranged from 2 to 27 percent. Fees therefore provided an important source of revenue flexibility for city officials as they coped with the declines in property taxes and new service demands. One might hypothesize that there was

Table 4. Correlations, Service Charges, and Expenditures

	Service Charges per Capita, 1979	*Service Charges per Capita, 1982*
Change in Expenditures	.119	.379*
Expenditures per Capita, 1982	.480*	.757**
Change in per Capita Expenditures	.165	.421*

*Significant at .05.
**Significant at .001.

a relationship between cities that increased fees and those that increased expenditures.

Table 4 correlates three measures of expenditure with per capita service charges in 1979 and 1982. Significant correlations occur between per capita service charges in 1982 and three expenditure measures: the percent change in expenditures, expenditures per capita in 1982, and the rate of growth in per capita expenditures. The unusually high correlation between expenditures per capita in 1982 and service charges per capita in the same year (.757) indicates that cities spending more were very likely to have a high level of fees. The increase in that correlation from 1978 to 1982 suggests that aggressive pursuit of income was most closely related to higher expenditures following passage of Proposition 23.

I examined the relationships between expenditure increases and changes in budget shares for each service and fees for that service, hypothesizing that aggressive department heads sought to increase their organizations by expanding their own revenue sources. No such relationships were found.

Explanations for Changes in Expenditures

Budget shares were altered significantly following the passage of "13." I assume that decision makers faced a radical change in revenue, much uncertainty about new revenue sources, constraints in their decisions, and little time to analytically assess several alternatives. Organization theorists maintain that when faced with a very complex situation, decision makers rely on simple procedures rather than complex analysis (March and Simon 1958: 178–179). Two such rules are proposed below.

1. Decision makers looked closely at voting patterns in their communities. The Proposition 13 issues was perceived as an ideological onc. Democrats generally opposed it and tried to label it as a measure under the influence of the extreme right; Republicans generally supported it. Ultimately voters of both parties favored it. Generally, trimming of the size of government is considered a conservative position. If decision makers

Table 5. Correlations of Changes in Shares of the Total Budget

	% Brown 1978	*% Carter 1980*	*% Yes Prop. 13*	*% Change in Budget Total*
Police	−.499	−.411	.181	−.627
Fire	−.149	−.112	.010	−.416
Public Works	.382	.385	.191	.628
Library	−.162	−.213	.121	−.270
Parks & Recreation	−.412	−.369	.201	−.272

followed the lead of conservative voters, one assumes that they favored cutting expenditures, and increasing public safety shares of the budget at the expense of libraries, parks and recreation, and public works. To follow the lead of liberal voters, budgets would be increased and nonpolice functions ought to fare better.

Three measures of city voting patterns were used: the percentage favoring Proposition 13, the percentage supporting Governor Jerry Brown in his successful reelection in the Fall 1978, and the percentage supporting President Carter in the Fall 1980. Each tests voting preferences in different arenas and points of time.

2. Decision makers reacted to the restrictions placed in the bail-out legislation by increasing police and fire shares when they perceived a need to cut back. In cities where budget totals were less, police and fire shares should increase if decision makers perceive a need to maintain a "similar effort" in public safety functions. The mandate became a simple cue to help them manage the decision process.

Correlations support both of these explanations (Table 5). Police share increases are related to support for Republican candidates. Public works share increases are related to support for Democrats. Parks and recreation share changes, however, proved to be related to voting support for the Republicans. Voting on Proposition 13 is unrelated to changes in any of the functions. Since the proposition ultimately enjoyed better than 2 to 1 support of the public, decision makers may have discounted it as an indicator of partisan policy preference. Indeed, the major study of public attitudes toward Proposition 13 argues that it was supported for a variety of reasons, and voter attitude toward it was not clearly related to political ideology (Sears and Citrin 1982: 220).

Likewise, increases in police shares of the total budget are related to decreases in budget totals. Decision makers, then, perceived that police expenditures should be given higher priority when cuts had to be made.

Table 6. Regression Equations, Determinants of Budget Share Changes, 1979–1982

Dependent Variables *Ind. Variables*	*Police Share Change*	*Public Works Share Change*	*Parks and Recreation Share Change*
Change per Capita Spending	−.742	.574	−.245
Per Capita for Function, 1979	−.389		−.541
% Brown, 1978			−.195
% Carter, 1980		.116	
Multiple R	.729	.637	.665
Significance	.0001	.003	.006

F values for all coefficients significant < .05.
Values are beta weights (standardized).

Fire budget shares, though they were treated similarly by the "maintenance of effort" clause, proved to be unrelated to budget totals. Public works shares increased as the change in the budget increased. Library and parks and recreation shares proved to be unrelated to changes in the total budget.

Multiple regression analysis was employed to evaluate the joint effort and relative influence of political and spending variables on budget shares. Table 6 lists the best equations that could be derived (assuming an F of .01 for all variables). The table contains standarized beta weights that reflect the relative influence of each variable. The three successful equations explain a significant portion of the variance, as indicated by the Multiple R.

Changes in police shares are best explained by spending variables. Shares increased with less change in per capita spending and a lower per capita police spending in 1979. Thus cities that increased total budgets less in this period proportionally increased the share of the budget devoted to police. Change in total spending was the more important of the two variables.

Public works shares increased as per capita spending increased and as the community supported liberal candidates. (Similar equations were generated substituting % Brown for % Carter). Thus when budgets expanded and residents supported liberals, budget shares for public works increased. The decision to increase spending was the more important variable.

Growth (or less decrease) in parks and recreation shares was related to less per capita parks and recreation funding in 1979, less per capita spending change, and conservative voting patterns. Since this function is a smaller proportion of the total budget, it may withstand cutbacks in cities with smaller budgets and a conservative ideology simply because a small cut in a small program more severely curtails its activities. Parks and recreation spending thus was likely to be cut in cities that had a comparatively large program prior to "13," felt a need to make budget reductions after "13," and contained conservative voters.

SUMMARY AND CONCLUSIONS

Proposition 13 appears indeed to have signaled a change in the California political system though not necessarily the kind of change that analysts predicted. Contrary to expectations, the typical California government budget has grown during this period. Some did experience declines, but others increased their expenditures considerably. Priorities have changed: Police expenditures have increased; parks and recreation spending has declined. Other services have generally held onto their shares of the budgets, expanding at a rate near or greater than the cost of living index. Public works expenditures have increased in cities where police and fire costs have experienced less of an increase. Service charges and fees increased and such additions are related to expenditure increases. The mandating of public safety "maintenance of effort" by the state seems to have influenced city expenditure patterns, particularly for police services. Police shares markedly increased in cities where budget growth was less. When forced to cut, then, cities spared the police department. There seemed to be no effect of the mandate on fire services.

Public works increases occurred when spending increased and the community granted greater support to liberal candidates. These cities were freed from the constraints of the maintenance-of-effort clause by growing resources, and less influence by the tax revolt, politically. Public works was the most frequent recipient of such spending increases. Both of these patterns suggest that changes were implemented by following simple decision-making rules. Leaders looked for cues in state legislation and community voting patterns and adjusted their budgets accordingly.

These cities, thus, did not necessarily experience declines in service levels. All managers did not need to implement a program of "cutback management." There is no common response to Proposition 13 other than a change from the previous budget. What explains the variations in budget changes among cities?

Underestimated in previous analyses is the ability of cities to insulate themselves from environmental shocks. Few city services or service levels are mandated by state law. Thus priorities can change as public officials respond to new concerns. Cutbacks thus could be made in functions like parks and recreation as city officials react to changed public priorities.

Likewise, increases in Police expenditures can be realized without altering other priorities.

Cities also have the ability to increase fee income to compensate for the loss of property tax revenue. Legislative approval was not needed to institute such fees, as it was in school districts, for instance. Thus city officials who sensed the need for change had the tools to respond to it.

The drop in service levels, and the layoffs that followed Proposition 13, were partially caused by declines in income directly attributable to Proposition 13. Altered priorities in city expenditures consciously directed by city officials in the aftermath of the initiative also contributed to cutbacks in some areas and growth in others. City officials perceived Proposition 13 as a mandate for change, or used it as one and altered priorities. The expenditure totals suggest that there was enough money generally to at least hold service at their 1978 level in the average city. The shock provided by the initiative, however, was the means to implement changes far beyond the need to cover costs.

City officials, of course, could not know that city income would increase steadily in the years ahead. An upturn of the economy and a lessening of inflation improved the financial setting of most cities from 1978 onward. Thus they may have changed priorities to prepare for a decline that did not materialize. Regardless, conscious choice seems to have led to changes in incremental spending patterns.

May and Meltsner, (1981), reflecting on the early "post-13" experience of several California jurisdictions, urged public officials to "demonstrate confidence in their enterprises by viewing the current unstable period as an opportunity for examining relationships with various constituencies, examining their organizations' functions and instituting positive reforms" (p 178). This research suggests that public officials may have done that. City officers perceived the "crisis" as an opportunity to redefine priorities. Flexibility in service delivery and revenue acquisition allowed them to pursue their own paths. Fear of decline permitted decisions that calmer times forbade. Cities were bounded but not constrained by the revenue limits of Proposition 13.

REFERENCES

Caltax. 1983. "Another Look at Local Fees," *Caltax Bulletin* (April): 1.

Crecine, John P. 1983. *Governmental Problem Solving: A Computer Simulation of Municipal Budgeting*. Chicago: Rand McNally.

Kemp, Roger. 1980. *Coping With Proposition 13*. Lexington, Mass.: Lexington Books.

Kirlin, John. 1982. *The Political Economy of Fiscal Limits*. Lexington, Mass.: Lexington Books.

Kirlin, John, and Anne Kirlin. 1982. "Public Choices—Private Resources." Sacramento: California Tax Foundation.

Levine, Charles H., Irene Rubin, and George Wologan. 1981. "Resource Scarcity and the Reform Model: The Management of Retrenchment in Cincinatti and Oakland," *Public Administration Review* 41 (November, December: 619–629.

Lowrey, David, and Lee Sigelman. 1981. "Understanding the Revolt—Eight Explanations," *American Political Science Review* 75 (December): 963–974.

March, James, and Herbert Simon. 1958. *Organizations*. New York: Wiley.

May, Peter J., and A. Meltsner. 1981 "Limited Actions, Distressing Consequences: A Selected View of the California Experience," *Public Administration Review* 41 (Special Issue): 172–178.

Nachmias, David. 1979. *Public Policy Evaluation: Approaches and Methods*. New York: St. Martin's.

Natchez, Peter B., and Irvin C. Bupp. 1973. "Policy and Priority in the Budget Process," *American Political Science Review* (September): 951–963.

Rabushka, Alvino, and Pauline Ryan. 1982. *The Tax Revolt*. Stanford, Calif.: Hoover Press.

Saltzstein, Alan, and Virginia Bott. 1982. "Personal Policy Making in Times of Crisis: California Personnel Directors Face the Aftermath of Proposition 13," *American Review of Public Administration* 16 (Summer/Fall): 195–208.

Schwadron, Terry, Paul Richter, and Jack Citrin. 1984. *California and the American Tax Revolt*. Berkeley: University of California Press.

Sears, David O., and Jack Citrin. 1982. *Tax Revolt: Something for Nothing in California*. Cambridge, Mass.: Harvard.

HOW WELL DO MAYORS ASSESS CITIZENS' SPENDING PREFERENCES?

Mark Baldassare

ABSTRACT

Citizens' preferences have an important role in urban policy decisions. This study examines the degree to which mayors perceive their own spending views as different from their citizens' and the extent to which mayors are accurate in portraying citizens' spending preferences. The Fiscal Austerity and Urban Innovation Survey and two public opinion surveys are analyzed using data collected in California. The findings indicate that mayors perceive citizens as wanting less spending than they themselves want with regard to education and public health but not other spending areas. Mayors also view citizens as wanting to spend less for education and public health than citizens indicate in opinion surveys. The reasons for these attitude discrepancies are explored and some conditions that lead to greater perceived similarity and more attitude accuracy are considered.

INTRODUCTION

This paper analyzes mayors' views of citizens' spending preferences as they relate to the mayors' spending preferences and the citizens' actual spending

Research in Urban Policy, Vol. 2, pages 159–174.

ISBN: 0-89232-534-8

attitudes. Citizens' preferences have been studied in the past but not with this particular focus on leaders' perceptions. The citizen characteristics that lead to certain policy preferences have been considered (Hoffman and Clark 1979) as has the role of citizen attitudes in the formation of urban policies (Baldassare and Protash 1982; Hatry and Blair 1976; Schumaker 1981). There is empirical evidence that citizen attitudes do affect policy decisions as leaders in various levels of government have shown responsiveness to their constituents' wishes (Erikson 1978; Miller and Stokes 1963; Page and Shapiro 1983; Kuklinski 1978, 1979). What is not known, and is addressed here, is the degree to which local elected leaders perceive agreement between their own views and citizens' spending preferences and the extent to which accuracy exists in the mayors' assessment of citizens' spending preferences. The conditions that facilitate perceived agreement and accuracy in perceiving citizens' views are also considered.

Elected leaders' views of citizens' attitudes are important since these perceptions have policy implications. Mayors may consider citizens as being at odds with their own preferences and with those expressed by other community interests. The elected leaders must then decide whether to pursue an urban policy that favors their own preferences, their views of citizens' preferences, or their views of the desires of others in the community. There may be other instances in which the mayors' views, the mayors' views of citizens' preferences, and the mayors' views of other constituents' attitudes may be similar. In such cases the elected leaders form urban policies that they view as being based upon broad consensus. Mayors' views of their citizens' preferences thus act as constraints in decision making. Therefore, how accurately elected leaders read their citizens' preferences, and in what areas they perceive the most disagreements, are essential aspects of policy formation.

Recent writings help to identify the conditions under which elected leaders may accurately perceive citizens' views and have views similar to their citizens. Clark and Ferguson (1983: 33–39) argue that political cultures exist that vary in policy preferences, sources of political input, and emphasis on public goods. One of these is "new fiscal populism," in which the conservative spending preferences of individual citizens are reflected in the fiscal policies of local leaders. This political culture provides evidence that the middle class has become more fiscally conservative and that the "new fiscal populist" leaders are operating with their support. It would seem that new fiscal populists leaders would view their spending preferences as being close to their citizens' spending preferences. Since their political future is linked to public opinion, perhaps they would also more accurately assess citizens' spending preferences. It will thus be important to contrast new fiscal populist mayors with other mayors. Another possibility to examine is that the political milieu may affect the mayors' ability to assess citizens' perceptions. Perhaps the mayor is most aware of the attitudes of citizens who belong to their party, especially when the mayor's party is in the majority. This would suggest that the mayors' accuracy is enhanced by partisan political factors.

There are many practical difficulties in studying spending preferences that should be considered. Previous research indicates that citizens often want more government spending in order to increase available services and to improve existing service deficits. Support for increasing service spending was found even among those who favored tax limitations in California, Massachusetts, and Michigan (Citrin 1979; Ladd and Wilson 1982; Courant, Gramlich, and Rubinfeld 1979, 1980; Gramlich, Rubinfeld, and Swift 1981). Citizens' spending preferences thus do not necessarily include a consideration of budget constraints or taxes. Clark (1974) has therefore devised the "budget pie" and others have argued for survey items that measure constrained spending preferences (McIver and Ostrom 1976; Scott 1976). The major conclusion drawn from spending preferences research is that citizens who are surveyed need to be reminded of the practical implications of their spending preferences. This problem may not necessarily be evident in questioning elected leaders. For instance, mayors may be very aware that spending increases have implications for existing budgets and future taxes, but whether mayors consider these provisions when giving their perceptions of citizens' spending preferences is not known. This suggests the need to cautiously analyze the comparisons between mayors' views and citizens' spending preferences. The contrasts of citizens' and leaders' views make up a most unique and most difficult task of this investigation.

The current study uses data collected in California where issues of citizens' spending preferences are especially salient. The statewide property tax reduction initiative, commonly referred to as Proposition 13, was passed by a two-thirds majority in the late 1970s. Many observers viewed this as a referendum against current spending—a "tax revolt"—and a call for limitations on local government activities (State of California 1980). Previous research in "tax revolt" states cited earlier suggests that citizens will prefer maintaining or increasing services for specific services if the tax implications are not presented. An important goal of this analysis is thus to explore whether California mayors believe that citizens favor spending reductions and, further, whether their views of citizens are congruent with their own spending preferences and citizens' actual spending preferences. The possibility that perceived agreement and accuracy in perceiving citizens' views varies across different service spending categories must also be explored. The potential for increased perceived similarity in mayors' and citizens' preferences and greater accuracy in perceiving citizens' views due to factors such as new fiscal populism and partisan politics should also be considered in the analysis.

DATA SOURCES

The source of information for mayors' views was data gathered as part of the "Fiscal Austerity and Urban Innovation Project." Mayors and city managers were reached through a mail questionnaire, though this research reports only the mayors' responses. The mailings commenced at the University of California at Irvine in April 1983. Several mail and telephone follow-ups were instituted to improve the response rate and the data collection ceased in June 1983. The universe included all California cities with 25,000 or more population, which amounts to 161 municipalities (U.S. Bureaus of the Census 1981). The eligible respondents were from 150 of the municipalities.[1]

Fifty of the eligible respondents returned a completed questionnaire. The response rate was 33 percent. The response was reasonable given the general difficulties in conducting mail surveys and the special problems in eliciting data from elected leaders (Frey 1983). The response rates within each type of place category were close to the 33 percent response rate for the total eligible respondents. The proportion of eligible respondents in each size of place category corresponded with the proportion of actual respondents in each size of place category. In general, the lack of response bias suggests that the sample is representative of California mayors in cities with 25,000 or more population.[2]

Twelve of the mayors who responded were in Los Angeles County, seven in Orange County, five in San Diego County, four in Riverside–San Bernardino–Ventura Counties, and 13 in the San Francisco Bay area. The remaining nine were in cities scattered throughout the state. Forty-seven percent of the mayors had served one term in office, 37 percent two terms, and 16 percent three or more terms. The median number of years in elected office was 7 years. On average, then, the mayors sampled began their terms prior to the Proposition 13 vote. Fifty-six percent were Democrats, 46 percent were Republicans, and 8 percent were independent, no party, or other political party. Eighty-three percent were male; 90 percent were white; the median age was 52 years; the median education was 16 years. There were two data sources for citizens' spending preferences. One is the California Poll conducted in March 1983. It involved telephone interviews with 755 adults and is representative of the state's adult population. This survey contained questions regarding public support for service spending increases. Further details about this survey are discussed elsewhere (Field Institute, 1983a). The other survey is the 1983 Orange County Annual Survey. This survey involved randomly selected adult residents of Orange County, California. In all, 1,003 respondents were interviewed in July 1983 regarding a number of subjects including their attitudes toward current

Table 1. Spending Preferences for Specific Services*

	Mayors' Preferences	*Mayors' Opinions of Citizens' Preferences*	*Significance*
Education	3.96	3.17	.02
Public Health	3.27	2.69	.02
Roads	3.69	3.56	NS
Parks and Recreation	3.09	3.13	NS
Police Protection	3.46	3.87	.001

*Lower mean scores indicate preferences to spend less money. Significance levels are based on paired t-tests.

levels of service spending. This survey and its methodology are discussed in detail elsewhere (Baldassare 1983).

MAYORS' VIEWS

Mayors were asked in one section of the questionnaire, "Please indicate your own preference about spending," regarding each of 13 urban services. Their answers were based on a five-point scale: 1 = spend a lot less, 2 = spend somewhat less, 3 = spend the same, 4 = spend somewhat more, and 5 = spend a lot more. Mayors were than asked, "Please estimate the preferences of the majority of voters in your city" for the same 13 urban services they rated for themselves. The Mayors' opinions of citizens' preferences were based on the five-point scale used for their own preferences. For the purposes of this analysis the spending preferences for which there are comparable public opinion data were selected. These include the service areas of education, roads, public health, parks and recreation, and police protection.

Table 1 presents a comparison of mayors' spending preferences and mayors' opinions of citizens' spending preferences. Mayors view citizens as wanting to spend less then they themselves want for two of the five specific service areas. These are in the areas of education and public health, where the differences in mean scores are significant in paired T-tests. With regard to roads and parks and recreation, mayors view themselves as wanting to spend about as much as their citizens prefer. However, the mean score differences for police protection are significant and indicate that mayors view citizens as wanting to spend more than they do. Mayors thus view themselves as wanting to spend less tan citizens for certain urban services but not for others.

Mayors were asked later in the questionnaire, "Please indicate your judgment about the spending preferences of several participants in city

Table 2. Mayors' Opinions of General Spending Preferences: Views toward Individual Citizens and Community Organizations*

	Mean Scores	*Citizens Want to Spend Less?*	*Significance*
Individual Citizens	2.77		
Low-Income Organizations	3.95	Yes	.001
Minority Organizations	3.92	Yes	.001
Elderly Organizations	3.30	Yes	.01
Civic Organizations	3.05	Yes	NS
Business Organizations	2.98	Yes	NS
Neighborhood Organizations	2.90	Yes	NS
Religious Organizations	2.82	Yes	NS
Homeowner Organizations	2.61	No	NS
Taxpayer Organizations	1.89	No	.001

*Lower mean scores indicate a general preference to spend less money. Significance levels are based on paired t-tests.

government affairs." These answers help to identify whether mayors view citizens per se as generally against spending. Responses were rated on a five-point scale: 1 = spend a lot less, 2 = spend somewhat less, 3 = spend the same, 4 = spend somewhat more, and 5 = spend alot more. Twenty in all were individually rated in order to allow contrasts in general spending preferences. Four were excluded because they were organizations at least partly external to the community, that is, political parties, the media, state agencies, and federal agencies. Six were not considered because they were in government, they included the mayor, city council, the city manager, the finance staff, department heads, and public employees. Table 2 presents the mean scores in column 1 for individual citizens and nine community organizations. A "yes" in column 2 indicates if, as expected, the mayors view the citizens as generally wanting to spend less than the organization. Column 3 presents the significance levels from the paired T-tests between the mayors' opinions of citizens' preferences and the mayors' opinions of the community organization. According to the mayors, individual citizens want to spend less than seven of the nine organizations. Three of these contrasts are significant. That is, individual citizens are more opposed to spending than low income, minority, and elderly organizations. Mayors view both taxpayer organizations and homeowner organizations as wanting even less government spending than individual citizens. Moreover, only taxpayer organizations are significantly different from individual citizens. The results thus indicate, in almost all instances, that mayors consider average citizens as generally wanting less government spending than do community organizations.

A multivariate analysis was then conducted in order to identify the conditions under which mayors' own spending views and their views of citizens' spending preferences were most similar. A difference score was calculated by subtracting the mayors' own view from the mayors' view of citizens for each of the five spending categories in Table 1. Then, seven factors were tested as potential predictors of the size of the difference scores in a stepwise multiple regression analysis. These predictor variables included age, race, sex, party affiliation, number of terms in office, attitude toward increasing the local tax burden, and perceived number of disagreements with constituents. Of course, these mayoral characteristics would help to distinguish mayors who are new fiscal populists who should, in fact, have spending views closer to their constituents' opinions.

The greatest interest was in explaining the larger discrepancies in spending opinions with regard to education and public health. The difference in education spending scores was smallest when the mayors did not favor an increase in the local tax burden (standardized beta weight = .46; $p < .01$).[3] In other words, the greatest differences were found in spending views when the mayors wanted to increase the tax burden. No other factor was significant and the effects of the local tax burden attitude remained significant when controlling for the other potential predictors. No factors explained the differences in public health scores. The findings offered some support to the view that new fiscal populists see less of a gap in spending preferences between themselves and their constituents.

Another finding was that the difference in police spending scores was the smallest when the mayor did not favor an increase in the local tax burden (standardized beta weight = .28; $p < .05$). The results are consistent when controlling for all other factors. This provides an interesting comparison with the education scores since, in the case of police spending preferences, mayors generally think their constituents want to spend more than they do while, in regard to education spending, they consider citizens as preferring less spending. In both instances, then, there is evidence that presumably new fiscal populist mayors view their own opinions as closer to their citizens' preferences than other mayors do. The remaining analyses offered little in explaining differences in spending scores. No factors predicted parks spending scores differences and only Democratic affiliation (standardized beta weight = .34; $p < .05$) was significantly associated with road spending scores. But the latter findings are not surprising since the mayors' opinions did not differ much from the mayors' views of citizens' spending preferences in these two realms.

CITIZENS' SPENDING PREFERENCES

The mayors' opinions of citizens' preferences are next contrasted with actual public opinions. The service spending categories reported in Table

Table 3. Citizens' Preferences to Reduce Spending: California Mayors' Opinions and Public Opinions*

	1983 Mayors' Opinions of Citizens' Preferences	*1983 California Poll*
Education	3.17	4.04
Public Health	2.69	3.52
Roads	3.56	3.63
Parks and Recreation	3.13	3.10
Police Protection	3.87	3.99

*Lower mean scores indicate preferences to spend less money.

1 are further analyzed. The first column of Table 3 contains the mayors' views of citizens' spending preferences. The second column reports the California Poll in which respondents were asked whether or not various service categories should have spending increased. The California Poll question wordings were similar to those used in the mayors' survey, though there were only three response categories instead of five for each spending preference. The responses were coded in order to conform with the coding scheme for the mayor's questionnaire: 1 = cut back, 3 = hold the same, and 5 = increase spending. There are no statistical tests that can judge the significance of differences across the survey of mayors and the California Poll. Thus, the size of the differences in mean scores for the comparable questions in the two surveys are analyzed.

The California Poll indicates that citizens are most favorable toward spending for education and police, somewhat less favorable in regard to roads and public health, and the least supportive of spending increases for parks. The mean scores indicate that mayors overestimate citizens' desires to reduce spending in the areas of education and public health. The differences in mean scores are .87 for education and .56 for public health. Mayors' views of citizens' preferences are more accurate with regard to roads, parks and recreation, and police protection. The differences in mean scores are .13 or less.

It is important to replicate and extend the results derived from the comparison of the survey of mayors to the statewide public survey. The California Poll may not be adequately comparable since, in its case, the unit of analysis is the individual while in the survey of mayors the unit of analysis is the city. It would be ideal to contrast the opinions of mayors in specific cities with the opinions of citizens in those same cities rather than one set of statewide statistics with another source of statewide statistics. This was not possible with the California Poll since information on the sampling areas was absent. Also, the analysis would have been improved if specific groups of mayors could be matched with subpopulations of citizens in order to identify the conditions under which mayors more accurately portrayed the views of their constituents. The level of detail available from the California Poll did not allow for this sort of analysis. For these reasons, actual citizens' preferences are examined with a second data source.

The 1983 Orange County Annual Survey contained among its 1,003 respondents 301 individuals who lived in the same seven cities in which the survey of mayors was conducted. The spending preferences of this subpopulation are contrasted with the seven mayors' opinions of spending preferences. The following approach was used in the data analysis. The spending preferences of citizens in each of the seven cities were separately aggregated[4] because the cities varied substantially in the number of interviews, and to do otherwise would have heavily weighted the responses to one city with a large sample. Then, the mean scores of each city were summed with all others, for each of the spending preference items, and a total mean score for Orange County was computed. The mean scores for the Orange county citizens were then compared with the mean scores for the Orange County mayors' views. This is an approach that much more closely links the mayors' views to the citizens' spending preferences. As is discussed later, this data source also allowed for the analyses of subpopulations of mayors and citizens in a search for greater closeness in spending attitudes.

The Orange County spending preferences are from a set of question that asked, "For each of these government services, tell me whether we should spend more money, spend less money, or no change." The items are similar in substance and wording to those used in the survey of mayors, though, again, there were fewer response categories than in the mayors' survey. The answers were coded in the following manner to provide comparisons with the mayors' data: 1 = spend less, 3 = no change, and 5 = spend more.

Orange County residents are most in favor of increasing spending for education and police protection, as indicated in Table 4. They are somewhat less supportive of spending more for roads and public health and are least favorable toward increasing spending for parks and recreation. Mayors' opinions of citizens' preferences are more anti-spending than Orange County public opinion with regard to education and public health. The differences in mean scores are .98 for public health and .90 for education. Mayors' views are more accurate with regard to roads, parks and recreation, and especially police protection. The differences in mean scores range from .26 to .02. Thus, the Orange County comparisons replicate the earlier

Table 4. Citizens' Preferences to Reduce Spending: Orange County Mayors' Opinions and Public Opinions*

Orange County Totals	*1983 Orange County Mayors' Opinions of Citizens' Preferences*	*1983 Orange County Survey*
Education	3.40	4.30
Public Health	2.71	3.69
Roads	3.57	3.83
Parks and Recreation	3.57	3.42
Police Protection	4.29	4.27
(N)	(7)	(301)
Huntington Beach Only		
Education	2.00	4.58
Public Health	2.00	3.75
Roads	3.00	3.49
Parks and Recreation	4.00	3.58
Police Protection	4.00	4.24
(N)	(1)	(130)
Republican Mayors, Cities, Citizens		
Education	3.30	4.03
Public Health	2.75	3.34
Roads	3.40	3.84
Parks and Recreation	3.20	3.38
Police Protection	4.20	4.15
(N)	(5)	(88)

*Lower mean scores indicate preferences to spend less money.

contrasts between the California Poll and the California mayors' data. Indeed, it is also interesting that Orange County is no more conservative, in terms of spending preferences, then the rest of the state.

The characteristics and the determinants of the Orange County spending preferences were also analyzed. Paired t-tests of all the possible combinations indicated that, with only the exception of roads and public health, the spending attitudes were significantly different for each other. Thus, the citizens' preferences for specific spending increases are fairly distinct. A multivariate regression was conducted to determine the factors that explained each spending preference.[5] The predictor variables included age, sex, income, length of residence, ethnicity, political attitude, and political party. Education was best predicted by age (standardized beta weight $= -.23$; $p < .001$) with younger residents desiring more spending. No other factor was significantly related to education spending preferences. Those wanting increased public health spending tended to be young, lower income, and liberal (standardized beta weight = −.14, −.13, and −.13; $p < .05$ for each). Younger persons also wanted parks spending increased (standardized beta weight = −.14; $p < .05$). No factors predicted attitudes toward police spending or roads spending.

The findings in Table 4 are replicated when analyzing the responses of the mayor and citizens from one Orange County city. The results from Huntington Beach are presented since there are sufficient respondents from that city to examine the citizens' spending preferences. Again, residents were most in favor of increased spending for education and police protection. The largest discrepancy between the mayors' perceptions and the citizens' preferences occurred with regard to education and public health. The score differences were 2.58 for education and 1.75 for public health. The mayors' perceptions were fairly accurate when considering police protection, roads, and parks and recreation. Here, the mean score differences ranged from .51 to .24. It should be noted that the mayor was Republican and that the city is predominantly Republican.

It is important to explore the conditions under which Orange County mayors have more accurate assessments of their citizens' spending attitudes. Unfortunately, the sample size and mayoral characteristics in Orange County are rather limited. All of the mayors are white and male. Six of the seven mayors are Republican. Six of the seven cities have a majority of Republican voters. Only two of the seven mayors (and they were Republicans) wanted to reduce or continue the current tax burden. Thus, new fiscal populism could not be explored. The possibility that is considered is that accuracy is improved when Republican mayors in Republican cities are compared with the Republican citizens in the same cities.

Table 4 indicates that most of the findings reported thus far are replicated. Republican respondents in the five cities with Republican mayors and Republican majorities favor education and police spending the most, as did the Orange County residents as a whole. Mayors' perceptions of citizens' preferences are most distinct from actual citizens' preferences, again, with regard to education and public health. The differences are smaller than for the total population, however, because Republican citizens are less favorable toward spending increases in these categories. The differences in education scores is .73 and in public health scores is .59. Mayors' accuracy continues to be best with respect to roads, police protection, and parks and recreation. The differences range from .44 to .05. There is some evidence, then, that mayors become more accurate about their constituents' views when their cities as a whole have a majority in the political party and when comparing their views with citizens who belong to their political party.

CONCLUSIONS

Citizens' preferences can have important implication for urban policies. Elected officials make decisions partly as a result of impressions about citizens' preferences. Their own preferences may be different from what they think citizens want. This perception about what citizens want can also vary in accuracy. This study found that California mayors view citizens' preferences as more anti-spending than their own with regard to education and public health. Mayors also were most inaccurate in judging citizens' preferences with respect to education and public health. There is evidence that the mayors' views of citizens' spending preferences may influence their fiscal policies. Two thirds of the mayors said they responded favorably to citizens' spending preferences "about half the time" or more. Only organizations for the elderly and business organizations had more perceived influence in the city. Also, mayors' spending preferences for education and public health fall between actual citizens' preferences and their perceptions of citizens' preferences. Some mayors may be shifting their own opinions based on their readings of citizens' preferences. All of this evidence suggests that mayors' views of citizens' spending preferences, whether accurate or not, do constrain spending policies.

There are several explanations for California mayors' views that their citizens are more opposed to spending for public health and education than they are. It is important to understand this finding in the context of mayors' also believing that average citizens were more opposed to spending increases than minority, elderly, and low-income populations. There is apparently a view among mayors that average citizens do not favor service spending increases when the services favor special or disadvantaged populations. This would be the case with regard to education and public health. Services that are viewed as for all citizens, such as police, roads, and parks, are not considered to have the same anti-spending connotations. The distinction that may account for the mayors' responses to different service categories is thus between general public services and special public services.

Another significant question raised by this analysis concerns the relationships between actual public opinions and mayors' views of citizens' preferences. Mayors' views were most dissimilar with regard to spending for public health and education. They believed that citizens wanted to spend less than citizens reported. Education had the highest spending increase ranking in California and in Orange County. Public health ranked fourth of the five service categories but had much higher scores than the mayors expected. Mayors were obviously overly conservative in their evaluations regarding education and public health for reasons noted above. Still, one should use caution in interpreting these results. It is likely that mayors and citizens approach the unconditional mention of "spending" very differently. Mayors asked about citizens' spending preferences for specific services may tend to think about increasing taxes as a necessity to implement a change for those services. Reckoning that citizens are opposed to new taxes, mayors note a weak desire among citizens for spending increases. Citizens asked about spending for specific services may thus not consider as many implications as the mayors did.

It is interesting to consider the factors that account for citizens' spending preferences and account for differences across service categories. There is indirect evidence from the public opinion surveys that spending preferences are partial reflections of service evaluations rather than the willingness to commit new tax monies. This interpretation is noted with the caution that, as Clark (1974) indicates, there are many factors that account for spending preferences. There has been a steady decline in perceived service quality, especially of education, as measured over time in the California Polls (Field Institute 1983b). This has coincided with an increase from 1979 to the present in the proportion of California residents desiring spending increases for several service categories (Field Institute 1983a). Yet, there has been no significant change in the proportion of California citizens who favor spending reductions to avoid increased taxes: 60 percent in 1980 and 56 percent in 983 opposed tax increases (Field Institute 1983a). Another example is presented in the Orange County Surveys (Baldassare 1982, 1983). The 1982 survey asked residents to rate the quality of education, police protection, public health, roads, and parks and recreation. Education, roads, and police protection had the worst evaluations. The same services, of course, had the highest rankings for increased spending in the 1983 survey. If the spending preferences partly reflect service evaluations rather than tax attitudes, as appears to be the case, then the finding that Orange County residents favor spending increases for certain service categories more than the California residents can be explained. The desire for spending increases is not a measure of fiscal conservatism but, instead, of service problems. The fact that Orange County residents want more money spent on education and roads than state residents do indicates little about their political attitudes and perhaps something about their community problems.

There are obviously some very delicate issues involved in measuring citizens' spending preferences. Future research needs to specify citizens' desires to improve services, pay additional taxes, and increase spending in different service categories. In order to link citizens' preferences with leaders' views, comparable data should be collected from leaders. Specifically, leaders' preferences to improve services, increase taxes, and increase spending must be gathered. As well, their views on whether citizens went to improve services, increase taxes, and increase spending are also essential.

Another important topic that was pursued in this paper is the degree of similarity between citizens across cities. Future studies ought to further examine the conditions under which mayors are responsive to their citizens' spending preferences. Mayors in this study varied in terms of the accurate perceptions of citizens' preferences and their agreement with citizens' preferences. These attitudes, in future studies, ought to be related to elected officials' favorable responses to citizens' preferences, their voting behaviors, and their policymaking. (See, for example, Clark and Ferguson 1983: Chapter 7; Kuklinski 1978, 1979; Page and Shapiro 1983). It would be interesting to examine the characteristics of mayors, cities, city governments, and citizens that result in more or less responsiveness. Several possibilities were explored in this study. Mayors who had some characteristics of new fiscal populists, that is, did not favor an increase in the tax burden and had service spending preferences closer to their perceptions of citizens' spending preferences. Republican mayors in Republican cities also seemed more accurate about the Republican citizens' views than all mayors were in evaluating all citizens. Of course, a future analysis of the similarities between citizens' and mayors' spending preferences should also consider other leadership styles and citizen group combinations, such as traditional Democrat and ethnic politician (Clark and Ferguson 1983). Such an expanded investigation would add new knowledge concerning the linkages between citizens and leaders.

It is important to note that elected leaders face many difficulties in gaining knowledge about citizens' preferences. Several factors may keep mayors relatively uninformed about these preferences. One possibility is that leaders may mistake general preferences about spending and taxes as evidence for policy decisions about specific services. Another is that past voting behaviors and preferences may be incorrectly extrapolated to the current circumstances. Elected leaders may also develop their impressions of citizens' attitudes in an insulated environment. Future research ought to thus carefully examine the elected officials' sources of information concerning citizens' preferences over a wide variety of urban policy issues.

It is obvious from this study that elected officials need to be better informed about citizens' preferences. Mass survey techniques are often used in local political campaigns but are rarely adopted to ongoing analyses of citizens' attitudes. Systematic and current opinion polls are necessary for local leaders engaged in urban policy formation and policy review (Hatry and Blair 1976). The time and effort involved in such public surveys are worthwhile given the difficult yet important task of accurately gauging citizens' preferences.

ACKNOWLEDGMENTS

This research was partially supported by a grant from the Institute of Governmental Studies, University of California, Berkeley. I thank Matt Davis for research assistance. Terry Nichols Clark and the anonymous reviewers provided helpful comments on an earlier draft.

NOTES

1. Ninety-three percent of the cities with 25,000 or more population were thus included. Eleven cities that were in the "Permanent Community Sample" (see Clark and Ferguson 1983) were excluded because they were involved in a separate research effort. The cities were Long Beach. Los Angeles, San Diego, San Francisco, San Jose, Santa Ana, Berkeley, Fullerton, Palo Alto, Pasadena, and Santa Monica.

2. The response rates and numbers and proportions of respondents within each size of place category are as follows:

	Eligible Respondents	*Actual Respondents*	*Response Rates*
Population under 50,000	51% (N = 77)	51% (N = 26)	34%
Population 50,000–150,000	43% (N = 65)	40% (N = 20)	31%
Population over 150,000	6% (N = 8)	8% (N = 4)	50%
Total	100% (N = 150)	100% (N = 50)	33% (N = 50)

3. The beta weights mentioned in this section are all derived from the final regression equations which include the 7 mayoral characteristics.

4. The number of respondents in each city is as follows: 130 in Huntington Beach, 25 in San Clemente, 15 in Tustin, 37 in Westminster, 30 in Yorba Linda, 33 in Fountain Valley, and 31 in Irvine.

5. The beta weights reported in this paragraph are all from the final regression equations which include 7 respondent characteristics.

REFERENCES

Baldassare, M. 1982. "Orange County Annual Survey: 1982 Final Report." Irvine: University of California, Mimeographed.

———. 1983. "Orange County Annual Survey: 1983 Final Report." Irvine: University of California, Mimeographed.

Baldassare, M., and W. Protash. 1982. "Growth Controls, Population Growth, and Community Satisfaction," *American Sociological Review* 47: 339–349.

Citrin, J. 1979. "Do People Want Something for Nothing? Public Opinion on Taxes and Government Spending," *National Tax Journal* 32: 113–129.

Clark, T. N. 1974. "Can Your Cut a Budget Pie? *Policy and Politics* 3: 3–31.

Clark, T. N., and L. C. Ferguson. 1983. *City Money: Political Processes, Fiscal Strain, and Retrenchment*. New York: Columbia University Press.

Courant, P., E Gramlich, and D. Rubinfeld. 1979. "Tax Limitation and the Demand for Public Services in Michigan," *National Tax Journal* 32: 147–157.

———. 1980. "Why Voters Support Tax Limitation Amendments: The Michigan Case," *National Tax Journal* 33: 1–20.

Erikson, R. 1978. "Constituency Opinion and Congressional Behavior: A Re-examination of the Miller-Stokes Representation Data," *American Journal of Political Science* 22: 511–535.

Field Institute. 1983a. "Taxes and Government Spending," *California Opinion Index* (April). San Francisco: The California Poll.

———. 1983b. "California's Public Schools," *California Opinion Index* (July). San Francisco: The California Poll.

Frey. J. 1983. *Survey Research by Telephone*. Beverly Hills: Sage Publications.

Gramlich, E., D. Rubinfeld, and D. Swift. 1981. "Why Voters Turn Out for Tax Limitation Votes," *National Tax Journal* 34: 115–124.

Hatry, H., and L. Blair. 1976. "Citizen Surveys for Local Government: A Copout Manipulative Tool, or a Policy Guidance and Analysis Tool?" Pp. 129–140 in T. N. Clark, ed. *Citizen Preferences and Urban Public Policy.*. Beverly Hills: Sage Publications.

Hoffman, W. and T. N. Clark. 1979. "Citizen Preferences and Urban Policy Types." Pp. 85–105 in J. Blair and D. Nachmias, eds., *Fiscal Retrenchment and Urban Policy*. Beverly Hills: Sage Publications.

Kuklinski, J. 1978. "Representativeness and Elections: A Policy Analysis," *American Political Science Review* 72: 165–177.

———. 1979. "Political Participation and Government Responsiveness: The Behavior of California Supreme Courts," *American Political Science Review* 73: 1090–1099.

Ladd, H., and J. Wilson. 1982. "Why Voters Support Tax Limitations: Evidence from Massachusetts Proposition 2½," *National Tax Journal* 35: 121–148.

McIver, J., and E. Ostrom. 1976. "Using Budget Pies to Reveal Preferences: Validation of a Survey Instrument." Pp. 87–110 in T. N. Clark, ed., from *Citizen Preferences and Urban Public Policy*. Beverly Hills: Sage Publications.

Miller, W. and D. Stokes. 1963. "Constituency Influence in Congress," *American Political Science Review* 57: 45–56.

Page, B., and R. Shapiro. 1983. "Effects of Public Opinion on Policy," *American Political Science Review* 77: 175–180.

Schumaker, D. 1981. "Citizen Preferences and Policy Responsiveness." Pp. 227–243 in T. N. Clark, ed. *Urban Policy Analysis*. Beverly Hills: Sage Publication.

Scott, D. 1976. "Measures of Citizen Evaluation of Local Government Services." Pp. 111–128 in T. N. Clark, ed., *Citizen Preferences and Urban Public Policy*. Beverly Hills: Sage Publications.

State of California. 1980. "The Growth Revolt: Aftershock of Proposition 13?" Sacramento: Office of Planning and Research, Mimeographed.

U.S. Bureau of the Census. 1981. "California: Final Population and Housing Counts." Washington, D.C.: U.S. Department of Commerce.

COMMENTARY:
DIFFERENT LEADERS PREFER DIFFERENT POLICIES

Richard Cole

This an interesting, and quite diverse, set of papers dealing with the general topic of fiscal stress and power in the urban setting. Mark Baldassare attempts to compare citizen policy preferences with those of mayors and with mayors' perceptions of citizen preferences. Relying on data obtained from his own survey of mayors in 150 California municipalities and available public opinion polls, he finds that mayors generally view themselves as willing to spend less on urban services than they perceive citizens are willing to spend. Baldassare also finds that mayors generally believe the "general public" wants to spend less in most cases than do "special-interest" groups. Comparing the views of mayors with public opinion polls, he finds mayors' views of citizen preferences were most inaccurate concerning education and public health issues. There, citizens were found to want to spend more than was perceived by mayors. This study has obvious policy implications as mayors' perceptions of public opinion may have a direct link to their support of various policy positions. To the extent that the results of this study are applicable to other cities, these perceptions may be significantly askew. This study would have been even more interesting, in my opinion,

Research in Urban Policy, Vol. 2, pages 175–177.

ISBN: 0-89232-534-8

if the author in his analysis had controlled for various categories of the public, such as the wealthy or the politically active. It may be that what appears to be a misperception of public opinion by mayors is in reality a very real and very shrewd evaluation of opinion among the most "influential" segment of the population. Also, it would be most instructive to know in which political and socioeconomic settings the attitudes of mayors and the public are most congruent. For example, some political structures may facilitate greater congruency between public opinion and that of elected or appointed officials. Baldassare has made an interesting start in addressing these issues.

Alan Saltzstein examines the changing nature of urban spending patterns in 25 large California cities following passage of Proposition 13. He finds that spending patterns have indeed changed, although not always in the direction analysts earlier predicted. Many cities in his sample experienced considerable budget *increases* in the period studied (1978–79 to 1981–82). Additionally, priorities were found to have altered in many cities. In general, spending on public safety functions increased and spending on parks and recreation declined. This research impressively shows that public officials may use a fiscal "crisis" situation to their advantage when their goal is the alteration of spending priorities. It will be interesting to see if these findings persist with more recent data. This sort of analysis would benefit from a consideration of public opinion, as suggested in Baldassare's contribution. Perhaps public opinion, or at least the perception of public opinion by public officials, has changed over this period and this is the real motive for spending changes.

Robert Stein and Keith Hamm, in what in some ways is the most ambitious of these articles, attempt to measure the influence of federal aid on political activity of blacks in American cities. Contrary to many previous studies, the authors show that federal aid programs indeed can have an impact on black electoral mobilization. This effect, they also show, is mediated by the size of the black electorate and the fiscal health of the city. These results will be of particular interest to those monitoring the implications of President Reagan's New Federalism and the general decline in federal money made available to local governments. One consequence of that, as suggested by the Stein and Hamm study, may be to affect minority political gains in many areas, particularly in terms of their proportionate share of the municipal labor force.

John Williams and Robert Shapiro offer a useful measure of mayoral power using structural variables. They compare their index of power constructed from a ranking of mayors' appointment and veto powers with reported mayoral power. They find modestly high correlations and conclude that researchers may use their (less-expensive) index as a surrogate measure. Indeed, their index should prove a useful tool. It only would be hoped that a structural index of even greater predictive power may ultimately be constructed. Such an index might include a measure of mayoral budget control. The authors find such a measure impossible to include in this study.

In an innovative essay, Harald Baldersheim examines the factors associated with municipal agency success in applying for *supplemental* appropriations throughout the fiscal year. This, of course, departs from our usual tendency to examine agency success in achieving *initial* allocations. The best explanations for success in this very important aspect of budgeting are found to be political ideology and strategic choice. Financial officers who know that governing boards will in large measure restore their recommendations for cuts will recommend large cuts. The process of supplemental budget requests is a vastly understudied area of the budget process, and Baldersheim has pointed the way in his inquiry to more important research.

Brett Hawkins, Mary Ann Steger, and Jean Trimble look at the success of nonprofit organizations to adapt to budget reductions. Examining 57 nonprofit organizations in Milwaukee, the authors find successful adaptation correlated with "success" in some other areas (such as the ability to attract specialists to board membership), and not necessarily related to size or budget strength. This should be of some comfort to many small nonprofits across the country as they struggle with budget cutbacks. One factor not considered, but which also may be of significance, is leadership characteristics and entrepreneurial style.

Again, this is a very interesting set of papers offering diverse perspectives on the urban situation. Almost all are confined to one or a few jurisdictions, and it will be very interesting to see the results of similar works conducted in the context of a national study. These papers suggest many important areas of inquiry for future, more broad-based studies.

PART IV.

CROSS-NATIONAL PATTERNS OF AUSTERITY

FISCAL AUSTERITY AND URBAN INNOVATION IN A WESTERN CANADIAN CITY

James Lightbody

ABSTRACT

The municipal finances of the City of Edmonton, Alberta, Canada, were severely impaired by the economic recession of the early 1980s. This factor, combined with a watershed municipal election in 1983, led to significant changes in long-standing municipal institutions in an effort to cope with fiscal austerity. In this case study, the author examines the conditions conducive to change and the process of its realization. A very preliminary assessment of the potential for efficiency, effectiveness, and responsiveness in civic operations is advanced.

Edmonton, Alberta, stands as Canada's sixth largest city with a population of roughly 560,000. A recent dramatic transformation of its form of civic governance provides a graphic example of how one set of urban policy-makers has attempted to come to grips with the exigencies of fiscal austerity. In this instance, the more general situation of a squeeze on municipal finances was worsened by the specific fact of an economic base inordinately dependent on a single primary resource extraction base—the petroleum

Research in Urban Policy, Vol. 2, pages 181–196.

ISBN: 0-89232-534-8

industry—and with the collapse of that industry in western Canada in the 1980s, municipal institutional adjustments were no longer an option but a necessity. Of course, Edmonton's councilors have not been unique in having to come to grips with austerity and across Canada the common strategies of layoffs, job reclassifications, wage rollbacks, privatization, and the implementation of user charges have been resorted to widely. A recent survey of over 300 municipal chief executive officers in Canadian municipalities with populations in excess of 10,000 found that just under 90 percent had cut back in more than three expenditure categories (Krause and Price 1985). But the situation in Alberta was arguably more severe, with the abrupt transformation from boom to bust economic conditions, than among central and eastern Canadian local governments where restraint and caution have of necessity been more habitual.

THE SETTING

The city of Edmonton was incorporated in 1904 generally employing the principles of good government then holding sway in the United States under the aegis of the American National Municipal League program. For Edmonton's leading citizens of the period, the role of municipal government was clear: It was to be an active adjunct of the local business community. This was the typical pattern across western Canada. Of Winnipeg, for example, Alan Artibise has written: "Winnipeg was established by businessmen, for business purposes, and businessmen were its first and natural leaders . . . the common outlook of Winnipeg's businessmen that the expansion of economic enterprise should be the prime concern of the local government is the dominant theme throughout the period." [1874–1914] (Artibise 1975: 25, 23). The same perceptions held true for Edmonton (Lightbody 1983: 256–258).

But, unlike most Canadian municipalities, Edmonton's "businesslike" governing principles were sufficiently broad to permit considerable state intervention. So to ensure conditions conducive to civic expansion, community leaders pressed for municipal ownership of utilities. A timid local electrical company established in 1891 was bought out in 1904, the same year in which the city bought up the local telephone system (which continued to function like any other private concern) and which is now the largest municipally owned system in Canada. Public transit (streetcars) were a necessity for realty developments and, naturally, ambitious water works and sewage systems were put into place (Lightbody 1984b: 14). The city was subsequently to take over and operate the municipal airport and ambulance system as state enterprises, and to build a major convention center.

The natural result has been that the City of Edmonton is one of Canada's largest corporations; for example, by the early 1980s it employed some 12,000 people, over twice as many as other comparably sized Canadian cities (Higgins 1977: 103) and, in 1983, ranked by expenditures for goods and services purchased it was the nineteenth largest corporation in the country, behind IBM Canada Ltd. (eighteenth), Shell (fifth), and Chrysler (tenth), but ahead of Kraft Foods (twenty-second) (*Small Business*, June 1984: 55).

The management of the municipal corporation was, from the outset, to be modeled upon principles of "good" government. A small, seven-man council would devise "policy," and professional managers would supervise "administration." This model departed from the more conventional Canadian experience, inherited from the United Kingdom, with the council-committee format. The unique feature in Edmonton's case, and the first appearance of the device in western Canada, was that the appointed managers were to be known as "commissioners" and section 41 of the city charter vested in them "a general executive jurisdiction over the affairs of the city [but] reserving to the council the right to direct and control the administrative policy of the commissioners" (R.S.A. 1913, chap. 23, sec. 41). Two commissioners were initially appointed and the mayor, from the outset, was also an ex officio commissioner. As the system expanded and matured, the management side firmed up as a "board of commissioners" which, by 1968, was composed of a chief commissioner with three others each supervising an array of functionally compatible civic departments headed by general managers. The commission board format has been described elsewhere as "a significant Canadian contribution to the art of local government" (Hickey 1972: 221). Regardless, to understand the apparent necessity for this managerial overburden, the size of the municipal corporation must be fully appreciated: Operating expenditures by 1983 had reached $434,891,000 and the capital expenditure program was $962,111,000. Hence, the commissioners were de facto managing one of Canada's largest corporations.

The discovery of massive petroleum reserves adjacent to the city in 1947, and the subsequent location of refining and manufacturing facilities in the metropolitan area, led, over the next 30 years, to a quadrupling of the city's population and a tripling of its area. Unrestrained growth appeared to be the order of the day to the public, the press, and the professional.

Reflecting the buoyant optimism of the late 1970s, a time in which there appeared to be virtually no limits to spatial and economic growth, in 1979 the Edmonton City Council was persuaded by its senior bureaucracy, principally the city commissioners and their corporate policy-planning branch, to attempt to annex some 467,200 acres which would have, in effect, quadrupled the city size. Concommitantly, and in retrospect, the civic administration appears also to have begun putting into place the municipal infrastructure and personnel to manage the anticipated growth of 110 percent to a population of 1,364,000 by the year 2020 (Mackenzie, Spencer 1979).

Certainly no one at the municipal level could have anticipated two events, the shake-up of international petroleum markets by the inability of OPEC to control international prices and the shakedown of the Canadian domestic industry in October 1982 by the national government through the policies of the National Energy Program. The impact on Alberta, and Edmonton, was considerable—and negative!

THE PROGRAM

The municipal election of 1983 appears to reflect a watershed in Edmonton's civic history (Lightbody 1984b: 11).[1] In an intensely bitter campaign, with nuances of national/provincial party identification impinging on the strong local tradition of civic nonpartisanship, Laurence Decore was elected the thirty-first mayor of Edmonton with 61.2 percent of the popular vote, defeating two-term (six-year) incumbent, C. J. Purves and securing in the process the largest margin of victory ever recorded in city history (54,000 votes) (Lightbody 1984a: 39–41).

Despite Decore's long-standing attachments to what would be called in the United States "ethnic politics" (he is himself a third-generation Ukrainian Canadian and served as the national chairman of the Canadian Consultative Council on Multiculturalism), in his approach to political activities he stands very close to Terry Clark's model of a New Fiscal Populist (Clark 1985: 73ff.). In the United States, Purves would have stood out plainly as a "Republican."

The significance of the victory for municipal institutional reform followed in two ways: (1) Decore accepted it as an endorsement of his election platform in which he had called for an end to the board of commissioners form of governance, and (2) the very enormity of his mandate endowed his program with an immediate legitimacy in the eyes of the 12-person council (two elected from each of six wards) which ultimately had to decide upon his recommendations. This latter proved especially helpful for, in the absence of clear party attachments either in elections or on the council, councilors stand as, and once elected behave as, independents. In this situation, any mayor attempting a series of major initiatives must assemble a series of floating coalitions for each pivotal vote. In the Edmonton case, employing Clark's topology of orientations as closely as possible while recognizing that we are faced with a different national political culture, Decore had to deal with a council composed of four Republicans, three

Democrats, three New Fiscal Populists, one "Ethnic," and a poujadist. This divergence, incidentally, suggests that the dominant expression of the city's political culture so solidly entrenched in the 1950s and 1960s (Lightbody 1983: 263–269) has been severely rocked by the massive influx of population during the decade of expansion and subsequently by the frustrations of retrenchment to the point where virtually any political appeal has *some* electoral salience. Consensus being improbable, coalition building escalated to the art of the possible.

With any radical structural adaptation being unlikely to proceed without some considerable impetus, local conditions must be strongly conducive to change. In the Edmonton instance two factors appear to have been pivotal.

First, the worsened circumstances of the area economy wrought havoc with civic finances and lent popular credibility to virtually any substantial measure that might bring significant economies to the municipal budget. Measures of the impact of the economic recession on the city are easily obtainable. For instance, the value of building permits issued declined from $1,157 million in 1981 to $334 million in 1984 (residential sector, $524M to $112M; commercial, $513M to $155M; other, $119M to $67M). A prospectus released in 1982 with respect to an issue of sinking fund debentures had proudly proclaimed, "Over the five-year period 1977–1981 the average annual value of building permits issued was $839,041,000." Situations change! For another example, in 1982 up to 20 percent of business and property taxes were in arrears (Edmonton *Journal*, November 14, 1982). Entrepreneurs are incidentally, if anything, entrepreneurial; one notable phenomenon of the period developed with the conversion of inner-city land to "farming," which by provincial law is taxed at roughly $13 an acre whereas other tax categories range from 50 to 2,000 percent higher. For 1984, for example, the city estimated that it lost about $4.2 million in municipal and school tax revenues to these schemes (Edmonton *Journal*, February 21, 1985).

In November 1982, Mayor Purves directed the city's chief commissioner to terminate some 977 civic job positions in order to reduce the budgeted property tax hike to 8 percent. Between 1982 and 1985, as well, the size of CURA (the association of nonunion employees and managers below department head level) was reduced by about 30 percent (to 700 people). These employees did not enjoy a pay raise for any of those three years (Edmonton *Journal*, February 25, 1985). For the 1983 municipal election, the incumbent mayor campaigned with a promise not to increase property taxes should he be reelected, a statement refuted effectively by his challenger with the observation that the incumbent mayor had voted for *every* tax and utility rate increase in his six years in office. Hence, the latter's call for substantive administrative reorganization as a vehicle for bureaucratic down-sizing and cost saving (for example, "Why do we need managers managing managers?") quickly became an attractive and easily understood political message.

But economic stress on the system would not likely be sufficient in itself to foster reform were the system itself not structurally conducive to it. Thus, a second key factor evolved with an erosion of the public perception of the commission board's legitimacy. This phenomenon had begun to develop in the 1970s as a wide range of articulate residents mobilized in opposition to bureaucratic designs for a comprehensive city-wide freeway system. As has been noted elsewhere, "they became increasingly cynical about their participation in a process so dominated by bureaucratic continuity, cohesion and apparent secrecy" (Lightbody 1984b: 16). The focus of the distrust was at the apex of the administrative pyramid—the Board of Commissioners—and came to a climax in a bitter council meeting in late 1981. Several councilors charged that the mayor, as chairman of the commission board, conspired "with the commissioners to keep information from them, of ensuring they were always the last to know about major developments"—and one, perhaps the most respected of the councilors, observed that "Mr. Mayor, I've come to believe you no longer represent me on the commission board and I say that with regret" (Edmonton *Journal*, September 25, 1981).

A month later the council established an external review of the administrative structure which, reporting in June 1982, concluded that "the most serious problem affecting the city of Edmonton is the lack of trust between council and administration" and recommended an executive committee format that was ultimately approved in principle but never implemented. The problem here was simple: The proposal had been referred to the administration (ultimately, the commission board chaired by Mayor Purves) for an operational design. Still, the credibility of the system in place for 80 years had been seriously challenged.

In his opening campaign statement, and relying on the closet advice of his friends on the council, the challenger, Decore, called for the creation of an executive committee for the council (May 1983) and, ultimately, for the abolition of the commission board and its replacement by a city manager (September). The incumbent responded "that the executive committee idea was illegal and impractical" (Lightbody 1984a: 38).

Being clearly among the most significant of his campaign promises, structural reform assumed an immediate priority status in the newly elected mayor's postelection political agenda. But it was also very much a part of a larger policy package! In his State of the City address to the Edmonton Chamber of Commerce in January 1985, Mayor Decore reflected upon several of his council's achievements in its first year in office in coming to grips with an era of fiscal austerity:

> In January, 1983, the City of Edmonton employed 10,944 non-management employees, and 1,520 management people. Those numbers have been brought down to 9,704 employees and 1,292 management employees, reductions of 12.8 and 17.7 per cent respectively. . . . We have shrunk the number of civic departments from 23 to 13. . . . We have done away with an entire level of senior and very expensive management by eliminating the Commission Board.

But the central accomplishment was certainly the last.

To implement this significant campaign promise in an environment in which the mayor's power is restricted to but one of 13 council votes, and in which a municipal council may undertake no action that is not specifically permitted by provincial government statute (in this case Alberta's Municipal Government Act), [2] required a shrewd calculus of political and bureaucratic intent and support. Within a week of winning the election, thus even before his inauguration, the mayor-elect publicly reaffirmed his plans to introduce the executive committee concept after meeting with the city's chief commissioner: "[I intend] to ensure that the mayor and council are seen to be and are in fact the people in control of city hall" (Edmonton *Journal*, October 20, 1983). On the one hand this tactic provoked an anticipated shrill reaction from some long-term councilors who were closely aligned with senior administrators (e.g., "I think it would be disastrous to move in that direction," or "Getting elected representatives to do the work of administrators would only lead to chaos"—Edmonton *Sun*, October 21, 1983), or who held political ambitions of their own, or who were ideologically ill-disposed toward the mayor, or who because of the proposed method of selection of members to the committee would not themselves be members, or for all four reasons. However, with the exception of a single local columnist with an apparent personal long-term vendetta against Decore ("There's precious little benefit to be gained from the Frankenstein's monster that an inexperienced mayor relying on bad advice is trying to foist on this city"—Edmonton *Journal*, January 18, 1984), the local media and opinion leaders were universally supportive of change.

Still, one of the disgruntled councilors requested an administration investigation of municipal executive structures across the country which provided a wealth of comparative data, but not his anticipated negative conclusions.[3] For the record, of the 12 Canadian cities, with populations of 100,000 to 300,000, nine operate with a city manager–chief administrative officer structure; all four cities in the 300,000 to 500,000 range have a city manager structure; and of the six with 500,000-plus population, three employed commission boards and three some form of executive committee. Of the 57 Canadian cities with populations in excess of 50,000, 48 (or 84 percent) function with either a city manager or a chief administrative officer. An unintentional finding was that Edmonton had the largest number of administrative departments (26) of any Canadian city. Montreal, with almost precisely twice its population, had three fewer. This finding did not hinder the new mayor's efforts for departmental and managerial consolidation (Edmonton 1983).

On the other hand, the paucity of negative reaction, the tacit support of the electorate for change, plus a general behind-the-scenes approval by senior city department heads—many of whom had themselves become frustrated with the duplication, duplicity, and delay now entrenched in the system (and directly experienced during the period of frenetic city expansion)—all strengthened the mayor's initiative. A city commissioner subsequently observed, *after* the changes had been effected, that "the commission board system had done all it could do; its time was up, given the views of the public. . . . Decore's changes are more evolutionary than revolutionary" (Edmonton *Journal*, January 25, 1984). Beyond the pale of public purview, moreover, the mayor's staff moved quickly to sensitize an existing external review of the civic management and departmental structure, Project 30 (whose terms of reference had been previously set by the commissioners), to the new set of priorities at City Hall. Consequently, the first "confidential" report of that review, released less than a month after the election, began with the words, "It is our understanding that the City intends to operate under a City Council/Executive Committee/City Manager form of governance." The Rubicon had been crossed.

By late December the mayor's private personal powers of persuasion with his fellow councilors had produced such a scenario that one of his confidential political advisers was able to write: "There seems to be universal acceptance of the City Manager concept. This is reflected in the Administration's report." Hence, by the time the mayor's proposal for *A Municipal Corporate Management System for the City of Edmonton* went to a special meeting of council for approval (January 23, 1984), only two fundamental issues were unresolved: (1) the range of powers to be granted the executive committee and (2) its size and method of selection. Only two councilors voted against the demise of the commission board, and only three against the executive committee concept. (None of the three would have been eligible for membership on it.)

The new executive committee was intended to exercise only those powers delegated it specifically by the council, under the authority of Section 47 of Alberta's Municipal Government Act. The intent was to streamline both council's own decision making and that of the corporate administration. In brief, its functions included "the areas of corporate policy formulation and recommendation, specific financial, personnel and land matters, directing the flow of information and city business, and in controlling the administration. . . . It would, in short, generally assume the authority delegated by Council at present." *And*, importantly, "The administration [i.e., department managers] would be responsible to Council through the Executive Committee" (Edmonton 1984: 7). Eight months after the committee was created, a consulting team summarized the powers granted the committee under Bylaw No. 7449 under three functional areas: financial and real estate matters, administrative control and direction, and a "steering function" with respect to council business (Kyle and Hinings 1984: 2–3). These are detailed as Appendix A, with the powers and duties of the city manager, as defined by bylaw 7450, as Appendix B.

It has been noted above that Canadian municipalities are very much the statute creatures of their respective provinces; they are precisely no more and no less than what provincial legislation permits them to be. Consequently, one curious finding by the team that assembled the new mayor's proposal to council was a two-year-old legal opinion provided to the former mayor, at a time when the bylaw defining the commission board's duties and powers was being considered, that had raised serious doubts concerning the basic legality of certain powers the council had in past delegated to it. In short, the opinion held that under the authority permitted by the Municipal Government Act there was no provision to permit the commissioners to enter into contracts, as they had been doing: "It would be very difficult to draft a section which allows the board of commissioners to enter into contracts." But, at the same time, the advice held that "council may delegate to any executive committee that has been created the power to enter into contracts."

A series of 61 votes as to detail were debated in the council (51 passed; 10 were defeated) but, despite some limited dilution of the proposed powers of the committee to make of it more of a monitoring and advisory body than the management group Mayor Decore had recommended, the principal question of delegation of authority to elected councilors was firmly established. Additionally, the council unanimously agreed to a review of the new structure "no sooner than 12 months from its adoption by Council, and not later than 18 months." Hence the review would be completed comfortably in the middle of the council's three-year mandate: All legislative assemblies have electoral time horizons!

A thornier problem by far was the less-significant question of committee composition: Hell hath few furies like a politician about to be cut from the limelight. On the advice of his campaign aides, candidate Decore had advocated a committee comprising the mayor plus the top vote getter in each of the city's six two-member wards.[4] This campaign promise *had* to be taken to council as his initial gambit. But, with the major battle having been won (i.e., the existence of the committee itself), the mayor was equipped with four "fallback" options on representation, the first of which he won. Thus, responding to concerns that a majority of the council at any one time would be committee members, councilors reduced the size of the committee to four plus the mayor; *but* the four were to be selected from among the six "senior" councilors, each to serve eighteen months during their three-year terms in office.

AN EVALUATION

It is, of course, far too soon following the reforms to offer a comprehensive, or fair, evaluation of their impact. One must also be very wary of a too-rosy assessment by those anxious to prove the success of an experiment. Over a decade ago, the Economic Council of Canada offered a now-familiar warning to students of policy analysis: "Policy scientists warn that organizational change as a substitute for change in substance is a typical disease of bureaucracies" (Economic Council 1971: 33). For the practitioner as well as the scholar, the operational question in assessing administrative reorganization in the context of governmental fiscal austerity is, as put so succinctly by Norton Long in discussing the matter of who governs, "what difference does it make?" So, for example, the cynical observor might note that the easy acquiescence of the city commissioners in January 1984 to the new city manager style of governance was, essentially, "bought" at the expense of optimal reorganization. Thus, the chief commissioner and three line commissioners were to be replaced by a city manager and two assistant managers.

As well, the potential for institutional sabotage of reform initiatives by strategically located individuals, in either bureaucratic or political positions, can be lethal. In his classic study of prairie radicalism in Saskatchewan, S. M. Lipset alerted us to the fundamental problem:

> The failure to change key members of the civil service had important consequences for the future work of the government. . . . The deputy ministers, realizing that there was no danger of being discharged, fell back into the traditional bureaucratic pattern. A number . . . were able to convince their ministers that certain changes were not administratively feasible or that they would incur too much opposition. Some deputy ministers exchanged information with other deputies on their techniques of controlling their ministers (Lipset 1967: 263).

The much-learned lesson seems to be that in order to effect substantive or radical reorganization it is usually necessary to alter the personnel as well as the basic institutions themselves, while appreciating at the same time that what might be most desirable is not always politically feasible.

In this Edmonton case, in the short term, the chief commissioner was destined to become the new city manager, the commissioner of public affairs became an assistant city manager, the commissioner of utilities and engineering was essentially placed on a consulting retainer as a second assistant manager until his early retirement, and the corporate resources (i.e., finance) commissioner was given a "golden handshake."

The initial salvo against the proposed shake-up of their institutional applecart from these skilled bureaucratic survivors, who well appreciated the writing on the wall, was an attempt to muffle and delay. In a confidential preliminary report to the chief commissioner and the mayor less than a month following the October election (November 15, 1983), a team of consultants working under the direction of senior management had advanced the proposals for a single manager and two assistants. They suggested:

> To facilitate the transition to an Executive Committee the evolutionary approach should be considered. That is, initially to expand the advisory role of the combined legislative and corporate resources committees and progressively add decision making responsibilities and authority as the Committee gains the confidence of Council.

While these recommendations were certainly not illegitimate in any way, neither did they upset any real applecarts.

In each of his reform initiatives, this being the most significant institutionally but only one of a half-dozen city-wide, Mayor Decore was abetted by his "seven sages," a kind of voluntary kitchen cabinet that had, more or less, been his election policy committee. One of them made two private, but pithy, observations about the report to the mayor:

> 1. The frantic worrying about "span of control" problems in administrative structure stems from the very real failure to accept that the commission board structure is to be ended. What they have done is to replace the board with the city manager who, on paper here, simply performs the old board's functions. . . . There is no appreciation of your commitment to having general managers directly accountable to the executive committee of elective personnel. . . .
> 2. Transition: Again the weakest alternative is advanced. . . . Your preferred option should be to make the transition to a powerful executive at the outset, and in total, providing the council votes are there, and build confidence through 2 years of performance. I doubt that council would surrender powers over time as the consultants suggest, and every time they were asked to do so there would be a policy debate in council and possible discrediting of the executive structure. . . .

Ultimately this was the advice that conformed best with the mayor's perception of policy and political realities and represented the position he took to the council, compromising with the chief commissioner by accepting the latter's demand to appoint two assistant city managers. Six months after his own appointment the city manager suffered a heart attack and triple-bypass surgery. Although he was physically able to return to office in early 1985, a significant majority on the council had by that time come to the conclusion that a manager–single assistant manager arrangement was appropriate. Hence, the council was prepared to terminate his contract with the city (two-thirds would be required) should an appropriate buy-out agreement not be negotiated. It was, and Edmonton's first city manager has resigned (Edmonton *Journal*, March 26, 1985). At the same time, the city manager's office endeavored to mount what was in effect a holding action to focus control of the civic administration there.

To evaluate insofar as it is possible at this point: As would be expected, much of the first year of executive committee activities appears to have been devoted to what functionalist theorists would label adaptive and integrative behavior or, in other words, problem solving while building the overall legitimacy of the system. After all, functionalists like Parsons do focus on issues about how "order and stability emerge from disorganization and dissension" (Kaplan 1967: 9–13). To the extent, naturally, that the attempts to perform these functions become conflicting activities, tension is built into the system and the potential for failure escalates. Kaplan, for instance, says: "A system may fail because it overemphasizes problem solving and tries to move too fast, because it excludes certain groups from policy making, or because it fails to reconcile conflicts among the internal segments of the system. In these cases the integrative function was not adequately performed" (Kaplan 1967: 27). So, while in academic terms you *can* have your cake and eat it too, in practical consequences the institutions fail!

Ten months into the new system, its basic principles are no longer debatable—only the extent of its practical policymaking powers—so it appears that the integrative function here has been well performed. For example, one of the two councilors who had voted against the original concept has said: "I'm not disputing the committee, I'm disputing the committee having too much power" (Edmonton *Journal*, October 14, 1984). Even former Mayor Purves "sees nothing wrong with an executive committee style of government" (Edmonton *Journal*, December 26, 1984).

Perhaps a more concrete index of integration lies in what has recently happened to the evaluation originally proposed for the system. First expected to involve a team of outside consultants and councilors and a budget in excess of $55,000, the budget was successively reduced by the council to $21,000, then $13,500, and it now appears that it will only entail an aldermanic task force of two, plus the mayor, with a single outside consultant. " 'Council is pretty much content with the executive committee,' [Mayor Decore] said after Tuesday's council meeting. He said aldermen just want a decision on how executive members should be chosen" (Edmonton *Journal*, March 27, 1985).

Although the mayor has conceded, publicly, that the body may have too much autonomy in some policy areas such as land transfers and tax concessions, and the council has acted in a few singular cases to restrict its powers, these adaptive-type problems pose no real threat to the new organizational form. "This isn't a war to grab and control. It's to determine a process of more effect and control. There is no more 'we' and 'they' at city hall," Decore said . . . " (Edmonton *Journal*, April 10, 1985).

The eventual form and power of the city manager's position will be a function of both personality and perceived structural need on the part of the elected mayor and council. The most scarce political resource is always time and it can be reasonably hypothesized that when time consumption by administrative matters begins to impinge too seriously upon more important political activities, interest in the former will wane, for elections are not evanescent. More than one alderman voted *for* the executive committee principle to free himself of the more tedious aspects of council duty. And, since political life (in the broadest sense of policy making) seldom permits a vacuum, it can also be hypothesized that the permanent officials will be prepared to expand their scope to take up the void. City Bylaw 7450, which established the office of city manager on January 24, 1984, for example, in its 11 specific job directives very clearly outlines the role as a policy *implementer*. Yet some trial balloons suggesting an expansion of the position have already been sent aloft by, among others, consultants retained by the senior administration. If adopted these would, for instance, make the city manager an ex officio member of the executive committee, have him establish an "administrative management committee concept" (presumably this would be a regularized meeting of the department heads), appoint for him a "director of corporate administration . . . to coordinate and direct all administrative support requirements in the city manager's office" (i.e., an executive assistant), and utilize the (presumably expanded) "support services" of the city manager's office to staff the city's three independent agencies: the city clerk, the city solicitor, and the auditor general. Thus far the balloons are still aloft.

But it must also be appreciated, in the most practical of all terms, that the current Edmonton city council *has* terminated a system of governance that *had* existed for four generations! Superficially this may not seem remarkable for there have indeed been significant innovations in municipal institutions in Canada in the twentieth century. But, in cases like the introduction of metropolitan government to Toronto (and regional government across the province subsequently), the consolidation of Winnipeg's metropolitan area governments into "Unicity," or the provision for regional districts in British Columbia, these have almost always been at the instance of *provincial* authorities. To its credit, the Edmonton City Council, notwithstanding the divergent political perceptions of its members, bit the bullet itself.

So, in an era of fiscal austerity for local government, this much at least is clear. In one Canadian city where the impact of the squeeze between revenue shortfalls and expenditure responsibilities was severe, the council was motivated to a position of direct hands-on management by *elected* officials. Allocative decisions previously the more-or-less secure domain of senior administrators acquired a high-profile political currency necessitating resolution by an elected executive. The direct consequences of the transformation have yet to be properly measured but, for the moment at least, this seems to be responsible behavior for the times by those electorally accountable.

NOTES

1. The author was senior campaign policy adviser to the successful challenger for the mayor's chair, Laurence Decore.
2. For those not familiar with the Canadian system, constitutionally municipalities are the statute creations of the 10 provincial governments. Such relative autonomy as they may possess is that *permitted* by the respective province.
3. The report thoughtfully included a direct reference to an essay by the mayor's publicly identified campaign policy adviser (Lightbody 1983): "It [the commission board] is a highly efficient bureaucratic form, well suited to the administration of a major corporate enterprise."
4. The model for this format was the manner in which the City of Toronto designates its representatives to the Council of Toronto's Metropolitan Government. The method was intended to avoid the various problems that would be associated with either the mayor's personal nomination or an election/recall by the council as a whole.

REFERENCES

Artibise, A.F.J. 1975. *Winnipeg: A Social History of Urban Growth, 1874–1914*. Montreal: McGill-Queen's.

Clark, Terry Nichols. 1985. "Choose Austerity Strategies That Work for You." In Terry Nichols Clark, ed., *Research in Urban Policy, Vol. I*. Greenwich, Conn.: JAI Press, Inc.

Economic Council of Canada. 1971. *Design for Decision-Making*. Ottawa: Information Canada.

Edmonton, City of. 1983. *Report on the Commission Board Style and the City Manager System of Administration in Canada*.

———. 1984. *A Municipal Corporate Management System for the City of Edmonton*.

Hickey, Paul. 1972. *Decision-Making Processes in Ontario's Local Government*. Toronto: Queen's Printer.

Higgins, D.J.H. 1977. *Urban Canada: Its Government and Politics*. Toronto: Macmillan.

Kaplan, Harold. 1967. *Urban Political Systems: A Functional Analysis of Metro Toronto*. New York: Columbia University Press.

Krause, Robert, and Trevor Price. 1985. "The Impact of Financial Restraint on the Provision of Municipal Services in Canada." Paper presented at the annual meeting of the Canadian Political Science Association.

Kyle, J. T., and R. Hinings. 1984. *City of Edmonton Study: City Manager/Executive Committee Inter-relationships*. Edmonton: Touche Ross & Partners.

Lightbody, James. 1983. "Edmonton." Pp. 255–290 in Warren Magnusson and Andrew Sancton, eds. *City Politics in Canada*. Toronto: University of Toronto Press.

———. 1984a. "The First Hurrah: Edmonton Elects a Mayor, 1983," *Urban History Review* 13: 35–41.

———. 1984b. "The Political Tradition of a Prairie Canadian City," *Local Government Studies* 10: 11–24.

Lipset, S. M. 1967. *Agrarian Socialism: The Cooperative Commonwealth Federation in Saskatchewan*. Berkeley: University of California Press.

Mackenzie Spencer Associates. 1979. *Long Term Planning Analysis*. Edmonton: City of Edmonton.

Plunkett, T. J., and James Lightbody. 1982. "Tribunals, Politics and the Public Interest: The Edmonton Annexation Case," *Canadian Public Policy* 8: 207–221.

APPENDIX A
POWERS OF THE EXECUTIVE COMMITTEE (FROM THE CITY OF EDMONTON BYLAW NO. 7449)

Finance and Real Estate

- defines and recommends budget guidelines, financial policies and spending priorities
- causes budgets to be prepared
- recommends rate charges for various public services
- authorizes contract awards and enter agreements on conditions directed by Council
- authorize settlement of claims in accordance with Council set limits
- determine tax rebates
- recommends on civic grants
- monitors financial performance and authorizes budget adjustments within limits established by Council and reports major changes
- makes decisions and enters contracts on real estate projects within limits established by Council, budget, by-laws and policies. Expropriation decisions are made by Council on recommendation from Committee

Civic Administration

- responsible to Council for ensuring the execution of Council policies, by-laws and directives
- controls the Administration through the city manager
- accountable to Council for the general performance of the Administration
- appraise the performance of city manager
- make decisions and enter collective bargaining agreements within by-laws, budgets, policies
- formalize legal contracts within limit established by Council

- direct the administration on matters involving Corporate Management policy
- instruct City Solicitor on required legal action
- issue general orders not requiring by-law authority

Steering Function

- establish Council agendas
- ensure that all items are properly documented
- direct and coordinate information flow to Council, Committees and Administration
- refer matters for specified action to Council, Committees or Administration
- undertake studies as required with approved budget

Source. Kyle and Hinings 1984.

APPENDIX B
THE CITY MANAGER (CITY OF EDMONTON BYLAW NO. 7450)

Powers and Duties of the City Manager:

- appoint, suspend or remove any assistant City Manager or General Manager (Department Head) subject to the advice of the Mayor. Executive committee to act as appeal committee in the event of City Manager–Mayor disagreement
- direct, supervise and review performance of the Administration except as limited by other statutes or by-laws
- implement all policies and programs approved by Council
- recommend annual capital and operating budgets
- report on municipal works and operations of all departments as required by Council and/or Committees
- advise and make recommendations to the Executive Committee on financial condition and future needs
- monitor and control civic expenditures in accordance with approved budgets
- organize or reorganize the civic administration as required
- develop and recommend change in service delivery in the best interest of the community
- attend all Council and Committee meetings unless excused
- prepare and submit any reports required by Council or Committees

Source. Kyle and Hinings 1984.

FISCAL STRESS IN LOCAL GOVERNMENT:

RESPONSES IN DENMARK AND THE UNITED STATES

Poul Erik Mouritzen and Betty Jane Narver

ABSTRACT

This article attempts a systematic comparison of certain causes and responses to fiscal stress in Danish and American local government. The authors suggest that the degree of vulnerability to fiscal stress as well as the nature of the responses are a function of the incentive structures of citizens and political leaders within the two countries. Certain contextual factors in each country have helped shape these incentive structures such as the degree of governmental consolidation and dependency, the visibility of the revenue system, mechanisms for individual political action and the formation of interest groups, and the structure of the electoral and party systems. In the Danish case, the contextual factors encourage a relatively predictable though unadaptive fiscal policy-making process; American local government is perhaps more adaptive to environmental changes but less predictable and less able to provide protection for its citizens from economic and social changes.

INTRODUCTION

A conscious program of reform in the 1960s created in Denmark a system of uniform local governments carrying out similar programs and functions.

Research in Urban Policy, Vol. 2, pages 197–218.

ISBN: 0-89232-534-8

Instead of 1,300 units differing in size and responsibilities, the reform created 275 relatively standard units. In the United States, even the term *local government* conjures up a myriad of distinct and separate entities. There are over 77,000 units of subnational governments including states, counties, cities, school districts, and special districts delivering a wide range of services. The relationships between these various jurisdictions is not uniform and often are in a state of flux reflecting the constant redefining of the American federal system.[1]

This article attempts to engage in a systematic comparison of certain causes and responses to fiscal stress in Danish and American local government.[2] The assumption underlying the analysis is that vulnerability to fiscal stress as well as the responses it generates are a function of the incentive structures of citizens and political leaders who are themselves influenced by certain contextual factors related to basic governmental structures.

Despite the stark differences between local governments in Denmark and the United States, we have chosen to risk the dangers of oversimplification and the injustice to variation within the countries in order to gain certain broad understandings. By emphasizing the differences between Denmark and the United States, we hope to provide insights that will be useful to academics and practitioners in reexamining their own systems. This seems important at a point when changing conditions in both countries have produced stress at national and local levels. Although the difficulties are obvious, we have chosen local government as the unit of analysis because of the common function of service delivery. In addition, the shape and nature of the incentive structures for citizens and political leaders are more clearly defined at the local level in both countries.

We have chosen periods of fiscal stress in part because those are the times in which we live, but also because it is our contention that during such times, natural tendencies within a country or a community may become more sharply drawn and therefore more visible. We believe that in the United States a natural fiscal conservatism rooted in individualism is reinforced by a set of fiscal and political structures that play a strong role in determining the way local political leaders respond to fiscal stress. Fiscal constraints, for instance, put into place during times of stress, may be as much a function of citizen response to the stress as of the severity of the stress itself. Often it requires the appeal of a strong leader to intervene in the natural tendency toward protection of individual interests.

In Denmark, on the other hand, policies tend to reflect a societal consensus on the importance of equity and the collective interest. In this case, the contextual factors we discuss serve a kind of mediating function to protect governments and their citizens from external forces. The electoral system and the political party system as well as the system for financing local government have been consciously designed to mitigate the effects of major economic or social change. Our belief is that in both countries certain contextual factors play a critical role in determining the way in which political leaders deal with fiscal stress.

From these basic assumptions, we have concluded (1) local governments in the United States appear to be more vulnerable to change in national economic conditions and shifts in local environment than in Denmark where a number of protective mechanisms have been devised to protect local governments from a turbulent environment; (2) in Danish local government, citizens have few strong incentives and few means to protest against taxes while in the United States the high degree of fragmentation, the finance structure, and the decision-making processes of local government tend to encourage a more fiscally conscious population group with several channels of strong influence; and (3) local political leaders in the United States have strong incentives to build visible coalitions through the distribution of tangible benefits (in the form of increased services or lower taxes depending on circumstances), leading to independent, entrepreneurial behavior in relation to interest groups. In Denmark, the incentive system for leaders is geared to the rewards of successful implementation of policies and strong, disciplined national-local political parties.

We generally conclude that American local governments and their leaders are highly adaptive and responsive to changes in their economic and political environments. However, their actions tend to be relatively unpredictable. The costs of this kind of system tend to be individualized as the full impact of social and economic forces are borne by politically weak groups and individuals in periods in which the system is in the midst of change. In contrast, Denmark has built a governmental system that, in relative terms, protects both its structures and the individuals within those structures. Even in periods of transition, fiscal policies tend to be marginal adjustments to existing policies that are clear reflections of party positions. This clearly has a cost which in the Danish case is borne collectively and institutionally. The cost may appear in the relative inability of the governmental sector to adapt to changes in national conditions, particularly the economy.

FRAMEWORK OF ANALYSIS

For this discussion, fiscal stress is defined as: "a gap between the needs and expectations of citizens and government employees for government services and benefits and the ability and willingness of taxpayers to support those services and benefits."[3] Gaps between needs and expectations and available resources will always tend to exist, at least in the long run (cf.

Schick 1980). Matters of degree become the essential issue in this case. We have been able to observe in Denmark as well as in the United States that under certain circumstances and during certain periods the gap seems to be widening. In explaining why this is true, the discussion centers on causes of fiscal stress. However, gaps between demands and available resources, especially growing ones and those extending over time, put political leaders under pressure. In both countries, local governments are bound by requirements of balanced budgets. In discussing the decisions made by politicians and administrators under those circumstances, we are dealing with responses to fiscal stress.

Local governments in Denmark and the United States are exposed to the same general environmental forces that may create fiscal stress.[4] In terms of revenue, a declining, weak, or unstable tax base is generally considered one of the most critical sources of strain. Reductions in grants from upper levels of government in both countries have provided the impetus for several analyses. On the expenditure side, the literature discusses various and changing "objective needs" grounded in economic conditions and population characteristics as well as political pressure from employee unions and special-interest groups. With respect to policy responses to fiscal stress, numerous studies have documented the strategies of various leaders.[5] These include traditional responses that may seek to close the gap through new revenues and/or cutbacks in expenditures, transfer responses that shift functions or clients to other units of government or the private sector, and innovative ones that focus on increasing productivity and attempting to influence underlying mechanisms that determine demands and resources.

Our analysis focuses on a limited number of contextual factors to better understand the influence they have on the degree to which local governments are exposed to fiscal stress as a consequence of environmental changes, and the general strategies adopted by political leaders and administrators in coping with fiscal stress. We concentrate on the degree of territorial, functional, and programmatic consolidation; the system of financing; and the structure of decision making. We perceive of public policy as a result of the actions of individuals acting in accordance with their perceptions of their best interests, combined with a pluralistic bargaining process in which groups compete for scarce resources. Our framework is inspired in part by two of the dominant approaches of behavioral political science—public choice theory and pressure group theory.

We start from the assumption that a certain perception of reality and a set of expectations affect the way in which citizens calculate the costs and the benefits of particular political action. More specifically, we are interested in structural properties of the two systems that may affect the degree to which a "fiscal illusion" exists for citizens. How visible to citizens is the system of public services and the means by which they pay for these services? We also assume that the particular contextual factors in both countries have led to a different set of incentives to take political action. The political action taken will also differ. Perceptions of reality and incentives can offer certain explanations for political action at the individual level. In order to have an effect, these individual preferences must in some way be aggregated and communicated to political leaders creating certain group-level explanations.

We look at the conditions that must exist for interest groups to form and examine the way the contextual factors affect the possibilities for individuals with similar preferences to form groups to attain political goals. For these groups to be effective, the opportunities for access and channels of intervention will be dictated in part by the factors identified. Individual and group-level activities explain the scope, content, and intensity of demands that are exerted upon political leaders. For several reasons, we assume differences exist between the two countries at this point. If, however, political leaders in the countries were exposed to exactly the same kinds of demands from individuals and interest groups, there is no reason to expect the same kind of responses. We expect the contextual factors to have an independent influence on the way local political leaders calculate the costs and benefits of their actions. We maintain that the differences in the contextual factors operating in Denmark and the United States change the stakes and the dynamics of the process in moving from perceptions of reality to actions by political leaders.

CONTEXTUAL FACTORS

Consolidation and Dependency

Local government reforms initiated in Denmark in the late 1960s drastically altered the degree of territorial and programmatic consolidation in local government. New boundaries were drawn according to the principle of "one city, one municipality." Except for the metropolitan area (City of Copenhagen and surrounding municipalities), the boundaries can now be considered "natural" ones. The number of municipalities was reduced from about 1,300 to 275.[6]

Since 1970, a number of changes in the distribution of tasks has moved the Danish system toward even greater programmatic consolidation. Several programs previously administered by local agencies or bodies of the central government have now become the responsibility of municipalities or counties.[7] Also, in functional terms, the Danish system is highly consolidated in that the delivery of services is for all practical purposes taken care of by local government institutions.

Another issue that is related to consolidation is the degree to which tasks that might be performed by the private sector in the United States are performed by the public sector in Denmark and are considered the responsibility of all regional or local governments. This is true, for instance, for day-care centers, leisure-time education for children and adults, dental care for children, visiting health programs for families with children, and so on. It is safe to say, therefore, that with minor exceptions, Danish local government is a highly consolidated system on all dimensions, delivering a broad range of services to citizens. It also represents a relatively standardized system with each unit of local government financing and delivering the same services throughout the country.

In contrast, services in the United States tend to be delivered through a system that is fragmented and noncentralized with formal authority for policymaking, financing, and actual provision of services dispersed among a variety of public and private entities. On territorial, functional, and programmatic dimensions, the American governmental structure is far less consolidated than the Danish one. Underlying this fragmentation are the complicated dynamics of federalism which are reflected with unending variation from state to state.[8] Even with tremendous variation within the United States, as a whole the system presents a model in sharp contrast to that in Denmark.

As to territorial consolidation, although there has been some move in a number of states toward more uniform standards in annexation and the determination of boundaries,[9] in many states territorial limits of governments are decided by a primarily political process with scant attention paid to "natural" boundaries. For instance, functionally, policy may be set at the federal level in the case of education for the handicapped, with financing being shared by federal, state, and local jurisdictions. Monitoring responsibilities may be at the state level, but actual services are delivered by a school district that may be a separate governmental entity from the local city government. Location of authority and accountability are often blurred. Similarly, several governmental units as well as private entities on contract may be responsible for various (or the same) aspects of job training, for example.

We propose that *the more consolidated a local government system is, the more individuals will be highly dependent and the more biased the local fiscal policymaking process will tend to be in favoring public expenditures.* In Denmark the high level of consolidation on all the dimensions mentioned tend to promote a high degree of dependency on local services. We suggest that more than 50 percent of the electorate in a Danish municipality will be highly dependent on municipal services.[10] Around 8–10 percent of the population is directly employed by the municipality.[11] Probably around 20 percent of the electorate will be directly dependent in that either husband or wife is a municipal employee. Approximately 20 percent—persons 67 years or older—is similarly dependent on the municipality and receives help through old-age pensions, visiting health nurses, and home help and eventually may live in a nursing home or sheltered home.

In addition, it is assumed in Denmark that at least 10 percent of the electorate is permanently or will periodically be highly dependent, requiring public assistance or a sick allowance, or will participate in municipal employment programs for young people or the long-term unemployed.[12] Citizens who are not highly dependent nevertheless receive relatively visible benefits from their municipality in the form of schools, day-care facilities,[13] library facilities, leisure-time education, and so on.

The high degree of fragmentation in the American system has important consequences for the fiscal policymaking process. It is difficult to find completely valid, comparable figures as to the size of the sector of those who are highly dependent in the American and Danish systems. It is possible to point to some gross figures to indicate the degree of difference between the two countries. The Advisory Commission on Intergovernmental Relations figures for 1982 indicate that 33 full-time equivalents per 1,000 population can be identified as employees of local government.[14] This number falls far short of the approximately 95 full-time equivalents per 1,000 population in the local government sector (municipalities and counties) in Denmark. This indicates a marked difference in the number of people who are directly dependent on local government for their employment in the two countries.

Even more difficult to compare is the size of the sector of service recipients who are also highly dependent on local government. The range of services financed and delivered at the local level in Denmark is almost comprehensive and the client group is universal for many services. As a general rule in the United States, however, services targeted to the poor and dependent have been initiated by and often paid for by other levels of government. Assistance to the most dependent sector (through Aid for Families with Dependent Children, Medicaid, care for the elderly, etc.) is not perceived as a local responsibility. Even the most universal of services, elementary and secondary education, is often provided by a jurisdiction separate from city government and is financed by a varying combination of local, state, and federal funds. The range of public services financed and delivered by local government is relatively common throughout the United States with notable exceptions[15] and has not changed dramatically since the turn of the century.[16]

Public Services as a "Free Good": The Visibility of Revenues

The benefits of public expenditures are private in nature. In contrast, the costs are public and the benefits of restricting public spending are a public good: The costs and benefits appear in changing tax rates which are "consumed" in identical amounts by the taxpayers (Kristensen 1980: 259). While this observation holds true for both Denmark and the United States, we suggest that the incentive for citizens to oppose higher taxes (or favor lower taxes) is generally higher in the United States than in Denmark.

We propose that *the more visible the revenue structure and the more fragmented the local government system, the more the fiscal policymaking process will tend to be biased in favor of lower taxes*. We start with a brief description of the revenue structure of Danish and American local government with special emphasis on tax revenues and a short note on the influence of intergovernmental grants.[17]

By far the most important revenue source for Danish municipalities is the income tax which in 1982 accounted for 41 percent of total revenues for localities. The system is based on proportional taxation and taxes are levied on the same base as the regional government's income tax (also proportionately) and the central government's income tax (progressive). Local and regional authorities are free to set their own rate of taxation. The local rate varies between 14 and 22 percent. For most income categories, the sum of the local, regional, and central rates varies between 50 and 60 percent.[18]

Income taxes are paid by the source in Denmark. Local, regional, and central taxes are collected together so that the employee is not made conscious on a regular basis of the proportion going to the separate jurisdictions. Property taxes in Denmark account for less than 3 percent of total revenues and are paid twice a year directly to the municipality by the owner. Danish local government derives no revenues from the sales tax. Nontax revenues account for 23.6 percent of total revenues in municipalities, with approximately one-third of this amount made up of current charges in public utilities. Other important nontax revenues are fees on day-care facilities and income from sale of municipal land.[19]

In contrast, in the United States in 1982–1983, local government income from property taxes accounted for 21.3 percent of total revenues while 19.1 percent was raised from taxes other than property taxes. Income from nontax revenues (including charges, interest earnings, and miscellaneous sources) was 31.8 percent.[20] As "creatures of the states," cities have limited control in terms of setting rates of taxation or developing untapped sources for tax revenues. In fact, the greatest degree of flexibility left to local governments is in the area of user charges and other nontax means of generating revenue. As MacManus (1983: 145) points out, state governments regulate the taxing, borrowing, and spending of cities as well as the financial administration of these separate jurisdictions.

Although income taxes are generally conceived as a relatively visible revenue source, the amount of money paid to a Danish municipality and the rate applied is obscured by the "withholding" provision and the system of tandem collection of central, county, and municipal taxes. In the United States, the major source of tax revenues for local government is the property tax. A single-payment property tax can be expected to "generate a high degree of tax awareness among property owners" (Goetz 1977: 180). Although the "installment plan" payment in which property tax payments are made monthly in conjunction with mortgage payments may diminish taxpayer awareness,[21] we maintain that the typical set of American local taxes is more visible to the average taxpayer than in Denmark.

The degree of fragmentation may also play a role in respect to incentives of citizens and employees to oppose tax increases. In a highly consolidated system, the relationship between the levels of taxation and of spending for an individual program is obscure and uncertain. If one is dependent on municipal services, it may be dangerous to oppose tax increases because resource scarcity may threaten those services.[22] In a highly fragmented system such as the United States, the awareness of which entity receives what level of funding is much greater. Higher or lower taxes for the school district have no direct impact on the amount of resources going, for instance, to the municipal fire department. There is some evidence that public employees primarily support higher spending in their own unit of government (Courant, Gramlich, and Rubinfeld 1980), which may also suggest a difference within local communities in levels of support for various local governmental units. In other words, when public employees in one sector look at total governmental resources within their community, their preference may well be to keep the overall level of taxation at current levels (or reduce the level) by supporting an increase in their own sector at the cost of reduced expenditures in other sectors.

The incentive structure of citizens, therefore, based on their preferences and perceived best interests, tends to produce different results in the two countries. In Denmark, we suggest, these factors create a fiscal policymaking process that favors the expenditure side. In the United States, however, citizens (or a large sector of citizens) have a strong incentive to oppose local government expenditures.

From Incentives to Action: Individual Preference and Organized Interests

The next stage in our explanatory framework focuses on the mechanisms through which citizens manifest their interests in political action. These actions are visible and can influence political leaders. In this section we focus on the process by which individual preferences are articulated through organized interest groups. We propose that *the higher the degree of consolidation, the greater are the possibilities of strong interest groups forming around expenditure issues and the more the fiscal policymaking will tend to be biased in favor of expenditures.*

In Denmark, citizens and employees mobilize when particular programs are threatened. This is due in part to a high level of organizational membership in employee unions, a high degree of professionalism, and the existence of user-councils within various service delivery institutions. There tends to be a strong congruence for maintaining municipal expenditure levels. The high degree of territorial and programmatic consolidation results in a union structure in which a number of relatively strong unions operate within the same territorial boundaries. Although they are affiliated with different programs, they have a strong incentive to form coalitions that cut across the various service areas.

In addition, the fact that service delivery is taking place within local government institutions (functional consolidation) may tend to produce a process biased in favor of the expenditure side. It has been suggested that department heads and bureaucrats within the departments are more likely to defend the interests of the service delivery employees in a setting in which they are directly in charge of operations. In fact, one of the arguments for privatization of service delivery has been that the incentives of bureaucrats will swing toward efficiency and productivity as a result of privatization (cf. Kristensen 1983: 258).

In the United States, interest groups that form at the local level tend to focus primarily on local concerns. With increasing frequency these have represented the nonpoor and the nonproviders who are frustrated at growing public expenditure levels and rising tax rates. In part this may be seen as a reaction to the period beginning in the 1960s when important national leaders and influential groups had insisted that attention be turned to poor and minority populations, particularly in the nation's urban areas. Continuing economic prosperity permitted a seemingly unlimited flow of resources from the federal level to states and localities encouraging a coalition between benefit recipients, an army of public and private producers, and a generally sympathetic middle class. A strong vertical relationship grew up between the interests concerned with civil rights and poverty at the national level and the providers of services at the local level.

With the shift from categorical programs to block grants, more authority was vested in local officials. The interest groups representing local, county, and state officials changed the emphasis from programs and their clients to greater concern with maintaining funding levels for governmental units. When these units were faced with retrenchment in the late 1970s and early

1980s and with major cuts in federal assistance, the special-interest groups of various professionals and their clients suffered from the fragmented, competitive nature of the system. With scarcer resources, various interest groups worked to enlarge or maintain their share, rather than forming natural coalitions to increase total expenditure levels. The fact that services are often provided and financed by different units of government and various private organizations serves to blur the point of authority. Often there is no single unit on which pressure can be exerted to increase the level of expenditures for a particular program area.

While there are strong forces in the Danish system that tend to encourage the creation of interest groups around expenditure issues, there are very few organized channels of influence for citizens who are dissatisfied with taxation interests. In Danish local government, revenue decisions (taxing, borrowing, and the use of liquid assets) are made solely by the political elite, that is, the councils. There are no provisions for binding referendums upon council decisions.[23] This particular characteristic of the decision-making structure makes it very difficult for the individual opposing high taxes to voice a protest.

This is not to say that Danes do not protest taxes. The anti-tax Progress Party, headed by Mogens Glistrup, became an important element in the national political scene in the so-called protest election in 1973. This movement, however, never gained influence at the local level and is significant in our discussion more as an exception than a rule. Citizens who protest taxes at the local level tend to do so individually; no institutional arrangements have developed to encourage a rapid, powerful mobilization of those who are dissatisfied.

Although there is no hard evidence, it is commonly recognized in Denmark that organized labor on occasion has put pressure on local governments to stop rising levels of taxation. This has probably been a more frequent phenomenon in the last few years, when many citizens have experienced a reduction in their take-home pay. To the extent that the local labor movement is the fiscally conservative sector of the community, local political leaders will probably respond in particular ways. It is highly unlikely that organized labor will accept major reductions in redistributive programs. One may therefore hypothesize that those pure public goods and divisible goods that mostly benefit the middle and upper classes will suffer most from the fiscal pressures that organized labor imposes upon local government.[24]

In the United States, growing economic constraints on state and local governments coincided with Reagan's domestic program reductions and the attempts to shift new responsibilities to subnational units of government. In a number of states citizen groups forced limitations on expenditures and taxes. California's Proposition 13 and Massachusetts' Two and

One-Half were the most visible and successful examples of citizens' assuming authority to legislate expenditure and revenue policies.

One of the major differences in the conditions of decision making between Denmark and the United States lies in the role played by citizens and by organized groups in the delay, modification, or reversal of policies. Citizens' involvement in the United States takes many forms ranging from the formal variety required by federal mandate to litigation to spontaneous protest in the streets. Special-interest groups can elect (or defeat) candidates or propositions through extensive campaigns and highly organized, well-financed lobbying efforts. Intervention is increasingly exercised through the use of initiatives and referendums that allow citizens to write legislation or override the actions of their elected representatives.[25]

Local Political Leaders: The Importance of the Party System

In the preceding sections we have pointed out a number of factors that have tended to create a fiscally more conservative environment for American local political leaders and an environment in Denmark that tends to favor expenditures. In this section we focus on the incentive structure of local political leaders. The findings suggest that there are different reward structures in the two countries which in the Danish case tend to *modify* the strong pressures that favor expenditures but in the American case tend to *reinforce* the pressures in favor of taxation concerns. We will briefly examine the political party systems in the two countries and the influence they have on fiscal policymaking.

In Denmark, local elections are held every fourth year. The system is based on proportional representation; that is, each party or nonpartisan list obtains seats in the council in proportion to the votes carried. In addition, representation on the important finance committee and various standing committees is based on proportional votes in the council. Each municipality is one district in electoral terms. While nonpartisan lists used to play an important role in many small municipalities, the national political parties have gradually gained a near-monopoly via their district and municipal organizations. Today, only 15 percent of all elected officials in local government are not elected in a partisan list, but they are generally identifiable in terms of position on the traditional left-right continuum. The major lines of cleavage are clearly between the political parties.[26]

Local political parties are parties in their own right, but they are also segments of national parties. Parties with parliamentary representation are numerous. The large, national parties have an organizational structure that closely mirrors that of national, regional, and local governments with district, municipal, county, and national elements. Two of the national parties tend to dominate local politics: the Social Democratic Party and the Liberal (or Agrarian) Party.

Considerable variation exists in American cities in terms of the election of local officials. Clark points to the differences that result from the two predominant forms of government in the cities. Communities that went through reform movements tend toward at-large constituencies, the presence of professional city managers (with weak or no mayors), and nonpartisan elections. These changes were designed to reduce the influence of organized groups and to encourage "efficient and honest" city government. Cities that did not undergo these reform movements tend to be older, with more heterogeneous populations, and generally retain the mayor-council structure with partisan election by wards. Almost two-thirds of American cities can now be characterized by the reform elements.

Nationally, American political parties have never had the strength of those in Europe. Party switching and cross-party voting are increasingly common practices in the United States and a growing number of voters classify themselves as independent. At various levels of government, party loyalty and discipline are much less important political factors than in many European countries, including Denmark. Political issues form an undercurrent in virtually every local election, but there are few mechanisms to tie those issues to national political debate. Because so many American cities have purposely chosen a nonpartisan electoral system in order to keep politics out of "good government," it is difficult to build local platforms or evaluate the performance of local officials on the basis of national political goals and programs.

At the local level, even in cities with nonpartisan governments, political parties exist to elect other officials at the county, state, and national levels. At all levels, but especially at the local one, political parties appear to have diminishing control over candidates. As voters tend to cluster around special issues or particular individuals, candidates become increasingly entrepreneurial and competitive. Parties have fewer and fewer mechanisms to reward the party faithful or punish mavericks who run on independent issues.

The existence of strong political parties is likely to create types of rewards and pressures that do not operate in a nonpartisan setting and that may have important consequences for determining fiscal policies. We suggest that *the existence of a strong party system in a country tends to give local political leaders a relatively high degree of freedom to pursue policies that run against or that differ from the dominant and manifest interests in a particular community. Further, the stronger the system, the more protected political leaders tend to be from interest-group pressures.*[27]

In addition to its capacity to shield political leaders from the influence of pressure groups, major interests are generally represented by parties in Denmark's highly developed, differentiated political system. These groups may, in a sense, be coopted as they are systematically brought into the decision-making process.[28] Consensus within one party or among a coalition can be built more easily in a system in which parties display relative internal coherence.[29]

A question arises as to how much political leaders can control their election and reelection. In Denmark's strong party system, there are very few chances for an independent political entrepreneur to be elected. Nomination from within the party is normally a prerequisite to a seat on the council. Nominations come from party recognition which is usually the result of years of loyal party activity. The individual owes more to the party and its platform than to his or her particular stand on issues. Often the newly elected or reelected local politician does not depend on the local party for success at the polls. Election results are more likely to be a function of the success of the party at the national level. A landslide in a national election may have important consequences in the next local election. Newton's (1974) observation of English elections holds true for Denmark: "What determines the election success of any given local party and its candidates is not their particular record in community politics but the record of their national party in national politics" (p. 67).

In Denmark, interest groups at the local level are more likely to gain influence through either the formal channels of the national political parties or national professional associations. Influence on local leaders, therefore, tends to be relatively predictable and flows down from the top of the system. The electoral system discussed earlier tends to protect leaders from the shifting demands of local concerns and allows them greater freedom in considering long-term decisions based on interest-group consultation and comprehensive planning. These leaders are most constrained by their need to make their decisions conform to the goals of national parties rather than various local constituencies. As a result, when a municipality is feeling the effects of fiscal stress, the actions of a leader are more likely to correspond to the directions taken by his or her political party. Because the primary focus is on the system, where the rewards for appropriate decisions originate, the Danish political leader can look upon local constituencies as necessary collaborators in developing and carrying out policies consistent with national goals.

Responses to fiscal stress by Danish political leaders fall within a relatively narrow range. There is little possibility or benefit in trying to transfer responsibility to another level of government or other actors because of the comprehensive nature of the municipal delivery system. The structure mediates against transfer either governmentally or to individuals since they are universally protected against the loss of benefits. The possibility exists for better management and innovation in service delivery. However, the most likely response is to seek new sources of revenue, primarily by increasing tax rates. Since local governments have the discretion to do this and since resistance to the practice tends to be on an individual rather than a group basis, Danish political leaders can often meet fiscal stress by increasing local revenues.

Political leaders and administrators of local governments in the United States remain in power as long as they are able to respond to the needs and preferences of their constituents, particularly those who have organized and gained power. However, the fact that these interest groups can mobilize rapidly, around changing issues, and can directly influence the fiscal decisions of leaders has a tremendous effect on the way leaders behave. The major share of political activity at the local level takes place outside of the formal party structure either because of the design of nonpartisan reform or because of weak ties to state and national parties. Without the discipline of a formal structure, groups proliferate, further exacerbating the fragmentation of interests. Consultation prior to decisions is difficult because of the competitive nature of the many actors. In order to respond to the multiple demands of this fragmented set of constituencies, a political leader must be prepared to shift positions. More important, since a temporary coalition of these groups can elect or defeat leaders, they must be able to produce satisfactory, visible benefits in the short term. This places the focus of attention on the development of new policies and budget items rather than on the implementation of programs and the attainment of long-term benefits.[30] In this uneasy, dynamic environment, political leaders must adopt an entrepreneurial approach with a vast repertoire of responses to constituent demands and to environmental forces.

In times of fiscal stress, leaders in American local government tend to listen to the more powerful sectors of the community which have in recent years coalesced around issues of taxation. Responses, therefore, tend toward cutting expenditures by curtailing services, cutting taxes, and transferring responsibilities to other levels of government. User-fees have become an increasingly important source of local revenues. When federal assistance has been cut, most state and local governments have not replaced lost federal funds with own-source revenues, but have instead passed the cuts along to lower levels of government, private nonprofit organizations, or directly to individuals. Those who have been most affected by economic downturn are therefore most likely to be hit again by reductions in federal assistance. At the same time, some political leaders have used this opportunity to institute new practices that can lead to greater efficiency in the management of resources, to develop new means of leveraging public and private funds, and to create more efficient ways to provide services. Probably the least used response has been to raise revenues from existing tax sources or to find new sources of taxation.

CONCLUSIONS

Local governments in Denmark are consolidated and they provide a comprehensive, universal system of services. When fiscal stress strikes, its effects are muted by a set of legal and political mechanisms that ensure stability both for governments and for individuals. Political leaders have considerable freedom in developing policies and implementing programs that are consistent with national party goals, local planning, and the preference of citizens. They can assume tenure in their positions even if particular actions create opposition and protest. Because the weight of public preference has inclined toward maintaining or increasing the level of municipal services, political leaders are safe in responding to stress by generating additional revenues.

The emphasis in the incentive structure of Danish political leaders is to successfully carry out programs that reflect national political goals. They are able to respond rationally to environmental changes and are not required to make immediate concessions to various interest groups. Rewards come from successful administration and from party recognition. For the ambitious, upward mobility in the party ranks is the primary reward. The dynamics of power and change are best seen, even at the local level, by looking upward in the system. The local government system that has developed from these various factors tends to be relatively insulated from outside forces, stable and predictable, and characterized by incremental growth.

In the United States, local governments are marked by fragmentation in the responsibility, financing, and delivery of services. When fiscal stress strikes, especially when it is in part precipitated by major cuts in federal assistance, local governments are vulnerable to the full impact of the strain. Local leaders are constrained in their ability to act by legal mandates to provide services and by prohibitions on generating revenue. They are especially vulnerable to the emergence of strong, ad hoc groups centered around a particular issue that can play a major role in the leader's ability to be reelected. These groups usually operate outside the traditional political party channels and often have unusual access to the press. In the last few years they have often reflected a middle-class impatience with high government expenditures, especially those targeted toward the poor. Therefore, American political leaders faced with stress are far less likely than their Danish counterparts to respond by generating additional revenues. Instead, they will find a variety of other mechanisms including cuts in service levels, increased user-fees, and management innovation to bring their governments back into equilibrium.

For American political leaders, by necessity, reelection is a primary driver in their incentive structure. In order to be reelected, they must develop an array of short-term responses to various, sometimes conflicting and usually competitive, interest groups. Long-range planning and concern with program implementation do not fit comfortably into this entrepreneurial approach. Although in some American cities political parties are still a strong factor in local-level decisions, for the most part loyalty to party platforms is not a major determiner in decision making. Attention of leaders is focused downward to the dynamic shifts of power among the constituents who elect them. The local government system in the United States can be seen in uneasy relationship with other competing levels of government, vulnerable to various environmental forces but with the capacity to adapt quickly to the effects of these forces through informal, often ad hoc, mechanisms.

In the broadest terms, Denmark has built a governmental system that protects both its own structures and the individuals who live within those structures. The cost, however, may appear in a certain stagnation and inability to adapt to new forces. In the United States, however, the system is unprotected and vulnerable, but extremely adaptive. The cost, in this case, may be paid by the individuals who suffer from the full force of social and economic forces while the system is in the midst of change.

The level of governmental intervention is higher in Denmark than in the United States but may well be less obtrusive. Danish government takes greater initiative in planning the collective life of citizens and provides a higher level of protection against threat. These government actions may be less intrusive because citizens have consented that government should ensure certain qualities, particularly that of equity. Governmental intervention appears at a lower level in the United States, allowing more leeway for individual action and greater exposure to risk. However, government intervention may be more marked and perhaps more obtrusive when it does come.

We have tried to describe, too briefly, certain factors that affect the way local governments experience and respond to fiscal stress. In the United States, the strong strain of individual rights creates structures based on competition and entrepreneurship. This assertion can be traced from the country's constitution, across its expanding frontier, and through its uneasy history of federalism. In Denmark the values of equity and collective responsibility permeate the structures of government and shape its policies.

NOTES

1. Advisory Commission on Intergovernmental Relations, *State and Local Roles in the Federal System* (Washington, D.C., 1982).

2. The unit of analysis is "local government" both in Denmark and in the United States. By local government we mean not only all-purpose governments; rather, we are extending the definition, by focusing on a total system (1) by which public services are provided to a local community, (2) that is governed by (one or more) democratic structures controlled by the local citizenry, and (3) whose revenues stem mainly from taxes or from grants from other levels of government. In the United States this could mean a composite of governmental units such as a county government, a city government with a separate but coterminous school district, and a number of special-purpose governmental or quasi-governmental structures that carry out services for that community. In Denmark local government comprises counties and municipalities.

3. For almost similar definitions, see Schick (1980) and Levine's discussion in the introduction to Levine (1980). The working definition presented is explicit on two points. First, fiscal stress is a condition imposed on a political system by the environment. (This condition is, however, not unaffected by the actions taken by the political system previously.) Second, the definition emphasizes both *resources* and *demands* as factors that may independently or simultaneously affect the degree of fiscal stress.

4. See, for example, Levine, Rubin, and Wolohojian (1981); Clark and Ferguson (1983); Rubin (1982); Bahl (1978); Nathan and Adams (1976); Mouritzen (1983b, 1984); Clark et al. (1976); Nathan and Doolittle (1983); Levine and Rubin (1980); Howell and Stamm (1979); and Burchell and Listokin (1981).

5. See references in the preceding note and Wolman and Davis (1980); Mouritzen (1985); and Brink and Guss (1982).

6. The number of counties was also reduced from 24 to 14.

7. Local state agencies handle police, vocational training, job placement, and the administration of unemployment cash benefits.

8. For a discussion of federalism, see Reagan (1972) and the ACIR's 11-volume series, *The Federal Role in the Federal System: The Dynamics of Growth*, 1980, and *The Federal Influence on State and Local Roles in the Federal System*, 1982.

9. Jane F. Roberts, "Intergovernmental Perspectives," Advisory Commission on Intergovernmental Relations (Washington, D.C., 1984), p. 22.

10. We refer to the municipalities in order to illustrate the general point. In the counties, the largest share of the work force is employed in the hospitals and certain social institutions.

11. The number of employees in a Danish municipality is by American standards very large. One illustrative example is that some of the largest organizations found in Denmark are the social and health departments in the large cities.

12. Public assistance (*kintanthjealp*) is the "lowest" part of the welfare net in Denmark. It is administered by the municipalities which have a minimal (although some) degree of autonomy with respect to eligibility standards, amount of cash benefits, and so on. The program costs are reimbursed at the 50 percent level by the central government (open-ended). The importance of the program is highlighted by the fact that approximately 600,000 citizens— or 12 percent of the population— (including children who are counted if their parents receive benefits) received public assistance in 1982.

13. Municipal day care now covers around 45 percent of children between birth and six years. It is financed via general revenues, state reimbursements, and fees, which each account for approximately one-third of the costs.

14. Advisory Commission on Intergovernmental Relations, *Significant Features of Fiscal Federalism* (Washington, D.C., 1984), p. 127.

15. There is wide variation in the United States with New York City, for instance, providing welfare, public education, public health services, and hospitals, while the city of Los Angeles provides almost none of these (Clark and Ferguson 1981).

16. See Stephens (1974: 50–51) for a discussion of this fact.

17. See the description of the role of intergovernmental grants in affecting the causes and responses to fiscal stress in Denmark and the United States in Mouritzen and Narver (1984). The paper discusses the critical role of the Danish intergovernmental grant as a means of triggering assistance during periods of stress and equalizing revenues for local governments with different sources of income and different needs. The intergovernmental grant is a device of the central government to carry out a national economic policy.

18. Denmark: Kommunal Budgetredegorelse, 1983.

19. Borrowing accounted for 1 percent of total revenues in 1982. It is controlled by the central government, and it has been restricted to the financing of certain specific purposes. It is, however, difficult to assert the effects of these restrictions. It is a matter of fact that municipalities that have a high rate of taxation and that have experienced increased rates of taxation have a relatively high debt. While the lowest quartile (in terms of taxation) paid 50 kr. per capita in interest on the principal on debt, the figure for the high quartile was 367 kr. per capita in 1983 (cf. Mouritzen 1985: Table 3).

20. Advisory Commission on Intergovernmental Relations, *Significant Features of Fiscal Federalism* (Washington, D.C., 1982–1983).

21. Other factors affect the visibility of property taxes such as the frequency of assessments and full-disclosure provisions.

22. This argument has an interesting parallel in a recent U.S. study of the voter response to three tax limitation proposals in Michigan. Freiman and Grasso (1982) observe that the most drastic tax limitation proposal would cut property taxes substantially. "However, the further actions necessitated by this cut were left unspecified. Substantial spending cuts might have resulted, but it was not clear in which programs" (p. 59). They see the degree of *uncertainty* as to the effects of tax limitation as a major determinant of voting behavior.

23. One exception, however, is an initiative clause which may come into effect if a council wants to close down a school.

24. An insider from the Social Democratic Party revealed a few years ago that the chief union leader of the biggest plant in one of Denmark's big cities went to the mayor and demanded that taxes be frozen because of the increasing pressure on the take-home pay of his union's membership. For several years following this incident the city did not increase personal income taxes.

25. Jane F. Roberts, "States and Localities in 1983: Recession, Reform, Renewal," *Intergovernmental Perspectives* (ACIR: Winter 1984), p. 12.

26. The chief administrators in 40 municipalities were asked about the cleavage lines in a 1982 survey. While 80 percent found the partisan dimension to be important, only 23 percent reported important splits based on territorial affiliation of councilors (cf. Dilling Hansen 1983: 203).

27. Similar hypotheses have been formulated by Newton (1974: 65) and Levine, Perry and Demarco (1977: 173).

28. Major interests tend to be coopted due to a number of features of the decision-making system: relatively large councils, many parties, institutionalized laymen, consultatory committees, and highly institutionalized hearings procedures for local government employees. Cooptation creates a relatively large but (once coopted) relatively closed policymaking system. While external interest groups demand publicly, coopted interests take and give in secret.

29. While 76 percent of the local political elite indicated that they had proposed amendments to the budget within their party group in the most recent budgetary period (1981), the low extent of party splits is suggested by the fact that more than 50 percent indicated that

their party was split only two or fewer times a year on issues of appropriations (a frequent item).

30. See Gustaffson, Hargrove, and Elmore (1984) for their discussion.

REFERENCES

Administrationsdepartementet. 1982. *Statslige forskrifter for kommunernes virksomhed*. Delredegørelse om regelforenkling. København.

Bahl, R. 1984. *Financing State and Local Government in the 1980s*. New York: Oxford University Press.

Bahl, R., ed. 1978. *The Fiscal Outlook for Cities: Implications of a National Urban Policy*. Syracuse: Syracuse University Press.

———. 1981. *Urban Government Finance: Emerging Trends*. London: Sage.

Brink, D. R., and M. B. Guss. 1982. *Cutback Management in Local Government: A Selective, Annotated Bibliography*. Chicago: CPL Bibliographies.

Burchell, R. W., and D. Listokin, eds. 1981. *Cities under Stress: The Fiscal Crises of Urban America*. New Brunswick: Center for Urban Policy Research, Rutgers University.

Clark, T. N., and L. C. Ferguson. 1981. "Fiscal Strain and American Cities: Six Basic Processes." In K. Newton, ed., *Urban Political Economy*. London: Frances Pinter.

———. 1983. *City Money: Political Processes, Fiscal Strain and Retrenchment*. New York: Columbia University Press.

Clark, T. N., I. S. Rubin, L. C. Pettler, and E. Zimmerman. 1977. *How Many New Yorks? The New York Fiscal Crises in Comparative Perspective*. Chicago: University of Chicago Press.

Courant, P. N., E. M. Gramlich, and D. L. Rubinfeld. 1980. "Why Voters Support Tax Limitation Amendments: The Michigan Case," *National Tax Review* 33.

Dilling Hansen, M. 1983. *Marginaler paa kommunaldirektorskema*. Rapport Nr. 17, Statslig styring, lokalsamfund og kommunalpolitik. Odense: Institut for Offentlig okonomi og politik, Odense Universitet.

Dommel, P. R. 1974. *The Politics of Revenue Sharing*. Bloomington: Indiana University Press.

Freiman, M. P., and P. G. Grasso. 1982. "Budget Impact and Voter Response to Tax Limitation Referenda," *Public Finance Quarterly* 10: 49–66.

Friedland, R., and H. Wong. 1983. "Congressional Politics, Federal Grants and Local Needs: Who Gets What and Why?" In A. M. Sbragia, *The Municipal Money Chase: The Politics of Local Government Finance*. Boulder, Colo.: Westview Press.

Goetz, C. J. 1977. "Fiscal Illusion in State and Local Finance." In Borcherding, ed., *Budgets and Bureaucrats: The Sources of Government Growth*. Durham: Duke University Press.

Gustafsson, G., E. Hargrove, and R. F. Elmore. 1983. "Comparing Implementation Processes in Sweden and the United States." Unpublished paper, Institute for Public Policy and Management, University of Washington.

Howell, J. M., and C. F. Stamm. 1979. *Urban Fiscal Stress: A Comparative Analysis of 66 U.S. Cities*. Boston: Lexington Books.

Kristensen, O. P. 1980. "The Logic of Political-Bureaucratic Decision-Making as a Cause of Governmental Growth," *European Journal of Political Science* 8: 249–264.

———. 1983. *Om privatisering*. København.

Levine, C. H., and I. Rubin, eds. 1980. "Fiscal Stress and Public Policy." *Sage Yearbooks in Politics and Public Policy*, vol. 9. London: Sage.

Levine, C. H., ed. 1980. *Managing Fiscal Stress: The Crises in the Public Sector*. New Jersey: Chatham House.

Levine, C. H., I. S. Rubin, and G. C. Wolohojian. 1981. *The Politics of Retrenchment: How Local Governments Manage Fiscal Stress*. London: Sage.

Levine, C. H., J. L. Perry, and J. J. Demarco. 1977. "Collective Bargaining in Municipal Governments: An Interorganizational Perspective." In C. H. Levine, ed., *Managing Human Resources: A Challenge to Urban Governments*. London: Sage.

MacManus, S. A. 1978. *Revenue Patterns in U.S. Cities and Suburbs: A Comparative Analysis*. New York: Praeger.

———. 1983. "State Government: The Overseer of Municipal Finance." In A. M. Sbragia, ed., *The Municipal Money Chase: The Politics of Local Government Finance*. Boulder: Westview Press.

Markusen, A. R., A. Saxanian, and M. A. Weiss. 1981. "Who Benefits from Intergovernmental Transfers." In R. W. Burchell and D. Listokin, eds., *Cities under Stress: The Fiscal Crises of Urban America*. New Brunswick: Center for Urban Policy Research, Rutgers University.

Mouritzen, P. E. 1983a. "The Resource Squeese in Danish Local Government," Report No. 25. *Central Control, Local Communities and Local Politics*. Odense: Institute for Public Finance and Policy, University of Odense.

———. 1983b. "Consequences of Fiscal Strain," Report No. 19. *Central Control, Local Communities and Local Politics*. Odense: Institute for Public Finance and Policy, University of Odense.

———. 1984b. "Kommunerne og den finansielle klemme." In Skovsgaard, ed., *Kommunernes servicepolitik. Fra udbygning til omstilling*. København: Samfundsvidenskabeligt Forlag.

———. 1985. "Local Resource Allocation: Partisan Politics or Sector Politics?" In T. N. Clark, ed., *Research in Urban Policy*, vol. 1.

Mouritzen, P. E., and B. J. Narver. 1984. "Fiscal Stress: Comparisons of Danish and American Local Governments." Paper presented at the Mid-Continent Regional Science Association Meeting, Chicago, May.

Nathan, R. P. 1983. "State and Local Governments under Federal Grants," *Political Science Quarterly* 98: 47–57.

Nathan, R. P., and C. Adams. 1976. "Understanding Central City Hardship," *Political Science Quarterly* 91.

Nathan, R. P., and F. C. Doolittle. 1983. *The Consequences of Cuts: The Effects of the Reagan Domestic Program on State and Local Governments*. Princeton: Urban and Regional Research Center, Princeton University.

Newton, K. 1974. "Community Decision Makers and Community Decision-Making in England and the United States." In T. N. Clark, ed., *Comparative Community Politics*. New York: Wiley & Sons.

Odden, A. 1984. *Education Finance in the States: 1984*. Denver: Education Finance Center.

Reagan, M. D. 1972. *The New Federalism*. New York: Oxford University Press.

Roberts, J. F. 1984. *Significant Features of Fiscal Federalism*. Washington: Advisory Commission on Intergovernmental Relations.

Rubin, I. S. 1982. *Running in the Red: The Political Dynamics of Urban Fiscal Stress*. Albany: State University of New York Press.

Schick, A. 1980. "Budgetary Adaptations to Resource Scarcity." In C. H. Levine and I. Rubin, eds., *Fiscal Stress and Public Policy*. Sage Yearbooks in Politics and Public Policy 9. London: Sage.

Shannon, J., and B. Wallin. 1981. "Fiscal Imbalance within the Federal System: The Problem of Renewing Revenue Sharing." In R. W. Burchell and D. Listokin, eds., *Cities under Stress: The Fiscal Crises of Urban America*. New Brunswick: Center for Urban Policy Research, Rutgers University.

Stephens, G. R. 1974. "State Centralization and the Erosion of Local Autonomy," *Journal of Politics* 36: 44–76.

Walzer, N. 1985. "Fiscal Austerity in Mid-Size Cities: Preliminary Findings." In T. N. Clark, ed., *Research in Urban Policy*, vol. 1.

Wolman, H. 1982. "Local Autonomy and Intergovernmental Finance in Britain and the United States." In Rose and Page, eds., *Fiscal Stress in Cities*. Cambridge: Cambridge University Press.

Wolman, H., and B. Davis. 1980. "Local Government Strategies to Cope with Fiscal Pressure." In C. H. Levine and I. Rubin, eds., *Fiscal Stress and Public Policy*. Sage Yearbooks in Politics and Public Policy 9. London: Sage.

SOCIALISM WITHOUT WELFARE? PRELIMINARY ANALYSIS OF POPULAR AND ELITE PREFERENCES ABOUT PUBLIC SPENDING IN YUGOSLAV COMMUNES

Peter Jambrek

ABSTRACT

This paper summarizes surveys of Yugoslav citizens that suggest they share many concerns of citizens in other countries: Government services are seen as deteriorating, but there is resistance to higher taxes, and ambivalence about how to deliver services more effectively.

Groups supporting government growth have been active for some years. A new block of groups has emerged more recently that is more fiscally cautious.

POLITICAL CULTURE

"The future role of government is clearly at stake. The 1960s prosperity and optimism seem distant; what to preserve under austerity is the more common concern. . . . Cities provide an opportunity to consider general ideas about growth of government and support for the welfare state" (Clark and Ferguson 1983:1). Although this statement refers to American cities in the 1970s and early 1980s, it also reflects public concerns in Yugoslav communes. And even if the observation no longer fully applies to the

Research in Urban Policy, Vol. 2, pages 219–226.

ISBN: 0-89232-534-8

United States in light of recent economic improvements, recovery of the Yugoslav economy is not predicted—even by her notoriously over-optimistic planners.

In Yugoslavia and most other socialist countries of Eastern Europe, the Soviet Union included, the issue of the scope of government versus the private sector and of central versus subnational levels of government has been a part of the political process from the beginning of the revolutionary establishment. Lenin's New Economic Policy and Stalin's bureaucratization, China's Cultural Revolution and recent modernization, the Yugoslav pattern of radical nationalization and subsequent decentralization are better-known examples of swings of the pendulum. Hungary, Poland, and Czechoslovakia also experimented with economic reforms, which were either self-aborted (Poland) or mortified by the Soviet Union.

This is not the place to examine reformist and counterreformist cycles across socialist states. We merely note that they occur regularly, and that they differentiate "liberals" and "conservatives," the two camps labeled in almost perfect assymetry to their Western, and especially American, counterparts. If the status quo is a petrified revolution, its defenders may be called "revolutionaries" or "conservatives" interchangeably, while the reformists are either "counterrevolutionaries" when persecuted or "liberals" when neutralized by softer, more political techniques.

DEPRIVATION AND STRAIN

In Yugoslavia, the 1960s represented the reformist cycle. The economy gained moderate autonomy, managers gained some political power, the state was federalized, and communes were granted some degree of self-government. In the 1970s the trend was reversed: Bureaucrats outmaneuvered technocrats, the federal government regained its grip, and Marxist class struggle and revolution were again the orthodoxy.

In the early 1980s, the reformist cycle reemerged, this time influenced by new developments. In the 1970s, economic growth was financed entirely by international loans, and 5–10% of public and private consumption was based on foreign accumulation. Around 1980, the country reached the limits of her solvency. At present, consumption is strained by several mutually reinforcing factors.

First, during the 1970s, old inefficiencies and bureaucratic privileges were upheld and new ones introduced: Political and public service bureaucracies grew and became further entrenched. Investment in the infrastructure of public services expanded their operative costs. Inefficient, politically motivated, or simply miscalculated investments contributed to negative growth. Only in 1984, when interest rates seem to be targeting the inflation

Table 1. Welfare under Strain: 1978–1983

"Is life in the listed areas now better, the same, or worse than it was five years ago?"

Life area	*Year of Survey*	*Better*	*Same*	*Worse*	*Don't Know*
Housing	1978	51.3	29.2	17.4	2.1
	1980	39.4	19.4	28.9	12.3
	1981	17.6	11.6	75.0	13.7
	1983	13.1	10.3	63.7	13.0
Employment	1978	54.8	27.6	15.9	1.7
	1980	47.3	18.3	27.7	6.7
	1981	11.8	12.1	68.4	7.8
	1983	3.0	7.5	84.4	5.1
Education	1978	86.7	10.4	1.9	1.0
	1980	83.9	7.8	3.4	4.8
	1981	57.2	23.5	12.7	6.5
	1983	38.6	31.2	22.3	8.0
Child care	1978	59.4	30.0	8.7	1.8
	1980	54.1	27.1	11.7	7.1
	1981	30.7	31.2	29.2	8.9
	1983	15.1	22.1	58.0	4.9

Source. Slovenia javno mnenje 1983.
N = 2,067.

rate, is capital slowly losing its curious status as the cheapest and best available commodity. Second, international loans, credit, and assistance are no longer available on the previous scale. And third, interest on foreign debt is being paid, diverting a sizable part of domestic consumption into exports.

These trends are reflected in opinion surveys conducted in Slovenia, an industrially developed federal unit in the Northwest. Some results for the transitional period from 1978 to 1983 are shown in Table 1. Dividing the sample into residents of Ljubljana (the largest city, approximately 300,000) and the rest of the surveyed population of Slovenia, we found that Ljubljana residents feel deprived not only relative to the previous five-year period (characteristic of all population blocs in Slovenia) but also compared with people in other regions of the republic (rural and urban alike). The difference is 18% in housing, confirming the assumption that city residents are harder hit than others.

AUSTERITY AND RETRENCHMENT

Let us further inspect how people react to deprivation and strain by examining opinions on acceptable versus unacceptable austerity measures.

Table 2. Attitude Formation on Austerity Measures: 1975–1983

"What kind of sacrifices and efforts are, and which are not, acceptable to help recover the Yugoslav economy?"

Austerity Measure	*Year of Survey*	*Acceptable*	*Unacceptable*	*Don't Know*
Lower incomes	1975	39.0	54.0	7.0
	1980	48.9	42.4	8.7
	1981	33.5	51.2	15.3
	1983	27.6	64.2	8.1
Spend less on education, health, and culture	1975	14.3	81.3	4.4
	1980	24.1	70.5	5.5
	1981	25.1	64.1	10.8
	1983	29.7	62.5	7.8
Spend less on new industrial construction	1975	45.9	46.2	7.9
	1980	50.4	40.7	8.9
	1981	55.9	27.1	17.0
	1983	55.4	32.5	12.1

Source. Slovenia javno mnenje 1983.
N = 2,067.

Table 2 shows that public support for welfare and industrial construction eroded over the last eight years, as shown by the increasing acceptability of austerity measures in those areas. The question did not specify, however, *who* should spend less on welfare functions: the government, public institutions, or private citizens.

The survey also showed that, regarding federal budget expenditures, half of respondents (50.9%) prefer reductions across all main areas of expenditure (defense, administration, foreign service, aid to underdeveloped regions, and pension funds for war veterans); a meager 4% alloted more. The remainder preferred no changes or could not decide. Correspondingly, when asked whether increasing federal sales tax was acceptable, 63.3% said no, 18.2% said yes, and 18.5% did not know.

Table 3 shows an indicator of support for private or public provision of social services for 1968, 1970, 1978, and 1983. A lack of support for private provision seems stable over the past 15 years. Somewhat surprisingly, however, fewer people support more public spending across all areas, and an increasingly higher proportion prefer no change. Thus, Table 3 does not indicate that attitudes are turning away from the welfare state and in the direction of private provision of social goods, but reflects instead a realistic assessment that less of everything will be available.

Table 3. Attitude Change about Public versus Private Provision of Social Services: 1968–1983

"Which services should to a larger degree than now be paid for by the citizens themselves, and which should be provided by public finds without fee or at a lower price?"

Public Service	*Year of Survey*	*More by Private Citizens*	*More by Public Funds*	*No Changes*	*Don't Know*
Health	1968	4.1	68.2	22.9	4.8
	1970	6.5	54.7	33.2	5.6
	1978	4.6	52.4	40.3	2.7
	1983	6.4	48.3	39.7	5.6
Education	1968	7.8	58.7	22.5	11.0
	1970	5.2	63.0	23.2	8.6
	1978	6.2	60.6	28.9	4.3
	1983	7.3	40.7	44.3	7.9
Child care	1968	15.2	50.8	21.9	12.2
	1970	17.6	54.8	18.6	9.0
	1978	10.1	56.4	26.9	6.6
	1983	8.7	47.2	35.3	8.9
Municipal services	1968	10.9	52.9	22.5	13.7
	1970	10.9	53.7	24.6	10.8
	1978	10.4	49.6	33.0	7.0
	1983	10.8	38.7	40.5	10.5
Housing	1968	25.4	39.5	23.6	11.5
	1970	28.4	40.5	21.8	9.3
	1978	19.7	48.4	26.4	5.6
	1983	21.2	38.9	27.9	11.9

Source. Slovenia javno mnenje 1983.
N = 2.067.

POLITICAL PROCESSES

In this section, we discuss preliminary results of a study of decisional processes in the 65 Slovenia communes, collected in an elite survey conducted in mid–1984. Responses below are from 10 top public officials in Ljubljana. They assessed sources of financial strain in the city and communes, strategies (preferred and actually employed) for reducing strain, attitudes of local and national decision makers toward public spending and their relative power, and aspects of local political culture.

When asked "What are the main sources of problems in providing funds for fiscal consumption and social services in your commune?" respondents ranked 12 items. The highest-ranked cluster combined low growth of the economy, foreign debt, and inflation and low growth of personal earnings. The second-ranked cluster included excessive demands for fiscal resources and social services. Listed third were pressures from employees of government, the courts, and social service organizations to increase salaries. Low taxes and increased demand for additional funds for social services received much less attention.

Among the 14 strategies used to reduce financial problems, the following were considered most important: seek citizens' contribution for nonbusiness investments, reduce noneconomic investments, give priority to specific programs, coordinate public service bureaucracies; and improve the organization and management of local administration. The following strategies were considered least effective: defer programs and payments, increase taxes, shift responsibilities from public-fund bureaucracies to local government, integrate local government bureaucracies, and reduce salaries of elected public officials.

It seems that, at least according to public officials in Ljubljana, the causes of fiscal strain are either out of local control (zero growth economy, foreign debt, inflation) or based in "excessive" spending of collective goods. This perception is matched by an orientation toward reducing strain by curtailing consumption of public goods or by instituting efficiency measures, but not by expanding public resources. Still, reducing salaries of public officials and employees of social service institutions—despite a preference for retrenchment in other areas—received only a low priority.

When asked to rank 18 local decision makers according to whether they prefer to increase, decrease, or maintain expenditures, the respondents considered public funds for social services, public service institutions and associations, and local administration to be pro-spending. (See Table 4.) All others were considered to favor retrenchment, especially private farmers, small businessmen, managers, the chamber of associated labor of the communal assembly, and all four political organizations (League of Communists, Socialist Alliance, Veterans' Association, and Youth Organization).

The main pro-spending actors are either active in the political process (public service funds) or influential (social service organizations). The local administration shares the pro-spending attitudes but seems to be an outsider; although moderately active, it has little influence. The executive council, the focus of local decision making, seems to occupy a position between pro-spending and retrenchment. The executive council is a coalition of business interests (private and public) and political organizations.

Among the retrenchment-oriented, the sociopolitical chamber of the Communal Assembly and the communal committees of the League of Communists and the trade unions are influential but less active in local

Table 4. Decision Makers Ranked According to Their Spending Preferences, Influence, and Activity

"Estimate for the below-listed local decision-making subjects (a) whether he/she prefers expenditures for fiscal consumption and social services to be lowered, stay the same, or be increased; (b) how active the subject is in pursuing his/her spending preference; and (c) how much influence he/she exerts upon decisions about the level of expenditures for general and collective consumption."

Subject	*Rank*		
	Pro-Spending Preference	*Activity*	*Influence*
Public service funds	1	3	6–9
Social service organizations	2	7–9	1–2
Voluntary organizations	3	17–18	16–18
Local government administration	4	7–9	12–13
Executive council of the Communal Assembly	5–6	2	1–2
Banks	5–6	2	1–2
Chamber of local communities of the Communal Assembly	7	11–12	11
Government at the national level	8	1	6–9
Sociopolitical chamber of the Communal Assembly	9–10	7–9	3–5
Youth organizations in the commune	9–10	14	16–18
Chamber of the associated labor of the Communal Assembly	11	11–12	12–13
Communal committee of the League of Communists	12–15	4–5	3–5
Communal conference of Socialist Alliance	12–15	4–5	6–9
Communal committee of Veterans' Association	12–15	10	10
Private craftsmen	12–15	15–16	15
Communal committee of the trade unions	16–18	6	3–5
Representatives of business organizations	16–18	13	6–9
Private farmers	16–18	17–18	15

decision making. Business representatives have medium influence, and the private sector (farmers and craftsmen) must be considered largely outside the political process.

The national government occupies the middle ground on spending attitudes and influence. It is an active mediator, setting the general course and making its power felt through the local executive council. The latter, presumably under the pressure of the local pro-spending actors, appears somewhat more pro-spending.

SUMMARY

We have presented an overview of finance-related political processes in Yugoslav communes. We identified a bloc of pro-spending actors composed of public service funds, social service organizations, and local administration, which also represents a formidable group. Next, we identified the retrenchment-oriented bloc of business interests and sociopolitical organizations (a new phenomenon). The political component (especially the League of Communists, the trade unions, and the political chamber of the local assembly) are also at the top of the local power structure.

Decisions are shaped by the national government setting the general policies and by the local executive council. Both actors are clearly conservative; that is, they support the status quo. Local government appears a bit more pro-spending than the national and is also more influential.

This observation fits our introductory characterization of the political culture of the 1980s in Yugoslavia: a cautious reformist orientation, with political actors approaching the interests of economic institutions without delegating power to them. The motives are obvious: Political survival depends on economic recovery. Outcomes, however, are dubious. Some observers maintain that the present reform has even slimmer chances than any previously introduced—and never completed.

REFERENCES

"Slovensko javno mnenje 1983" ("Slovenian Public Opinion 1983"). 1983. Ljubljana: Raziskovalni institut FSPN, Univerza Edvarda Kardelja, June. Mimeographed research report.

Terry N. Clark and Lorna Crowley Ferguson. 1983. *City Money: Political Processes, Fiscal Strain and Retrenchment Policies*. New York: Columbia University Press.

COMMENTARY:
INSTITUTIONAL DIFFERENCES

Edward C. Page

Ultimately, I suppose that the bad shape of national economies and their changing spatial constitution can be held responsible for urban fiscal stress. The questions addressed by Lightbody, Jambrek, and Mouritzen and Narver are concerned with how these feed through the political system to produce the scale and nature of austerity in urban policies and the reaction to this among citizens and policymakers.

Lightbody's interesting account of organizational changes in Edmonton sets out some rather casual links between reorganization and fiscal austerity. However, it is not clear from his research so far how strong these links are. At least we need to know how far the reforms he writes of were aimed at producing substantial savings and how far they have produced them. As Lightbody himself recognizes, the record of organizational change's helping produce desired substantive outcomes is a poor one.

Moving away from possible prescriptions, Jambrek's discussion of extensive surveys in Slovenia offers some tantalizing findings about the scale of austerity and how it comes about. The perceptions among the survey respondents have changed remarkably over a five-year period. In 1978,

Research in Urban Policy, Vol. 2, pages 227–230.

ISBN: 0-89232-534-8

between 2 and 17 percent of respondents felt they were worse off in housing, employment, education, and child care than they were five years previously. By 1983 this had increased to 22 percent for education, 58 percent for child care, 64 percent for housing, and 84 percent for employment. What have been the causes, in terms of actual changed services, of this massive shift in perceptions about life-styles? If the services have been as hard-hit as the perceptions imply, then how has such austerity arisen? Some of the answers are suggested by Jambrek's reference to the different groups involved in urban service decisions—some groups and institutions favor increased spending while others do not have such a commitment. Above all, in the brief discussion of the changes in the climate of government between the 1970s and 1980s, he suggests that in the 1970s "bureaucrats outmaneuvred technocrats" although this was reversed in the 1980s. This point might be crucial in understanding the causes of stress. Moreover, it offers an interesting comparison with many other nations in which the assumption is frequently made that bureaucrats and technocrats are virtually identical, or at least have identical interests, as far as the growth of government services is concerned. Even if one does not accept the "budget maximizing" assumptions about bureaucratic behavior in public choice theory, this similarity of interests between technocrats, service professionals, and bureaucrats is made explicit in many of the discussions of the "sectorization" of policymaking, such as Samuel Beer's concept of "professional-bureaucratic complexes" in the United States.

It is doubtful, however, whether either of these questions—the scale of retrenchment in different services and the conflicts within and between governmental institutions—can be addressed through survey research. On this point, one might query the validity of the question on which Table 4 is based. It is not only that it relies upon a reputational approach (and, it appears, on the reputations held by a mass sample), but the question appears to demand from its respondents a level of inside knowledge about diverse institutions that cannot usually be presumed to exist. The survey analysis has pointed to some important aspects of fiscal austerity that non-survey-based evidence, above all relating to institutional structures, relationships, and behavior, must elaborate and explain.

Mouritzen and Narver explicitly look at the impact of such institutional structures on the causes of austerity and reactions to it. Broadly speaking, they argue that vulnerability and responses to fiscal stress result from incentive structures created by institutional arrangements. Largely these institutional arrangements refer to local government structures, the system of urban finance, and the party system. While the mechanisms might appear to create such incentive structures in Denmark and the United States, do the hypothesized relationships between institutions and incentive structures work in a wider comparative context?

Consolidation is their first major institutional difference affecting incentive structures. Slightly confusingly, the term includes the degree to which local governments are ad hoc or ad omniam authorities with the territorial dimensions of local government units. The authors propose that local government systems dominated by ad omniam authorities that provide most services are likely to have less austerity. It is not altogether apparent why this should be the case—indeed, it is not altogether apparent that it *is* the case. In Britain, local government has suffered from greater levels of austerity than France despite the fact that France's proportion of public spending channeled through local government authorities is about one-third that of Britain's. Moreover, a counterhypothesis might be just as plausible: when local governments do more, they spend more, and the pay-off for a national government's cutting their spending is greater.

On the second institutional difference, the visibility of tax structures, Mouritzen and Narver appear to be arguing that where there is a direct link between individual services and taxation, there is less support—or less powerful support—for local spending. Again, this argument could profit from a more systematic exposition of the mechanisms involved. However, it would be equally plausible to argue that particular services can justify their existence more easily than can local government as a whole. Wildavsky's dictum, "Each part of public spending is wanted, only the whole is unwanted," suggests that the reverse effect might equally be expected. It is easier to justify spending on schools or public utilities in particular than on "local government" services in the abstract.

I think that the third institutional difference—opportunities for interest group activity—is probably the most crucial and probably might dwarf the other differences discussed in the paper. In the United States there are fewer routine opportunities for powerful, often fiscally conservative, groups to shape urban fiscal decisions: The points of access to such decisions are many in the United States (Washington, state capitols, and city halls), whereas the national as well as the local budgetary process in Denmark as in other European states is far more closed. Moreover, the closed nature of the systems is reinforced by party cohesion in national legislatures in Europe (Mouritzen and Narver's fourth institutional difference), and it is probably this, rather than the rewards systems that emerge from party structures, that accounts for the influence of party structure on fiscal austerity. Party cohesion has, however, a centralizing rather than a fiscally liberal effect. In Britain, for example, it was party cohesion that helped stifle effective Labour Council opposition the austerity introduced under a Labour government in the late 1970s, and it is party cohesion that has allowed the Thatcher government to pursue some of its more radical policies aimed at curbing local spending such as "rate capping"—property tax limits that, in effect, limit spending levels.

Perhaps two further crucial institutional differences could also be brought into the Mouritzen and Narver approach. First, the most striking difference in the nature of urban fiscal austerity between the United States and many European nations is that in many European unitary states the central government tries to control local spending. In the United States the federal government does not—it appears to concentrate on the contribution that it makes to subnational governments through grants. To put it another way, in the United States urban fiscal austerity at the federal level is concerned with reducing federal spending; in states such as Denmark and Britain urban fiscal austerity is concerned with reducing local spending directly. Whether or not this is a characteristic distinction between unitary and federal states remains to be seen. However, it means that from the perspective of a national government, the urban austerity goals are different, cutting grants on one hand and control on the other. This opens the possibility that one set of goals (control) is more difficult to achieve and politically even messier than the other (cutting grants).

A second important difference not elaborated by Mouritzen and Narver is the impact of the federal system. One of the possible impacts on the question that they address derives from the fact that it is consistent with widely held views of constitutional legitimacy (admittedly rather conservative ones) that the federal government should give greater power to the states, this includes reducing state and local "dependence" on the federal government. In Britain, and I suspect Denmark too, despite the doctrine of parliamentary sovereignty, centralization and the erosion of local self-government cannot claim the same legitimacy. Members of Parliament of all parties, Conservatives included, have expressed severe reservations about the manner in which urban austerity has been pursued. Yet such is the nature of the British party system that Mrs. Thatcher does not have to worry for the moment about things like that.

COMMENTARY:
REACTIONS AGAINST BUREAUCRACY

Vincent Hoffmann-Martinot

These are three very different papers, originating as they do from four different countries: Canada, Denmark, the United States, and Yugoslavia. Some are more advanced in their research than others. Yet, all focus on one and the same problem: How do urban authorities react to austerity?

All the various local governments have suffered the "economic turmoil" of the seventies. In their very interesting comparative study, Poul Erik Mouritzen and Betty Jane Narver underline that in both Denmark and the United States, "the same general environmental forces . . . may create fiscal stress. In terms of revenue, a declining, weak, or unstable tax base is generally considered one of the most critical sources of strain." The period of austerity for Yugoslav communes studied by Peter Jambrek belongs to quite the same pattern—but in accepting fiscal austerity without any further debate, is there not a risk of disregarding what at first seemed obvious? In this respect, we must be grateful to Mouritzen and Narver for their discussion of "fiscal stress." It would have been an asset to their paper to assess even briefly the repercussions involved in the countries under survey (with a few national statistics).

Research in Urban Policy, Vol. 2, pages 231–233.

ISBN: 0-89232-534-8

As strategists, stakes and policies were taking shape; the "growing awareness" of a radical change in a socioeconomic context became widespread among the public. And this is a real prerequisite: Had it not been the case, Decore might have had to wait a long time before he could become Edmonton's mayor, as James Lightbody shows.

Jambrek shows clearly that the Slovene population grew increasingly conscious (from 1970 to 1983) of the extremely severe economic difficulties and the necessity to accept sacrifices and efforts in certain areas, while at the same time refusing, and very cautiously at that, to alter the mode of financing public services. Mouritzen and Narver start a very perceptive inquiry into the "fiscal illusion": how the average citizen perceives services and financing. Comparing local fiscal systems (less obvious in Denmark as the income tax is predominant and its revenues are shared among local governments, regions, and the state) and service structures (much more integrated with the Danes) clearly illustrates the greater visibility of services offered by American local governments. Citizens are more aware of the problems and are more easily mobilized. Lobbying efforts can thus have more impact.

Once there is consensus for minimal support, or even once citizens feel committed to a local budget policy adapted to austerity, this policy will truly come into effect when there is a "deliberate political determination." "Let's all tighten our belts still a little more, and financial equilibrium will be restored." Such is the new electoral watchword in many countries, on a national as well as a local level (such as in the French municipal elections in 1983).

Organizational changes called for to improve urban policy represent an opportunity to redefine the sharing of municipal powers and start a "new deal." For some years, there had been many recommendations from experts and auditors: The City of Edmonton should be modernized and growth limited. (After the boom of the thirties, there was a constant expansion of the economic activities and significant population increase.) But beyond a deep reshuffling to meet this purpose, the then-candidate and future mayor, Laurence Decore, also wanted to end the overwhelming administrative power of the Commission Board that had ruled the city for some 80 years. Would such an attempt have been successful in a period of prosperity, before the 1980s?

Lightbody describes at length the fall of the bureaucratic empire. The reader cannot but be sorry not to learn more about the history of the creation and reinforcement of this administrative oligarchy and more about interrelations with the municipal council. The little credit that city commissioners seem to have enjoyed with public opinion and the local press, together with the new mayor's strategic skill when he gradually introduced his own executives, are not quite enough not to set the outside observer thinking. Were the shortcomings of the commission board so patent that the municipality had to do away with it? Was it not, rather, a symbolic measure meant to be paid for better managing the city—as it belonged to other times and could not be adapted to the new challenges in a period of austerity. The comeback of policymakers is obvious in this Canadian city, because of the setback in the economic growth.

This very intriguing question of relationships and equilibrium between elected officials and civil servants is barely mentioned in the other papers. In this respect, Yugoslavia is rather a case apart as local administrators do not have much influence in the local budget decision-making process; in large measure, it seems to depend on central government policy.

As Jambrek's paper is preliminary to an in-depth study, we are given the opinions of only 10 municipal officers concerning (unfortunately nothing is said about their positions) the budget choices of various pressure groups. Nothing can be inferred about the general trend among Yugoslav or even Slovene communes, but we will be very anxious to hear about the new developments linking the present-day atmosphere favorable to reforms and the more conservative resistance to changes, economic turbulence, and evolution of municipal policies within the federal framework. Mouritzen and Narver oppose the leeway of political leaders in Denmark compared with those in the United States. Denmark has a "protected" political system where norms and political standards of—essentially—the liberals and social-democrats are imposed on the local militants and politicians, relatively distinct from the national sociopolitical conflicts and bargaining. By contrast, in American cities mayors first must adapt and innovate when faced with many and intense demands from organized groups, but political entrepreneurs have more room to maneuver as political affiliation is scarce. To prop up their comparisons, Mouritzen and Narver may tend to exaggerate differences between the two systems. Despite consensus on equity and collective responsibility in Denmark, are there not tensions within the Liberal Party concerning the virtues of total or partial privatization of public services, as is the case with liberals and conservatives in France and West Germany?

BIOGRAPHICAL SKETCHES OF THE CONTRIBUTORS

Lynn M. Appleton is an Assistant Professor in the Department of Sociology and Social Psychology, Florida Atlantic University, Boca Raton, Florida. Her current research is on the causes and consequences of urban growth; she is presently completing a case-study of growth in one of the fastest growing Florida counties.

Mark Baldassare is Associate Professor, Program in Social Ecology, University of California at Irvine. He is the Director of the Orange County Annual Survey, which was begun in 1982 to analyze changing public opinions about community problems and local policies. His interests are in the field of urban sociology with recent research including the determinants of local growth policies, earthquake policies, and fiscal strategies. He has published numerous books and articles in sociology including *The Growth Dilemma* (1981), *Cities and Urban Living* (1983), and the forthcoming *Trouble in Paradise: The Suburban Transformation in America*.

Harald Baldersheim completed an M.A. in political science at the University of Oslo, 1971, and Ph.D. at the London School of Economics and Political Science, 1977. He is Professor of Public Administration, University of Bergen, and Director of the Norwegian Institute for Urban and Regional Research, Oslo. He has published and/or edited several books on public administration and local-city government subjects between 1975 and 1984.

John Bolland is a Research Associate at the Institute for Research in Social Science at the University of Alabama. His previous research focusing on social networks in local communities has been published in *Power and Elites* (Fall 1984) and in *Social Networks* (forthcoming). Other articles dealing with political analysis are forthcoming in *Political Behavior* and *Political Methodology*.

Terry Nichols Clark is Professor of Sociology and Director of the Comparative Study of Community Decision-Making at the University of Chicago and the National Opinion Research Center. He has taught at Columbia, Harvard, Yale, and the Sorbonne; and has worked at the Brookings Institution, The Urban Institute, U.S. Conference of Mayors, and Department of Housing and Urban Development. He has published over 100 articles and books, mainly concerning urban decision making and public policy.

Richard L. Cole is Dean of the Institute of Urban Studies and Professor of Political Science and Urban Affairs at the University of Texas, Arlington. Professor Cole is the author of five books and over 50 articles dealing with various aspects of urban affairs and policy. His current research interests focus on urban policy making in an era of fiscal constraints.

Richard C. Feiock is an Assistant Professor at the University of Miami Florida, and is completing his Ph.D. in political science at the University of Kansas. He has published in the area of urban service delivery and has forthcoming articles on judicial policymaking in an urban context and strategic organizational adaptation by local chambers of commerce. He is the editor of *Mid-American Journal of Politics* and is currently engaged in a comparative analysis of the effectiveness of urban economic development policies and the impact of local politics and policies on urban economies.

Roger Friedland is currently working with Donald Palmer on a corporate geography of America. They are analyzing both the organizational structures of the urban system and its impacts on that system, as well as the geographical structure of the corporation and its impact on its behaviors. Their most recent article, "Park Place and Main Street: Business and the Urban Power Structure," appeared in the 1984 *Annual Review of Sociol-*

ogy. Friedland is also working on a book with Richard Hecht on religion and politics in the city of Jerusalem.

Keith E. Hamm is an Associate Professor of Political Science at Texas A&M University. His research interests are in the area of state legislative behavior and urban politics. His work has appeared in *Legislative Studies Quarterly*, *Western Political Quarterly*, and the *Journal of Politics*.

Brett W. Hawkins is Professor of Political Science at the University of Wisconsin, Milwaukee. He has taught at Washington and Lee University and the University of Georgia and is author of numerous books and articles on public policy. His current research concerns state intergovernmental aid and city fiscal strain.

Vincent Hoffmann-Martinot is a researcher at the Centre d'Etude et de Recherche sur la Vie Locale of the Institut d'Etudes Politiques (Bordeaux) and the Centre National de la Recherche Scientifique. His doctorate was on French and German local government. He is active in the French Fiscal Austerity and Urban Innovation Project.

Peter Jambrek was born in Ljubljana (Yugoslavia) in 1940. He studied at the Universities of Ljubljana and of Chicago. He received his Ph.D. degree (Sociology) in 1971 from the U. of Chicago. Presently he is professor of sociology at the Law Faculty of the University of Ljubljana. He also taught at the Universities of Zambia and of Virginia. His published studies in English include topics on political development, legal dispute treatment, community decision-making, human rights, and ecology of urban deprivation. He serves as vice-president of the RC 10 of the ISA, as member of the board of the Institute of sociology of law for Europe, and member of the editorial board of the International journal of the sociology of law.

James Lightbody is Associate Professor of Political Science at the University of Alberta, Edmonton, Canada. His articles and research interests focus upon metropolitan reorganization and the urban political process. He has served as a municipal affairs consultant to both local and national governments, and as senior policy advisor to the mayor of Edmonton.

Poul Erik Mouritzen is currently an Associate Professor in the Institute of Social Science at the University of Odense in Odense, Denmark. At the time this article was written, Mouritzen was a visiting scholar at the University of California at Irvine. His fields of teaching include public administration, policy analysis, organizational theory, and intergovernmental relations. His research interests have included grass-roots political movements, local output analyses, and various aspects of intergovernmental relations. Mouritzen is the initiator and coordinator of an ongoing research project on local government involving researchers from a number of Danish universities. His most recent work has been on issues of fiscal stress and their impact on local governments.

Betty Jane Narver is Director of the Institute for Public Policy and Management at the University of Washington in Seattle. Her fields of interest have included educational policy and school finance, implementation of various governmental programs, and emerging policy issues in state and local government. She served as a field associate in the recently completed three-year study by Richard Nathan examining the impact of the Reagan Domestic Program on state and local governments. She is currently working on a 14-state study of the Medicaid Program looking particularly at the effects of the 1981 Omnibus Budget Reconciliation Act on state ability to administer the program with cost savings.

Irving Ostrow is a doctoral candidate in Public Administration at the University of Southern California. He is also program manager for the City of Los Angeles' Community Development Department. He formerly served on the Mayor's Human Resources staff. He was also a professor of urban studies at Moorpark College.

Edward C. Page, B.A. (CNAA), M.Sc., Ph.D. (Strathclyde), is a lecturer at the University of Hull. He has written extensively on local government in Britain and other western nations. His other interests include comparative politics and public policy. His latest book, *Political Authority and Bureaucratic Power: A Comparative Analysis*, was published by Tennessee University Press in 1985.

Barry G. Rabe is an assistant professor of Health Politics in the Department of Health Planning and Administration in the School of Public Health at the University of Michigan. He was formerly a Research Fellow at the Conservation Foundation and in the Governmental Studies Program at the Brookings Institution.

Alan L. Saltzstein is Professor of Political Science and Chair of the Department at California State University, Fullerton. He is the author of *Public Employees and Policymaking* and articles dealing with local government decision making, affirmative action, and personnel policymaking. He holds a Ph.D. from UCLA and an M.P.A. from the University of Minnesota.

Stephen L. Schechter is a Professor of Political Science at Russell Sage College.

Paul Schumaker is Associate Professor and Chairman of the Department of Political Science at the University of Kansas. He has coauthored with Russell Getter articles on the extent to which urban governments respond equally to the preferences and demands of various subpopulations; these articles appear in the *American Journal of Political Science* (May 1977) and *Western Political Quarterly* (March 1983). He has also written on the success of protest groups in the *Journal of Politics* (August 1975) and *Sociological Quarterly* (Spring 1978). He is currently examining the applicability of various models of community power to Lawrence, Kansas. Papers on the project are available on request.

Robert Y. Shapiro is an Assistant Professor at Columbia University and a Research Associate at NORC, University of Chicago. His research interests are American politics, the policymaking process, and public opinion. He has published recent articles in *Public Opinion Quarterly*, the *American Political Science Review*, *Policy Studies Journal*, and *Urban Affairs Quarterly*. He is now studying the impact of mass media upon Americans' policy preferences.

Raphe Sonenshein is Assistant Professor of Political Science at California State University, Fullerton. He received a B.A. in public policy from Princeton University and a Ph.D. in political science from Yale University. In 1975–1976 he served as a grants deputy to Los Angeles City Councilman David S. Cunningham; he previously served as an intern in a grant-funded division of Mayor Tom Bradley's office. His dissertation dealt with Mayor Bradley's political organization.

Mary Ann E. Steger received her doctorate from Southern Illinois University at Carbondale and is currently an Assistant Professor in the Political Science Department at Oakland University. Her research interests include organized and unorganized forms of collective action, the CDBG program, and the relationship between program rules and the distribution of program benefits. She has published in the *Urban Affairs Quarterly*, *Publius*, and *The Urban Interest*.

Robert M. Stein is Associate Professor of Political Science at Rice University. He is currently conducting research on the growth of federal aid programs. His articles have appeared in *American Political Science Review*, *American Journal of Political Science*, *Western Political Quarterly*, *Public Choice*, and the *Journal of Urban Economics*.

Jean Claude Thoenig is Senior Research Fellow at the Centre National de la Recherche Scientifique, and Professor at INSEAD (Fontainbleau, France). He is also Head of the Groupe d'Analyse des Politiques (Paris, Sorbonne), and Consultant to major French public agencies. His most recent publications concerning French administration and policy are *L'Administration en miettes* with Francois Dupuy (1985) and "*L'Analyse des politiques publiques*" in *Traite de science politique*, ed. M. Grawitz and J. Leca.

Jean Trimble holds an M.S. in Urban Affairs. Over the last few years she has acted as program coordinator and community organizer for two prominent Milwaukee agencies and she volunteers for several area organizations. Presently Mrs. Trimble is the Medicare Project Consultant and Outreach Coordinator for Southeastern Wisconsin Benefit Specialists.

Bruce A. Williams is an Associate Professor in the Department of Political Science, Florida Atlantic University, Boca Raton, Florida. This current research is on urban development policies and on the politics of hazardous waste regulation.

John Allen Williams is an Associate Professor of Political Science at Loyola University of Chicago, and Executive Director and a Fellow of the Inter-University Seminar on Armed Forces and Society. He received his B.A. from Grinnell College and his M.A. and Ph.D. degrees from the University of Pennsylvania. His publications have appeared in *Urban Affairs Quarterly*, *The Washington Quarterly*, and *Armed Forces and Society*, among other places.